MONTESQUIEU AND THE OLD REGIME

MONTESQUIEU
AND THE
OLD REGIME

MARK HULLIUNG

UNIVERSITY OF CALIFORNIA PRESS

Berkeley   Los Angeles   London

University of California Press
Berkeley and Los Angeles, California
University of California Press, Ltd.
London, England
Copyright © 1976 by
The Regents of the University of California
ISBN 0-520- 03108-3
Library of Congress Catalog Card Number: 75-22658
Printed in the United States of America

to A.L.E.

CONTENTS

PREFACE

In this book I have set forth an interpretation of Montesquieu which is at odds with widely held opinions concerning his intellectual stature and ideological identity. From an implicitly secondary position, he has been elevated to the ranks of the greatest political thinkers. And against the familiar rendering of his thought as conservative apologetics, I have contended that he was a foremost detractor of the old regime and the proponent of a radical alternative. When viewing England, Montesquieu dreamed of nothing less than a national republic and a democratic society in France which could displace a monarchical politics and an aristocratic society.

Montesquieu took to task both the theory and the practice of the old regime. In some of the chapters which follow, we shall see him attacking the factual reality of the old order directly and its theoretical backbone indirectly. Chapter II of this study is one such case. With uncompromising vigor Montesquieu depicts the misdeeds of the old regime; his sociological explanations of political absolutism and aristocratic society double as indictments. Yet the theories of absolutism, its ideologies, do not drop out of sight. Far from it, divine right and *raison d'état* also come under fire, if less directly, because theory is not something distinct from reality. The denunciation of Spain is a hit at divine right; the denunciation of the Orient is a hit at raison d'état.

In other chapters the factual reference is to something other than the old regime, but Montesquieu's attack on absolutism does not, on that account, abate — it simply becomes a more direct attack on the theories of absolutism. Chapter VI is an illustrative case. Here one finds Montesquieu addressing himself to ancient Rome: he does so, however, in order to disprove divine right and raison d'état.

Montesquieu is, so to speak, the *Aufhebung* of old regime thought. The political science, the historiography, the economic doctrines — he subjects these aspects, and more, of the old regime's consciousness to critical scrutiny. Almost always Montesquieu begins with an established genre of old regime thought; almost always he ends with that genre destroyed, perfected, or transformed.

For the most part, Montesquieu's thought is critical in nature, but he is not unwilling to put forth an ideal. As a partisan, he belongs to the republican tradition which includes Artistotle, Polybius, Machiavelli, Harrington and many others. Time and again Montesquieu draws his moral sustenance from the ancient polis; and in the national republic of his aspirations, he looks forward to the possibility of a renewed civic life. During the last few years, republican thought has received the attention of able scholars. So far, however, Montesquieu's republican sentiments have been inadequately appreciated — a shortcoming I have tried to remedy.

Admittedly, Montesquieu's intellectual concerns do not invariably have their origins in a desire to attack the old regime or to call for its successor. His efforts, for instance, to supplement a sagging natural law tradition with new types of moral proofs (chapters V and VI) are initially a response to the skeptical implications of Locke's epistemology. Originally, then, the problem is purely philosophical and nonpolitical. But even in this instance, as we shall see, the question quickly becomes one of how best to repudiate the theory and practice of absolutism. Montesquieu's thought is too complex to answer simply to any formula; but if a formula is to be cited, it should surely be this: down with the old regime, up with the new regime.

A note on procedure. *The Spirit of the Laws* is discussed early and not until later do *The Persian Letters* and *Considérations* appear. The justification for such a break with chronology is that Montesquieu's ideas were already mature in *The Persian Letters*, and underwent a change in development, but not in nature, as he aged. This frees the interpreter to organize chapters around ideas, and to draw his quotations on a particular topic from all three of Montesquieu's major works. Sometimes the chronological approach is mandatory, but not in Montesquieu's case.

Besides the major works, I have also made use of Montesquieu's unpublished writings, such as the *Pensées*. I have supplemented my findings with such minor works, but all interpretations are based upon his three major efforts. As the most comprehensive of Montesquieu's works, *The Spirit of the Laws* is my center of gravity.

I wish to thank Michael Walzer and George A. Kelly for commenting on my manuscript. Happy the author who has such able critics. Most of all, I wish to acknowledge my indebtedness to Judith N. Shklar for invaluable suggestions and encouragement.

PROLOGUE:
Montesquieu and Minerva's Owl

Montesquieu has long been abused by those who treat ideas as shadows "reflecting" the "real" world. All we need know — so the most prevalent interpretation implies — is the social situation in Montesquieu's day, and the proper understanding of his thought will readily follow. Accordingly, an intellectual "expression" of the fusion of Robe and Sword has been sought and discovered in fulfillment of the "materialist" canon. Arguments presented by Montesquieu in defense of intermediary bodies are seen as an apology for the upstart nobility of the Robe, and his history of feudal laws is designated as doing the same for the ancient nobility of the Sword.[1]

Ignored in this formulation, and fatally so, is the possibility that Montesquieu's mental activities are *"reflections on"* rather than *"reflexes of* the life process"; ignored is the unbudging reality that his thought "expressed" the old regime by explaining it, and in explaining condemned it. Aristocratic society and political absolutism are in intellectual shambles by the time his powerful criticism has taken its toll, and he has radical ideals to offer as well as a radical critique to deliver. Decades in advance of the French Revolution, he dared nominate a national republic and democratic society as worthy and possible successors to the *ancien régime*.

Formidable impediments to thinking radical thoughts did indeed exist in the *ancien régime*. That much, certainly, must be granted to those who have identified Montesquieu with conservatism. But the most serious stumbling blocks to radical opinions were not social, as has been assumed, but conceptual. As the present work progresses, Montesquieu's radical critique and radical ideal will steadily unfold.

At present it is enough to recount his conceptual revolution, the revolution in the form of political thought which cleared the way for a revolution in content.

More often than not, Montesquieu derived his inspiration from the works of Aristotle, Polybius, or some other classical author. In content, Montesquieu discovered, the classics were a storehouse of civic information, waiting to be adapted to the needs of modern political units. In method, the classics offered the notions of the "type" and the "whole," notions indispensable to the sociological mode of analysis which Montesquieu favored. But in philosophy the classics upheld the metaphysical fallacies of essentialism and naturalism which Montesquieu had to purge before the promise of neoclassical thought could be fulfilled.

It was England that Montesquieu had in mind when he proposed the ideal of a republic hiding under the form of a monarchy. (Montesquieu's republican sentiments are elaborated below in chapter II, section 4; chapter IV, section 1; and in the Epilogue, section 1.) Yet in itself England could merely furnish the raw materials of a possible and coveted French future. When Montesquieu dwelled on the possible rebirth of citizenship, civic spirit, and political participation in the modern age, or when he discussed the political system appropriate to a free people, he advanced ideals far beyond anything to be had by a simple description of England. At this point England became more abstraction than fact, more ideal than real. In Book XI, chapter 6, of *The Spirit of the Laws* "should" and "ought" constantly recur; "is" appears but irregularly. "It is not my business to examine whether the English actually enjoy this liberty or not." England is understood as what a country evolving from the feudal embryo might aspire to be, not as what she or any other country is. And the classics were indispensable in this process of idealization, for without them Montesquieu could never have begun to breathe the spirit of the polis into the monarchical body politic.

Montesquieu had to be selective in borrowing from the classics because they contained the rationalization of the old regime as well as the germ of the new. Among the radical elements were republicanism, civic virtue, and citizenship; among the conservative elements were essentialism and naturalism. Plato and Aristotle had conceptually treated the civic ethos as a "thing," a fixed entity, an essence; and an essence does not develop and grow or change over time.[2] It simply is. Eager to forget the republican content of the classics, apologists for the old regime remembered the philosophical exclusion of time, change, and history which was also characteristic of the ancient sources. Renewed and revised, the essentialist philosophy which began in Greece lived on in later thought and flattered the old order with intimations of immortality.

The naturalistic preconceptions of the classics were also to the liking of the ideologists of the old regime, and doubly so. Such notions were additional obstacles to historical consciousness, and they promoted a vision of society as integrated by a norm and law of domination-subordination. Confounded with a law of nature, inequality was inevitable, immutable, irresistible. Feudal society, born and bred on privilege and hierarchy, was bound, then, to marvel at the good sense of the classics. A wary Hobbes feared the enormous radical potential of the classics; but no less enormous were their conservative uses.

Montesquieu hoped to remove the unwanted offshoots of the classical tradition and then to transplant the remainder in fresh soil. To begin with, essentialism and naturalism had to be replaced by an historical point of view. Ancient thought, underwritten by a philosophy of essences, simply could not cope with becoming; for in essentialist philosophies the universal, unchanging, and timeless is alone cognizable. In direct contrast, the particular, changing, and historical is stigmatized as irrational and unknowable. Arbitrary, fortuitous, or demonic the particular might be; an object of knowledge, never. Naturalist preconceptions compounded the unhistorical cast of classical thought. Instead of man in history, Greek philosophers apprehended man in nature, and consequently they mistook human actions for physical events and historical for natural processes. History was regarded as cyclical and closed; indeed, necessarily so. Just as nature is filled with movement but ever the same, so must human history, as an extension of nature, be filled with happenings but barren of novelty. *Plus ça change, plus c'est la même chose.*

Conceptual recognition of how man differs from an object in nature is the most elementary of those procedures needed to expel the naturalist and establish the historical perspective. One way of marking the boundary between historical and natural is by subject matter: historical science studying a thinking and feeling subject, natural science a mindless object. Somehow the categories of investigation had to subsume the mental processes which distinguish the social and historical from the natural. Very much to the point, then, are "virtue," "honor," and "fear" — the subjective elements ascribed by Montesquieu to republic, monarchy, and despotism, respectively. These subjective categories signify his determination to see political and social phenomena internally as actions, no less than externally as events.

In taking a view from the inside, Montesquieu advanced beyond classical political science,* both in its earlier and in its later manifestations. Polybius, commentators have noted, was so busy tinkering with the institutional machinery of the polis that at times he lost sight

---

*By "political science" we mean the efforts of classical and modern thinkers to develop empirical generalizations about politics. By "political sociology" we mean the empirical generalizations ventured by those political scientists who study the social context of politics.

Some readers may wish to ask whether the term "political sociology" is appropriate in a study of the thought of the old regime. A distinction between politics and society, W.G. Runciman has contended [*Social Science and Political Theory* (Cambridge, 1969) ch. 2], is central to political sociology; but such a distinction was unknown before the nineteenth century. Reading modern notions into premodern authors is, admittedly, a common mistake, and we may be grateful to Runciman for putting us on our guard. Yet it is misleading to say that a distinction between politics and society is the exclusive property of modernity. Aristotle was not so much ignorant of such a distinction as morally opposed to it. Few men, he knew, could be "beasts" living outside human association, but many were abandoning political associations for private friendships. As a dedicated defender of the polis, Aristotle was adamantly opposed to such an incipient separation of politics and society.

Aristotle also came close to a distinction between politics and society when he examined the causes of political decay. So frequently, he explained, had the polis been torn apart by factional disputes and class struggles that the only question left was whether the rich or the poor, the oligarchs or the democrats, would use public office for private ends. Not so long ago citizenship had been a way of life; society itself had been political; politics and society had been one. But now, he continued, various social forces were contending for the political weapons they needed in order to conquer their social enemies. The social was still related to, but distinct from, the political.

Runciman is wrong, then, if he means to suggest that Montesquieu could not have been a political sociologist. But certainly Montesquieu does contrast in important respects with Saint-Simon, Comte, Durkheim, and various other modern writers who go by the name of "political sociologist." Montesquieu does not share their belief in the inevitability of progress, nor does he "anticipate" their efforts to reduce the political to a function of the social. Decay is an ever-present possibility within Montesquieu's world, and the political normally maintains a certain autonomy vis-à-vis the social. In all this Montesquieu is, of course, simply being faithful to the intellectual tradition to which he belonged, the classical school of political sociology — the school of Aristotle, Polybius, and Bodin, to mention a few of Montesquieu's ancestors, and of Tocqueville and Mosca, to name two of his possible descendants.

of civic virtue.[3] And Harrington, having magnified Polybius' polis to the size of a national republic, also magnified the defects of Polybius. Not only was Harrington totally engrossed in constitutional gimmickry, but he explicitly disdained the civic ethos, confident that the levers and cogs he had designed would constrain the most selfish men to act for the public good.[4]

Another heir to the classical tradition is Bodin. A sociology of class conflict and political decay was as marked in him as it was in Aristotle, as has often been pointed out. But again the internal dimension was missing. Fear, honor, and virtue do not figure in his account. Approaching politics from the outside, Bodin and Harrington both made the mistake of assuming that Oriental despotism was a stronger regime than Western absolutism. Neither penetrated the social psychology of those who lived under despotism. Neither understood the ubiquitous fear that reigned in the East. And not knowing this, Montesquieu complained, they were unable to appreciate why absolute power, omnipotent in external appearance, is impotent in internal reality. (See below, chapter II, section 3.)

Doubtless, one of the most exquisite exemplars of classical political science is the *Politics* of Aristotle. And against it, we must concede, the previously mentioned complaint does not apply. Unlike Polybius and the old regime heirs of the classical tradition, Aristotle attained mastery over the subjective side of socio-political phenomena. His skillfully articulated analysis of class ideologies and the civic ethos signifies nothing less. Yet even here, in its finest hour, classical thought is wearing blinders.

Aristotle had, indeed, staved off some of the ill consequences of naturalism, but he did not do the same with essentialism. He had thought the polis through the category of "substance," and a sub-

---

Montesquieu may also be called a "social scientist," since he held that it is possible to discover certain regularities which inhere in society. Notably, he came to realize that economics can and should be considered as a discipline in its own right, and not simply as the branch of political science which it was both in mercantilist thought and in classical republican thought.

Finally, it may be said that Montesquieu's is an "historical sociology." For he did not stop after giving an account of the nature of a given socio-political system, but went on to explain how an entirely new system could arise from the ashes, or the seedbed, of the old — how, for instance, a national republic could emerge from a feudal past. In this regard, he went beyond Aristotle, his master, who had outlined the course of change, indeed drastic change, within the polis, but whose reflections always presupposed the city-state as a fixed point around which political thought would forever revolve.

stance always was and always will be. Consequently, Aristotle could account neither for the origins of the polis, nor for its change into something else. Whatever else his political sociology might be, it was not an historical sociology. Aristotle conceived of the polis as a "whole," a "system," which was much to Montesquieu's liking; but this "whole" was petrified and atemporal, which was not at all to Montesquieu's liking.

Montesquieu's history of feudalism accomplishes all that the classics could not. The change of political regimes that classical authors were adept in charting is complemented in his writings by an unclassical conceptualization of the origins and growth of a sociopolitical system. To which comparison with England and the Orient adds a comprehension of the possible future transformations of French politics and society into something entirely new: either constitutionalism and democratic society or despotism and despotic society. Should the "nature" and "principle" of France continue to evolve along their present course without experiencing revolutionary change, reactionary Spain offers an idea of her ultimate destination. (See below, chapters II–IV.)

At times the self-enclosed essentialism and misplaced naturalism that compromised the classics gave ground to a worse offender, the outbursts of pagan superstition. Through the notion of *fortuna*, the idea of civilization wrestling with demonic forces recurred in intellectual and popular form. For every thinker, such as Aristotle, who could blot out the goddess of fate and fortune, there were several others, such as Polybius, Sallust, or Tacitus, who could not. So imperious was fortuna's reign that she was the object of a popular and official cult during much of Roman history. And when the classics were reborn in Renaissance Italy, fortuna was treated to a second life. Not even the likes of Machiavelli and Guicciardini could extricate themselves from her clutches.

Now and then the voices of antiquity decried the obfuscation latent in the catchword "fortuna." During these moments of lucidity, that ill-conceived term was known as nothing more than a bad way of expressing ignorance of causes, or as an obscurantist recognition of the contingency of human affairs — the role of chance and accident in shaping their outcome. As for the taming of fortuna, the best her ancient detractors could offer was the promise of natural science to nullify the irrational by making known the hidden causes of the apparently arbitrary. The shortcoming of this procedure was not only its lack of fulfillment, but also its retrenchment of naturalism in the sphere of the historical.

Actually, the most promising method of expunging fortuna was by adding causal analysis to historiography while refusing to retreat from the historical to the naturalistic point of view. In other words, historical causation had to expel its naturalistic cousin, often out of place in the historical world, and this was another of Montesquieu's achievements. Having begun "internally," he went on to search for causal explanation from the outside. By means of an historicized social science, he unraveled those "necessary relations arising from the nature of things" which pertain to man in time and society. Not that society is literally a thing or an object in nature, of course. But the web of social relationships is such that society is more than the sum total of the individuals composing it. Men make their own history, but not under circumstances of their own choosing. What they do is always more or less than what they intend. Process is complemented by structure, or what must be thought of as structure, and the unsolicited consequences of actions sustain or destroy social and political structures over time.

For an example of how the foregoing may be used in ascribing causal efficacy to an historical event, we need only preview our interpretation of the *Considérations*. (See below, chapter VI.) There Montesquieu begins from the inside by analyzing civic virtue, the social psychology of the well-functioning republic. Staying on the inside, he reproduces the mentality of a ruling class, discovering the reason for the senators' proposal of continuous war in their fear of the demos. But when searching out the causal antecedents of the republic's fall, Montesquieu approaches Rome from the outside. What matters is no longer the intentions of the senators, but the unintended consequences of their acts, and these must be judged externally. As the polis expanded, republicanism faded, its structures and functions ill-suited for empire, its civic virtue irreparably damaged.

Between republican imperialism and political decay the relationship is one of cause and effect. One of the more significant consequences of this conclusion is that fortuna is ousted from historical explanation. It was, moreover, a distinctively historical causation that purged fortuna, and not an intrusion of natural causation beyond its proper sphere. The regularities of nature postulated by natural science are universal and timeless, the regularities of history postulated by social science are timebound and limited to a particular "type." Thus the argument of the *Considérations* can be generalized beyond Rome but not beyond the ancient republican type. Montesquieu had rid the classics of *fortuna* without falling into the trap of naturalism.

And in charting a transition from essences to "ideal-types,"[5] he performed another vital service for the classical tradition. The "types" employed in Montesquieu's political sociology are not essences. Far from being reified into things, they are understood as ideas, as logical constructs of the investigator's own making. Abuse of generic terms — "the flaw," Montesquieu insisted, "of all ancient philosophy"[6] — was terminated by following in the footsteps of Locke and the epigoni of the *Essay Concerning Human Understanding*. Once universals were recognized as the products of mind, instead of the metaphysical gifts of heaven, they could be used more self-consciously and with greater force of creative imagination.

Montesquieu's ideal-types differ both from the concepts of traditional logic and from average types. The *per genus et differentiam* rule of Aristotelian logic fails to define monarchy, republic, and despotism. They are equally impossible to define in terms of the characteristics common to all monarchies, republics, and despotisms, or according to the average qualities of the various individual specimens that belong to each group. "In practice," a modern sociologist observes, "we carry out a 'stylization'; . . . we construct a type."[7] Ideal-types are not "things" seized upon by mind, but rather mind itself, mind knowing its own activities and conducting them the better for it. Therein lies the departure from essentialism.[8]

By the same token, Montesquieu had broken still further away from naturalism. Social and political situations presumed to be typical abound in the classics because the human world was thought to repeat itself endlessly, exactly like nature. In Montesquieu's writings, however, the "type" became a construct of mind, designated by the investigator as typical during an unrecurring historical era.

The most momentous consequence of the transition from nature and essences to ideal-types was that it opened up history as much as naturalism and essentialism had closed it out. Carried over into the thought of the *ancien régime*, naturalism and essentialism conferred conceptual eternity on monarchy, much as they had done earlier for the polis. Placed within time by Montesquieu, the old order was transient as all things human. Despotism, republic, and monarchy do not exhaust history. They merely convey what has been thus far, and not even all of that, for England — as we shall see — represents something entirely new.

Now that the ahistoricism of the classics has been given its conceptual cure, let us proceed to the second unwanted child fathered by Plato and Aristotle, the pattern of domination and submission they saw as integral to the natural order of things, society and politics included. Beneath nature thus idealized lay the reality of deep hostility to individualism and egalitarianism. In the eyes of the old regime, this was the most enduring, and the most endearing, feature of the classical tradition.

According to classical naturalism, "matter" was saved from madness by the "forms" which crystallized nature into structured wholes. Of all such wholes, the most humanly important was the polis. Through the polis, the individual found fulfillment and was what he was meant to be. In brief, the individual's lot was to belong, for he was nothing outside the whole. Nor was he anything within the whole if he was too physically unfit to benefit it; hence, the nonchalance of Plato's and Aristotle's proposals to do away with deformed infants.[9] So primary was the whole that for all the individual's importance when discharging his function, he could not boast an intrinsic worth.

Classical naturalists also justified a harsh inequality. Hierarchy, they contended, pervades everything. Gifted with reason, man is the highest of species and hierarchy does not stop there. Within the human species, some are more rational than others, men being superior to women and citizens to slaves. For non-Greeks slavery is "natural," as is woman's submission to man. Aristotle could not resist quoting Sophocles: "A modest silence is a woman's crown."

Citizenship involves both ruling and being ruled, Aristotle repeatedly asserts, and is shared among equals. But his is the equality and fraternity of the great and therefore has nothing in common with social levelling. Given the opportunity to turn back the clock, Aristotle would return to the Athens that preceded the democratic reforms of Solon. The ideal citizenship discussed in the earlier sections of the *Politics* pertains to that archaic period and is exclusionary in the extreme.

As defined by Aristotle, citizenship is an intensely aristocratic ideal, and for it to be possible, noncitizens must be dregs. Anything beyond gentlemanly agriculture is incompatible with a fully developed personality, so the great cannot provide their own leisure. Nor can leisure be had from an exchange economy since that would destroy the foundations of archaic society. Equality for the few great men, inequality for the remainder, is the only possible solution. Yet all is well since most men are unfit for citizenship but quite capable of economic plodding. Inequality is proper, then, in that it allows everyone to realize his potential.

The same is true of wives and domestic slaves. They, too, have a characteristic excellence toward which they should strive, and it is similarly manifest when they know their place and act accordingly. Outside the household they are out of place; inside they contribute to the well-being of the polis and experience such fulfillment as befits the lowly. Justice is theirs because they have been given their due. More, of course, is due the rulers, for justice is not just unless it is discriminatory.

Monarchy plunges the great into privacy, and that is why Alexander's imperial ambitions are inexcusable. By Aristotle's frank avowal, however, family structure is and should be monarchical, since nature and the needs of the polis have so ordained. Many tiny monarchies constitute a city-state republic, each one ruled by a paternalistic despot — the husband, father, and slave owner. At home a monarch and beneficiary of inequality, he is a citizen, brother, and equal among equals in the political assembly. His freedom, moreover, depends on the necessity of those subject to his kingly rule. For the father to act in public, wife and slaves must labor in the household, ministering to biological repetition as they endlessly replenish the supply of food, drink, and other necessities.

A republic for the few, the polis is a monarchy for the many who de jure or de facto are mere subjects. To the sanction of tradition, classical philosophers added their own approval of inequality. Lest hierarchy be misunderstood as oppressive, Plato and Aristotle were prepared to defend it as natural and just. Wanting to overturn the established arrangements was to rebel against all nature and to be guilty of injustice in desiring that unequals be treated as equals.

Read selectively by the apologists of the old regime, the classics were ready to aid and abet the existing social and political arrangements. Filmer, the patriarchalist, could claim as truthfully to be a descendant of Aristotle as could Harrington, the republican. And patriarchalism was not the only example of the conservative uses of the classical tradition. After deleting republicanism from the classics, the ideologists of feudalism lingered over the corporate and hierarchical vision of society evident in Plato and Aristotle. With the polis long defunct but corporatism and hierarchy feudally reborn, at least one-half of the classics had returned to life. As in antiquity, and with the express consent of the oracles of ancient wisdom, a law of domination and subservience was proclaimed to abide cosmically.

Taking another look, one may note that the tradition of classical naturalism was not one tradition but two. Whether society was seen as composed of several strata of matter, each shaped by its respective form, or as made up of just one bulk of matter, bearing the imprint of one overall form, was of utmost significance. The first road was travelled by the Greek theorists, the second found greater expression in Roman political thought. The former leads to corporatism, but the latter dissolves corporate bodies into the myriad individuals who compose society. Here was a conceptual difference within the family of classical naturalism fraught with the greatest socio-political import.

Clearly the Roman viewpoint was headed in directions foreign to the Greek. When all members of the polis are reduced to similar particles in one huge chunk of matter, two alternative conceptualizations can be distinguished. Either the levelling conception suggests democratization or it suggests a new form of domination and submission. In the first alternative the constituents of society are "the people," in the second "the mass." Not surprisingly, Machiavelli, whose classicism was highly latinized, exhibited both currents. First he eulogized the people and then he scolded them.

As seen in Livy, the Roman variant of classical naturalism was notably "Machiavellian." Politics was everything because it gave form to recalcitrant matter, transmuting society into body politic. From the beginning, then, Roman thought took a view from above, from the standpoint of the rulers, a view sustained by its lowly estimate of those below. For all the praise which Machiavelli occasionally heaps on the demos, their abuse is sure to follow when Livy's ghost rears his head. Then a sharp gap between mass and elite opens in Machiavelli's writings and with it, to borrow the words of Charles Norris Cochrane,

> a profound distrust of the commons, to whose merely animal impulses are ascribed cataclysms, the equivalent in human life to what in nature are the blind and erratic thrusts of matter-in-motion. . . . The

conclusion must be obvious: what Leviathan needs is a head. To supply that kind of head is the work of creative politics.[10]

Livy is bent on selling the Augustan prince, Machiavelli on utilizing the agency of the Renaissance prince.

Historians have seen fit to modify Burckhardt's formula of the Renaissance state as "a work of art." Nevertheless, its accuracy in describing Machiavelli's theory of the state remains uncontested. A favorite analogy of the great Florentine compares statecraft to sculpture. The prince is sculptor in *Il Principe*, the ruling class in the *Discorsi*. But no matter whether the state is principality or republic, it is the ruling elite who infuse the ruled with value, much as the sculptor shapes formless material to fit a largely preconceived design. Rulers act but the ruled are acted upon, passive, barren of character in their own right. Better than the most long-winded discourse, this analogy expresses the Machiavellian tendency always latent in classical naturalism, especially in the Roman variant. At one and the same time, it becomes clear that the supposedly egalitarian version of naturalism actually thrives on ruling class domination, and that the state does not grow but is made by a political superman before whom all must bow.

When alloting responsibility for Italy's plight, Machiavelli notes that "the people are not to be blamed for this, but rather their princes."[11] Even in such democratic moods, however, he still holds to a notion of differential rationality that underestimates the people and overestimates the political elite. Whenever corruption overtakes the body politic, it is the elite, in the Machiavellian view, who are at fault. The animal impulses, above which the mass rarely rises, are as functional in times of civic vigor as they are pernicious in times of civic degeneration. Virtually mindless, the mass continues to cling to its civic habits for quite some time after the elite has abandoned the old ways. At last the multitude betrays civic virtue but only because it always comes to imitate the ruling class. Glory belongs to the elite, as does shame, but those outside ruling circles, being mere objects in nature, are incapable of either. Reason of state is necessarily the reason of the rulers, for the ruled are without reason.

Unfair to the ruled, Machiavelli's differential rationality is so overly generous to the rulers that Machiavellian thought is often more ridiculous than "realist." Repeatedly it backslides into the worst excesses of "rationalism in politics."[12] Polybius, a forerunner of Machiavelli, was convinced that Sparta could aspire to immortality because, he fantasized, she was formed overnight and in exact accordance with a single man's blueprint design. A second example of the propensity of Machiavellian thought to attribute too much to the rulers may be derived from its attitude toward history. Knowing that the Romans had conquered the world, Machiavelli searched for the schemers responsible, purporting to find them in the Roman senators. That world conquest might have been decided by unforeseen and unintended accidents was totally unacceptable to him.

Equally embarrassing, Polybius, Livy, and Machiavelli had drastically misinterpreted Roman religion. Understood as something fabricated by the elite to restrain the herd, Roman religion was Machiavellian in the extreme. Once again it was the rulers who monopolized reason and the ruled who were devoid of the same. From the Roman perspective, political leadership was completely outside society and immune to its beliefs, which is another way of saying that Machiavellian thought was historically and sociologically absurd. So far as the people were concerned, the assumption was that they would never see through the machinations of the rulers, and this, too, was an act of faith historically and sociologically unfounded.

No less than the Greek, hierarchical, and corporatist brand of classical naturalism, the succeeding Roman, egalitarian, and unitary version raced to the defense of the old regime. When the corporatist ideology first lost the support of the Ptolemaic universe and then reeled from the blows ministered by a levelling absolute monarchy, Machiavellism stepped into the breach. Reason of state* became a mainstay of the monarchy.

More accurately, Machiavellism did not so much displace corporatism as coexist with it. After rendering feudal society governable and its corporate groupings functional, Richelieu had fulfilled all he had ever intended. The truth is, Machiavellism had neither the stomach nor the imagination to transform society. Reason of state was scarcely less conservative than its corporatist brother, both of them born of classical naturalism, orphaned, and adopted by the old regime. For even if Richelieu had managed to disabuse himself of the old regime's corporate bodies, his outlook would still be conservative. First, because the Machiavellian variant of classical naturalism filtered his every thought through the prism of political elitism. Second, because

---

*Throughout this study "Machiavellism" and "reason of state" will be regarded as interchangeable terms.

to naturalism change spelled trauma, the outrageous uprising of matter against form. Third, because naturalism's historical blindness aborted every thought of a new order; historical experience, it taught, is finite, closed, and a genuinely new politics and society impossible.

We are now in a position to appreciate the consequences attendant upon Montesquieu's expulsion of essentialism and naturalism from the classical tradition. In one fell swoop he could open history and end the logic of domination-subordination. To open the future, he transferred Aristotle's category of "potentiality" from nature to history: representing the best evolutionary possibility of feudalism, Montesquieu's British model is an historically possible ideal. To end domination-subordination, he used the classics to idealize England. Thus idealized, she was a national and assimilationist republic which had banished feudal, Machiavellian, and clerical exploitation.

Montesquieu's thought is remarkable for its methods of analysis and for its solutions of vexing intellectual problems. In his works the political theories of the old regime attain a fulfillment which is also a surpassing. And from the advanced outpost secured by his exceptionally fecund analyses, the new regime was visualized in advance of the demise of the old. Upon reading him, we learn that Minerva's owl left the roost well before dusk, notwithstanding rumors to the contrary.

CHAPTER I

Absolutism and Its Ideologies

1. Before and After 1685

Absolutism was a hybrid regime — half modern and half traditional; half all-powerful, half powerless. Before 1685, the modern and potent element was conspicuous; but after 1685, the traditional and impotent side staged a dramatic comeback. As a preparation for Montesquieu's antimonarchical strictures, we shall examine the early promise of absolutism and its later failure to keep its word.

On its ascent, absolutism was notable for its attempts to rationalize monarchical politics. Most such efforts pertained to the military, which in Louis XIV's reign had taken great strides forward organizationally. Uniforms and uniform wages were indicative of the new state of affairs, as were the artillery and engineering branches, which featured control on the basis of expertise. For its part, science was bent to political use when the laws of falling bodies were applied to ballistics, and again when information was centrally collected and stored with the help of statistics. Overall, a united front of bureaucratic rationalization and scientific rationalism elevated state power to unprecedented heights.[1]

Late in the seventeenth century, all was still well in the royalist camp. But from then on disaffection was unmistakable, as one class after another excused itself from the royalist consensus. Nobles frustrated the regal will by casting off the capitation tax (1695), and this particular episode was only the opening shot in a protracted struggle between Crown and Second Estate. Likewise, the bourgeoisie forgot who was master and who servant. The War of the League of Augsburg unleashed such potent hostility to mercantilism that in

1700 a Council of Commerce was instituted. Heretofore bourgeois participation in government agencies had been an excuse for royal intervention in business affairs. Now it meant the capture of government agencies by the bourgeoisie.

Society had broken loose from the polity's embrace, and that was not all. Increasingly it was obvious that the social order was not about to shed its traditional stamp. *Dérogation,** labor-intensive agriculture, and an abiding reverence for the claims of time and title suggested that reason of state was not matched by reason in society. Moreover, the state itself was inconsistent in its dedication to reason. Outside the army, the intendant was the only example of the modern administrator, professionally trained and subject to discipline, transfer, and dismissal. Other offices were usually venal, bought and sold as private property, and hence beyond central control. Never was the political realm strong enough to do as it pleased with society.

Sixteen eighty-five was a turning point in the career of royalty. In that year the Huguenots lost their homeland, France lost her most able producers, and the state lost economic power. Before the Revocation of the Edict of Nantes, the Gallican liberties of the church had one consequence; afterwards they had another. Previously national Catholicism spelled a political religion; now it spelled a religious polity — a retreat from modernity and a backslide into powerlessness.

Ideologically, the Revocation had been decisive. For it proclaimed, in effect, the defeat of raison d'état and the victory of divine right. An ideology of reason, raison d'état was embarrassed by the resurgence of mystification in politics. An ideology of power, raison d'état was discredited when it proved too weak to fend off divine right, the ideology whose effect was to drain absolutism of its powers. So crucial was the struggle between divine right and reason of state that the nature of the combatants deserves further attention.

2. Raison d'état and the Ascent of Absolutism

To Richelieu and his kind, the "rationalization" and "demystification" of the world (in Max Weber's sense) were not inevitable, nor was absolute power. Instead, "reason" and "power" were painstakingly pursued through the theory and practice of "reason of state" and "power politics." Advocates of raison d'état consciously endeavored to

---

Dérogation: the loss of noble status suffered by aristocrats who worked for a living.

render politics calculable and controllable. They aspired to rewrite Machiavelli's *Prince*, to create a science of politics, to issue a foolproof how-to-do-it manual. And all for the sake of bestowing absolute power upon monarchy.

Raison d'état first had to rid itself of several encumbrances with which Machiavelli had burdened Machiavellism, most notably historical example. The Florentine Secretary had saddled his writings with Greek and Roman exemplars, but Richelieu would have none of it.

> There are none more dangerous for the state than those who wish to rule the kingdom according to the maxims which they have learned from books. By this means they often ruin it completely, because the past bears no relation to the present, and because the relative disposition of times, places, and people is quite different.[2]

Cyclical history fared no better with Richelieu and the masterminds of raison d'état. Machiavelli was sufficiently pagan to believe in the inevitability of decline. Delaying actions can arrest the pace of degeneration, but sooner or later the ineluctable will have its way. From such a Sisyphean nightmare, the revised reason of state easily escaped, since no historical fatalism of any sort, optimistic or pessimistic, underlay its vision. When raison d'état did occasionally turn away from its natural home in the present, it was to plan future possibilities, and not to ransack the past. The emphasis was on voluntarism, organization, and planning here and now.

In his *Political Testament*, Richelieu stated the goals of raison d'état with stark simplicity: the king was to be first in France and France first in Europe. As for means, reason of state readily lent itself to a search for techniques and methods. Pamphlets discussing government procedures, rational decision making, and the new man of power politics became the common currency of absolutist thought.

Richelieu's writings belong to this genre, and he was especially attentive to the coterie of ministers that surrounded the king and who were chiefly responsible for policy advice. Administrative effectiveness of this select corps, he postulated, was a function of its size. Beyond the minimal few, growth of numbers merely exacerbated problems of coordination while conferring no compensatory benefits. As the final moment of decision draws near, even these few must yield to a single advisor, the Prime Minister.[3]

Whenever Richelieu's attention is not on the prince's advisors, it is on the prince. More than all other men, insists the Cardinal, the king must abstain from indulgence of private passions. At one and the same time, the crown is, or ought to be, the locus of the public interest and the visible incarnation of the reign of reason. First in grandeur, the prince must also be first in self-denial. The public self must repress the private, and reason must repress passion.[4]

In foreign policy, the practitioners of raison d'état used the idea of state interest to fashion policies. According to Rohan — a leading theoretician of the new diplomacy — international relations is a pluralistic universe in which each state has its particular interest. It is not enough, then, for the diplomat to be well versed in the interest of his own state. He must also calculate the interest of every other state, an exercise which demands repression of nationalist passions and empathy with the enemy.[5] At times Rohan's thought verged on what is known today as "game theory."*

The new man of power politics exuded mastery over the forces of history and over himself. History did not make him, he made history. Self-mastery was evinced in the exacting regimen of asceticism to which he voluntarily subjected himself. Mastery was also possible because the renovated raison d'état, unlike Machiavelli's original doctrine, was realistic in its goals. Hope for a revived civic virtue in Renaissance Italy was an idle dream, but the ends of European hegemony and absolute royal power were distinct historical possibilities in the France of the old regime.

Lastly, the proponents of reason of state claimed mastery over religion, that most impregnable stronghold of mystification. Gabriel Naudé, librarian of Richelieu and then of Mazarin, explicitly urged that religious conviction be manipulated in accordance with the needs of the state. From time to time, moreover, the raison d'état party boldly suspended Christian ethics and made the state a law unto itself. What better example of the Machiavellian can there be than Richelieu, Cardinal in the Catholic church and advocate of a network of alliances that supported Protestant potentates in Germany at the expense of Catholic Hapsburgs in Spain and Austria? Insofar as politics did, or did not, control religion, raison d'état was, or was not, a formidable doctrine.

---

*Game theory is a theory of conflict in which rational actors are presupposed. Each such actor calculates strategies by which he strives to achieve his objectives. To make an effective "move," a player must anticipate the moves of his opponents.

3. Divine Right and the Waning of Power

Ultimately the logic of royal absolutism was self-defeating. Unceasing effort, planning, and struggle were rewarded by the accumulation of total power within the hands of a single human being. But what was to assure that this one lonely figure, awarded absolute power because he happened to be born, would exercise his prerogative with wisdom, or indeed care at all for the labors of kingship? Louis XV saw little more in affairs of state than a cause of ennui and accordingly abandoned himself to the chase — of foxes and of women. Moreover, the residue of the medieval personal administrative regime which survived into the period of the bureaucratic state nurtured a dangerous tendency to wield a very unmedieval concentration of power as whim or fancy dictated. Distinctions between the royal dynasty, the crown, the state, and the nation were dissolved by the enveloping omnipresence of a single personality. As Albert Guérard has put it:

> For Richelieu, of comparatively modest origin . . . the state . . . was a sort of formidable idol, to be served by methods of terror. For Henry IV, and for lesser men like Francis I and Louis XIV, the State was no Leviathan but something accessible and personal — their own domain, their family, themselves.[6]

Everywhere the personal nature of royal government was in evidence. The king embodied the whole of authority; the law was often coterminous with his will; the military waved the personal banner of the house of Bourbon and sometimes the king graced the battlefield with his presence. Frederick the Great's description of himself as the "first servant of the state" admirably expressed the self-abnegating outlook of a raison d'état prince. Louis XIV's self-indulgent *"l'état, c'est moi"* was, however, more descriptive of the usual mentality of absolute princes.

Ideology was unable to restrain the monarch. Submission of the royal will to the state, to the nation, to reason, or to the public interest — the various ideals proposed in doctrines of raison d'état — suffered one and all a similar fate. The king proclaimed his will as identical to that of the state, the nation, the rational, and the public. Even the second level of raison d'état thinking — instrumentation and technique — fell into disuse. Both Louis XIV and Louis XV ignored a major aspect of Richelieu's advice: the necessity of delegating authority to a prime minister. Louis XIV, true to his character, wanted all affairs of state to be directly in his own hands; similarly Louis XV, absentee ruler though he usually was, acted at times as if the monarch alone should do politics. Not only did Louis XV refuse to name a successor to Cardinal Fleury, the prime minister, but he consistently obtruded into diplomacy. Perversely, he carried on a diplomatic correspondence behind the backs of his official negotiators. Centuries past, writes Garrett Mattingly, Louis XI of France and Ferdinand of Spain had been "too fond of secrecy, mystification and elaborate double-dealing to trust much to systematic organization."[7] Hence, the development of sophisticated diplomatic machinery, achieved in Italy as early as the Renaissance, was an inordinately prolonged process in the rising Leviathans. The example of Louis XV suggests that the new machinery was never really finished; at any time personalism could overtake rationalization in foreign affairs.

Another technique victimized by personal rule was the dispassionate calculation of the interests of the European states. A certain modesty had always been implied by Machiavellism; power politicians taught that overextension increased vulnerability by spreading power too thin. Heedless of these warnings, Louis XIV embroiled the state in war after war with the inevitable effect that the powers of Europe united against France. And to what end was Louis' policy aimed? — his personal quest for glory, which he assumed was necessarily France's as well. What is good for Louis XIV is good for the country.

Although miserable as obstacles to royal excess, doctrines of monarchical rule were never wanting during the age of absolutism. Imagine the potential power of a tutor charged with educating the dauphin. Here was an intellectual who might sway the fortunes of the most powerful nation in Europe. During the declining years of Louis XIV, an especially striking situation occurred which is an object lesson in the politics of personal rule. Rarely before or since have the disputations of teachers portended such drastic political import. Louis the dauphin was educated by Bossuet, who indoctrinated his pupil in a carefully articulated theory of absolutism. Upon the dauphin's death in 1711, Fénelon's pupil, the Duke of Burgundy, was elevated to the stature of heir apparent. Overnight the probable flow of France's future history seemed arrested, diverted, and reversed, since Fénelon taught that royal absolutism presaged despotism. As an "aristocratic liberal" or "feudal reactionary," Fénelon revived memories of "fundamental laws" and an "ancient constitution" whose venerable Gothic roots had been severed by a usurping prince. In the end, of course, the differences between Bossuet and Fénelon proved to be as transient in practical significance as they were eternal in doctrinal contradiction. Fénelon's candidate died after a mere year of eligibility and the episode came to a close. But who could forget what high drama had occurred within the study chambers of tutors? The race was on. He who captured the mind of an absolute prince could reshape the contours of history.

Independently of his quarrel with Fénelon, Bossuet is a man to whom the analyst of the *ancien régime* must return time and again. Remarkably, his *Politics Taken from the Very Words of Holy Scripture* is none other than a religious restatement of *The Prince*. On issues of staffing, flow of information, and control over advisors, Bossuet is, indeed, the equal of Machiavelli and Richelieu. Where he differs from them is in the source of his wisdom. Perhaps Machiavelli would have felt honored to have the instrumentalist side of *The Prince* adapted to the needs of seventeenth-century Machiavellism. Beyond a doubt, however, he would have been shocked to see the same techniques of statecraft derived from the words of Holy Scripture.

Bossuet was so near and yet so far from raison d'état. Cardinal Richelieu wore the robes of a cleric but spoke of absolutism from the vantage point of state interest; Bishop Bossuet defended absolutism while keeping the interests of the church uppermost in mind. Richelieu's thought begins and ends with the glorification of the impersonal secular state; Bossuet's revolves around the sacerdotal person of the prince. *"Tout l'état est en la personne du prince,"*[8] Bossuet wrote, and this is as close as any ideologue ever came to replicating Louis XIV's *"l'état, c'est moi."*

Given Bossuet's religious preoccupations, there is nothing contradictory in his movements to and fro between eulogies of personalism and impassioned declarations of princely duty. A secular ideal, the state hardly appealed to Bossuet in the same way it appealed to a Machiavellian. But in siding with the king he was allying himself with one of the most time-honored of Christian doctrines: the religious nature of kingship, the divine right of kings. After the coronation oath, the king was the Lord's anointed. His person was henceforth elevated above that of all other men, but more than all other men he was dutybound to honor and serve God's holy church.

Likewise, Bossuet's oscillations between utilitarian and anti-utilitarian sentiments can readily be explained in terms of his religious convictions. A Hobbesian judgment of royal absolutism as the most stable form of polity was the utilitarian element in his thought. But he could never be a complete Hobbesian, since he was unwilling to extend utilitarianism to religion. Bossuet was the ideologue of the national church, but that did not make him an advocate of a political religion. Quite the contrary, he was determined that France would be a religious polity. He reminded the king of what the regal memory was most eager to forget — that under pain of mortal sin the crown was obliged to fill vacant ecclesiastical posts using the criterion of religious fitness rather than political expediency.[9] Bossuet's dreams were the nightmares of Machiavellians. If he had his way, the church would possess the absolute prince, body and soul.

And it did. From 1685 onward the religious policy of the crown was an unmitigated disaster and can be regarded as a case study in the decline of royal power. First came the Revocation of the Edict of Nantes, a measure totally inimical to the interests of the crown. The primacy of the unitary state was no longer at issue. Huguenot cities, once a kind of anachronistic state within the state, had long been disarmed by Richelieu. The king, therefore, had no cause to purge the Huguenots; and he had excellent cause to cherish his Protestant tradesmen. In expelling the Protestants, Louis was crippling the economic foundations of his power. Hundreds of thousands of industrious craftsmen fled France. Bossuet proclaimed Louis a new Theodosius, a new Charlemagne; church leaders, Jansenist and Jesuit alike, gave thanks to God. Machiavellians wept.

If nothing else, the Revocation was at least popular, but the next religious battle coalesced popular opinion around opposition to the crown. The papal bull *Unigenitus* (1713), politically a pronouncement against the national church, split France and aligned Jansenists, Gallicans, *parlements*, and the mass of the population on one side, with the king, the Jesuits, and a few ultramontane bishops isolated on the other. The smoldering ashes of religious strife which Richelieu had tried to smother were fanned into a conflagration by the newly discovered religiosity of an old king.

Some time back into the past, divine right produced consequences that were beneficial to an ascendant absolutism. Linked as it was to the tradition of Gallican liberties and a national church, divine right facilitated the break with Rome and ended the era of politically divided loyalties. At the same time, it served to popularize the notion of sovereign power,[10] which in Bodin's version was a doctrine fit only for a bookish few. But had he lived longer, Bossuet would have soured eventually on the resurgence of divine right in the later years of Louis XIV. In accepting and enforcing *Unigenitus*, Louis not only abandoned the Machiavellians but Bossuet as well. Leaving the national church behind, Louis upset both the hopes of Machiavellians for a politically controlled religion and the aspiration of Bossuet for a polity religiously controlled by the French bishops. Louis' reversion to a situation of divided loyalties — Pope and nation, Pope versus nation — would have disturbed Bossuet as much as Richelieu, although not for identical reasons.

Bossuet, however, unlike Richelieu, could have offered a convincing explanation of how this course of events had come to pass. Not the least of Bossuet's insights was his penetration, mystifying in rhetoric but marvelously naturalistic in its explanatory powers, of the logic by which religion ultimately overtakes the mind of an aging prince. A man of deeper perception than is often appreciated, Bossuet knew why the Christian influence would outlast the other doctrines contending at the foot of the throne. However fickle the personality of the prince, it could not escape the furies of conscience and remorse. The person of the king enveloped all the external means of controlling regal conduct, but he could not rid himself of the controls built into his personality by the Christian ethos. Bossuet portrayed God in frightening terms: "he lives eternally; his wrath is implacable, and always alive; his power is invincible; he never forgets; he never tires; nothing escapes him." God is the most powerful of all absolute princes and before him worldly absolute monarchs stand in fear and trembling. "The fear of God is the true counterpoise of [royal] power; the prince fears God all the more since he need fear no one but him."[11]

Political dynamics propelled princely guilt and bad conscience to the forefront of conscious awareness, where they festered as open sores in need of assuagement. The logic of the political situation was inexorable: both the constant princely pursuit of *gloire* in warfare and the continuous practice of raison d'état were sins against Christianity which no amount of casuistry could explain away. *Gloire* was pride, and nothing better. Had not Bossuet sketched the rise and fall of empires, in his *Discours sur l'histoire universelle*, so as to teach the prince humility? If the grandeur of empires was nothing in the sight of God, how puny was an absolute prince and how scandalous the deaths he caused by unnecessary wars.[12] As for raison d'état — the suspension of Christian ethics for the purposes of power — it was a sin by definition. The king might temporarily ignore Christian morality, but he could not eradicate its psychological imprint, and never did he live beyond good and evil. Eventually his embattled conscience would seek expiation in acts of extraordinary piety.

Now Bossuet knew exactly the kind of grand gesture that would propitiate God. The good Bishop's opposition to raison d'état is evident in many particulars — for instance, his belief in the inviolability of treaties.[13] But it is especially in his harangue against a political religion that Bossuet assaults power politics. The king must not feign piety for power's sake but sacrifice everything, power included, to piety.[14] Case in point: the Revocation. Bossuet's paeans to Louis were not ex post facto apologies. Already in *Politique tirée des propres paroles de l'écriture sainte*, begun long before 1685, Bossuet demanded that the king destroy false religions domiciled in the state.[15] The Revocation was Bossuet's vindication, God's joy, and the king's relief from the harpies of remorse and bad conscience. What Bossuet failed to appreciate, and what subsequent events (*Unigenitus*) clearly dramatized, was that a troubled regal conscience could opt as easily for the much hated ultramontanism of Jesuit confessors as for the very popular Gallican liberties of the national church.

The religious policy of Louis XIV reads as a point-by-point reversal of the Machiavellian program. Advice-giving had become the province of Mme. de Maintenon, leader of the *dévot* party, and of the Jesuits, who as confessors at court infiltrated ultramontanism into the highest circles of government, not excepting the king. Policies of political toleration of Protestants and of a politically inspired moratorium on intra-Catholic quarrels were abruptly terminated. Politics became the instrument of religion and not religion the instrument of politics. And all at the cost of dissipating power. Raison d'état was the ideology of absolutism emboldened, assertive, and self-confident; divine right the ideology of absolutism faltering, repentant, humble, and humiliated.[16]

"Reason of state" and "power politics" were phrases in an ideological vocabulary that portrayed absolutism as progressive and state-building. But when both reason and power were spent, it was time for a thoroughgoing re-evaluation in the form of a vigorous indictment. As the *praxis* of absolutism grew steadily ineffectual, its theory lay increasingly open to challenge. The stage was set for Montesquieu.

CHAPTER II

Political Sociology as the Indictment of Absolutism

1. Political Science in the *Ancien Régime*

Gropingly and with hesitation, something vaguely resembling a science of politics stole its way into the consciousness of the *ancien régime*. It was political science in the form of policy directives, rationalization of power techniques, and shreds of organization theory. Yet, for all its pretensions, the revised and augmented "realist" theory of politics was curiously abstract and truncated. Reason of state was always reason as it belonged to the state and therefore a strictly circumscribed and abrasively partisan reason.

Much was amiss in what was said by absolutists; even more was amiss in what was not said. Neither bureaucratic structure nor the social context of politics made its way into the rarefied atmosphere of theoretical generalization. Once extracted from empirical existence, absolutist thought never returned to its point of origin.

Oppositions drawn by Machiavellians between reason and passion, public and private interest, the general and particular, were common polemical antitheses that downgraded the feudal mentality and upgraded the royalist persuasion. The idea of functional utility, injected into the body politic by both Richelieu and Bossuet, was an antibody combating the aristocratic mores of leisure and play. Nevertheless, a statist rhetoric is a far cry from a theory of bureaucratic politics.

Obviously the notion of a bureaucratic theory implies the development of propositions that explain the whole of bureaucracy, the entire maze of personnel, offices, and practices. From the outset it is clear that Machiavellism is wanting in this crucial prerequisite. In absolutist thought the only bureaucrats regarded as worthy of theoretical comment were the king's immediate advisors. We hear nothing of policy as the output of competing bureaucratic agencies, each with its interest and fragmented perspective, nor do we see anything of middle level bureaucratic chiefs wheeling and dealing power. Absolutists were silent on the subject of bureaucracy, and strangely so, since they desperately needed to demonstrate how personalistic weakness could be converted into institutional strength.

Absolutists did have something to say about society, but not enough. The nobility was to defend the state, the bourgeoisie to spur commercialism, and the peasantry to support the weight of the agrarian economy.[1] Economic activities were to provide a rich tax base and to divert energies that might otherwise go into political activism. Yet even as they wrote of the objective social factor of classes, absolutists missed the subjective factor of class values. Sociologically, absolutists knew not what they were doing: that in codifying the existing mode of stratification they were leaving intact the aristocratic ethos that runs counter to bureaucratic and economic vocations.

What general explanations can be adduced to account for the failure of royalist thinking to evolve into a science of politics? One of the most important is the deleterious effect of the personalized polity. If the politics of absolutism stimulated visions of a political science, it was also responsible for the myopia with which the subject was conceived. The concentration of power in the frequently irresponsible and incompetent person of the prince drew attention to the highest rung of ministers and advisors, the Richelieus and Mazarins whose brilliant politicking behind the throne was the difference between chaos and efficiency; hence the profusion of pamphleteering by, for, or about the occupants of ministerial office. Similarly, what regime was more apt than a personalized one to produce a body of literature on rational decision making? When the specter of irrationality looms large, such writings come as an urgent antidote to reality. The words Bossuet whispers to the prince are telling: "the less you have to give reasons to others, the more you must have reason in yourself."[2]

Moreover, Machiavellian thought was congenitally antibureaucratic and nonsociological. For if, as Mannheim said, "the fundamental tendency of all bureaucratic thought is to turn all problems of politics into problems of administration,"[3] then the fundamental tendency of Machiavellism is to turn all problems of administration into problems of politics. In its pure form, Machiavellism concedes nothing to bureaucratic procedures and necessities, those impersonal processes which can only obstruct the efforts of political leadership to manipulate everything by clever stratagems, techniques, and force of personality. And like Machiavelli himself, the neo-Machiavellians were unsociological creatures in their mental processes. For them, as for him, "the autonomy of politics" signified something more dubious than discarding metaphysics and natural law. Also included was a depiction of the political realm as free from sociological or historical determination. Personalities were the only actors on a Machiavellian political stage; impersonal forces counted for nothing.

What makes the absence of sociology so glaring is that it was not for lack of availability that the subject was neglected. Educated as they were in the classics, absolutists could have found much to edify them in the *Politics* of Aristotle. Nowhere before or after had the causes and cures of instability been better discussed. In his sociology of class struggles and ideological conflict, Aristotle isolated the seeds of destruction; and in his formula of mixed government, he fashioned an institutional remedy. A revised and royalist Aristotelianism, an Aristotelianism that endeavored to adapt lessons of the city-state to the needs of feudal monarchy, was a distinct historical possibility. That absolutists failed to embark upon such an intellectual undertaking was their loss, and when the dormant wisdom was finally reactivated, it was for Montesquieu's purpose of indicting absolutism.

2. The Critique of Monarchy

Bits and pieces came within the purview of the new political science, but the whole eluded it. Now it is precisely the search for a comprehensive vision that characterizes all of Montesquieu's work. Against the methodological individualism of the utilitarians and social contract theorists, he held that society is more than a conglomerate of individuals, that institutions have a life of their own, that the whole is greater than the sum of its parts. To be sure, Montesquieu upheld the sanctity of the individual and felt that institutions should serve humanitarian ends, but these were his moral postures, not his methodological premises. For purposes of empirical research and adequate explanation, society must be methodologically approached as a structural whole, the integrity of which is assured by the functions that institutions serve and the roles that individuals play.

Montesquieu's political analysis features a methodological presumption against the causal efficacy of historical accidents.

It is not chance that rules the world . . . . There are general causes . . . and [all] accidents are controlled by these causes . . . . In a word, the main trend draws with it all particular accidents.[4]

The relevant general causes are linked with the newly conceived socio-political whole as its creators, its supports, and finally, through their malfunctioning, its decomposition. Peculiar to each age and differentiating each nation within an age is a totality, an *esprit général*, the character of an age and a series of national characters respectively. Soil, territorial expanse, climate, religion, laws, maxims of government, customs and mores — these and more forge the complex chain of causation, "physical" and "moral," whose outcome is the *esprit général*.

The explanatory power of these causal factors increases when joined to another of Montesquieu's generalizing concepts, the distinction between the "nature" and the "principle" of government. Essentially Montesquieu meant the political system when he spoke of the "nature" of government, while the social system is the referent of the "principle." In studying the political system, the number of rulers and the manner in which power is exercised are decisive. For example, monarchy is one-man rule, but arbitrary power is obstructed by intermediary bodies. The "principle" is the structure of social values — honor in monarchies, virtue in ancient republics, fear in despotic states — that activates a society, the "spring" that sets its parts in motion. Political science is the study of the interactions of the political and social systems.

Description, analysis, and criticism participate simultaneously in Montesquieu's political sociology. Any adequate discussion of his model of monarchy must be prefaced by the caveat that he is to be read on more than one level. Each crisp, almost staccato, concatenation of sentences is both description and stricture, analysis and indictment. Now a series of damaging close-ups of particular institutions and groups, now a landscape showing the hideous relationship of these particulars, Montesquieu's political sociology is a radical critique of politics and society in the *ancien régime*. King, ministers, nobles, and clergy are ridiculed first as individually absurd and then as collectively odious in their complicity with absolutism. On still another level, Montesquieu's criticism extends to the entire ethos of aristocratic society, regardless of its immediate political significance. By the time he finished his sociological exposé, very little of the *ancien régime* remained immune to his accusations. Thinking in sociological terms about the actors of the old order meant reducing them to the puppets of a system too pathetic to be tragic. To understand all is to forgive nothing.

We shall begin by reviewing Montesquieu's pitiless description-critique of the aristocratic ethos and then allow the other planes of his criticism to filter into the discussion, always mixing analysis with criticism as Montesquieu himself did.

Measured by the yardstick of civic virtue, "honor," the motor force of aristocratic society, withers to an embarrassingly diminutive stature. Aristocratic society "subsists independently of the love of our country, of the thirst of true glory, of self-denial, of the sacrifice of our dearest interests, and of all those heroic virtues which we admire in the ancients, and to us are known only by tradition."[5] Mandeville's fable equating private vices with public order was acceptable to Montesquieu with the single revision that it is much more relevant to aristocratic France than to bourgeois Britain. Ambition fires aristocratic society which, on careful examinations, turns out to be an ever so courteous footrace for preferences. Self-interested action is the rule, and the honorific ethos is highly individualistic — a corporate individualism wherein the focal points of selfish calculation are personal glory and the interest of the family dynasty. Huizinga remarks, by way of modifying Burckhardt, that a species of individualism was already full-blown in the late feudal ethos,[6] an insight which represents a recovery of lessons already taught by Montesquieu.

Following the feudal ethos costs nothing emotionally, but how painful was the acquisition of Greek and Roman civic virtue. Anticlerical though he was, Montesquieu could express the marvel of republican self-repression only through a comparison with the fanaticism of the monastic order.

> The love of our country is conducive to a purity of morals, and the latter is again conducive to the former. The less we are able to satisfy our private passions, the more we abandon ourselves to those of a general nature. How comes it that monks are so fond of their order? It is owing to the very cause that renders the order insupportable. Their rule debars them from all those things by which the ordinary passions are fed; there remains therefore only this passion for the very rule that torments them. The more austere it is . . . , the more it curbs their inclinations, the more force it gives to the only passion left them.[7]

In its arduous self-renunciation, its dedication to duty and "constant preference of public to private interest,"[8] the concept of civic virtue is a kind of Kantianism before Kant and is unique among systems of social values in deserving designation as moral. "In well-regulated monarchies, there are good subjects, and very few good men, for to be a good man a good intention is necessary, and we should love our country, not so much on our own account, as out of regard to the community."[9] To someone of Montesquieu's temperament, civic virtue is actually much more awesome than the categorical imperative. Individualist, universalist, and disinterested, the categorical imperative undershoots and overshoots socio-political content and is the negation of life-giving human passion. Civic virtue, contrariwise, once had an historically concrete existence and reaffirmed the grandeur of emotion through its very denial. There is something staggering about the thought of an entire society consecrating itself to the communal good. "Every man is capable of doing good to one man, but it is like playing God to contribute to the well-being of a whole society."[10]

Honor is defined as "the prejudice of every person and rank."[11] Feudal in origin, honor is "both child and parent" of the nobility.[12] As a lifestyle, it features "a certain nobleness in our virtues, a kind of frankness in our morals, and a particular politeness in our behavior." None of these qualities are esteemed for their intrinsic worth, however, but rather as conspicuous marks of pre-eminent social status. Supposed grandeur of soul is linked with haughty disdain for the habits and ways of the multitude: "in proportion as [aristocratic] frankness is commended, that of the common people is despised, which has nothing but truth and simplicity for its object." Or consider the motive behind politeness: "[Politeness] arises from a desire of distinguishing ourselves. It is pride that renders us polite; we are flattered with being taken notice of for behavior that shows we are not of a mean condition." Nobility, then, means having someone to look down upon and being in a perpetual race with one's peers for distinction, but it does not preclude an egalitarian impulse of sorts within the aristocracy proper. There is a second motive behind politeness: "One man excessively great renders everybody else little. Hence that regard which is paid our fellow-subjects."[13] Refusing to traffic in the impersonal bourgeois market of goods and services, the members of the nobility are nonetheless preoccupied with exchanging symbols of personal esteem.

At bottom honor is sham, conceit, and pretense. Where its presides over societies "the actions of men are judged, not as virtuous, but as shining; not as just, but as great; not as reasonable, but as extraordinary."[14] For all its inconvenience, however, honor has one enduring positive trait: it is a barrier to the incursions of arbitrary royal power. Subjects of the highest rank defer to the royal will but with the stipulation that the king's dictates may not transgress the code of honor.

By itself honor cannot withstand the prince. It is formidable only if its inegalitarian social psychology is rooted in institutions that perpetuate hereditary inequality. Which is to say that monarchy rests on privilege, the privilege of the nobility, church, and cities. The nobles have their fiefs, the clergy their immunities, and the cities their residues of medieval autonomy. Montesquieu was perfectly candid in his description of French society. He described privilege as the abuse it was instead of having recourse to organic language or the Great Chain analogy, whose evocation was a sure means of masking harsh social realities. "Far am I from being prejudiced in favor of the privileges of the clergy . . . The question [, however,] is not whether their jurisdiction was justly established, but whether it is in fact established."[15] Any kind of bulwark to absolutism is better than none at all.

Honor has a centripetal side that draws the nobility into the service of the king. "There is nothing that honor more strongly recommends to the nobility than to serve their prince in a military capacity. And, indeed, this is their favorite profession, because its dangers, its success, and even its miscarriages are the road to grandeur."[16] But even as honor impels the nobility into the service of the state, it promotes conduct in office that is totally unbecoming to the bureaucrat. Modern objectives of a dispassionate sense of duty, conscientious execution of routine procedures, and rigid discipline — the mainstays of bureaucracy — were incompatible with the honorific ethos. One or the other had to retreat, and very often the nobles in the officer corps sacrificed the new to what was time-honored and aristocratic. Consider the habit officers had of temporarily abandoning their regiments to run off and frolic in Paris for a few days.[17] Such actions belittled the bureaucratic state and emitted the scent of feudal anarchy.

From the standpoint of Machiavellism, the identifications inculcated by honor were at once too general and too particular, too cosmopolitan and too localistic. The rhythms of Corneille's *Le Cid*, a timeless embodiment of the feudal ethos, were penned in exquisite French nuances, but its epic content is Spanish. A European-wide passion of aristocracies, honor overreached the national boundaries and statist crystallizations of social sentiment so crucial to raison d'état enthusiasts. And when it was not squandering its energies supranationally, honor rushed to the opposite extreme, subnational and hence antinational identifications: personal pride, the family dynasty, fiefs, provincial assemblies, and "particular liberties" that were really particular abuses. In 1757 the French army, under the inept leadership of Soubise, sustained a disastrous defeat at Rossbach. Bernis, a minister, reported that "The Court was very interested in the lost battle insofar as it affected M. de Soubise, but ignored its effects upon the State."[18] There is the spirit of honor.

Monarchy, then, is both too diffuse and too fragmented, but neither of these saves it from being too centralized. Monarchy becomes harmfully centralized "when the prince . . . calls the state to his capital, the capital to his court, the court to his own person."[19] And he is issuing such a call, whether he knows it or not. Mute but sociologically perceivable forces have their own logic of centralization, a logic whose ultimate results are political irresponsibility and social malaise.

The fate of monarchy is to experience centralization in the form of a court and capital which flourish at the expense of the provinces. Living in the countryside without access to Paris, Frenchmen feel, is a form of bleak exile. Each and every road leads to the capital: "In the province Paris [is] a boreal pole to attract you; the intendant an astral pole to repel you."[20] Domination of the capital city over the agrarian hinterland is so dramatic because "a great capital creates the *esprit général* of a nation; it is Paris that makes France."[21] And Paris, like everything else, is merely a way-station along the road to the court at Versailles. The court takes its opinions from the king, the capital from the court, and the countryside from the capital.

Worse still is the aggravation of centralization brought about by the economics of monarchy. Once again the king is gratuitously awarded influence he does not need and should not have; and more than ever, the provinces lose to the capital and other cities. How monarchical economics combines short-term good with long-term evil is worth examining in detail.

Under monarchy, luxury is the primary stimulant of economic production.[22] Trade of luxurious items grows in direct proportion to the populousness of cities, especially in the capital. In a compact urban environment desires, wants, and fancies multiply rapidly because "the inhabitants are filled with notions of vanity and actuated by an ambition of distinguishing themselves by trifles."[23] Ornate carriages, gold and silver plate, perfumes, wigs, and headdresses are objects representative of those exchanged on the market of superfluous goods. Changing whims of women's fashion signal the rising fortunes of some craftsmen and the bewildering decline of others. In short, the analogue of the monarchical state is an aristocratic society, and consequently economic demand stems from the noble caste and its *bourgeois gentilhommes* imitators.

This aristocratic thirst for luxuries is as old as the Middle Ages and yet as new, in one regard, as the ascendancy of the monarch. For in the eighteenth century the king is upstaging the privileged orders. All eyes are on the prince; his preferences of fashion and style are so paramount in the social psychology of monarchy that soon the nobles are seen mimicking the king's latest fancy. "The prince impresses the character of his mind on the court; the court, on the city; the city on the provinces."[24]

In sum, every time the king indulges his taste for a luxury, he also asserts, knowingly or not, that he is the pinnacle of French society. And every time the bourgeoisie produces a luxurious good, it asserts two things about its particular social situation: one, that it has economic virtues which an aristocratic society needs but disdains, and, two, that it aspires to aristocratic status. The ethos of honor does not permit the noble or the *bourgeois gentilhomme* to engage in productive activity; but the ordinary bourgeois, spurred by the venality of offices bearing noble titles, does display a capacity for economic prowess. Hence Montesquieu favored the very venality that *philosophes* and royal ministers alike denounced as scandalous. Montesquieu knew better: "the method of attaining to honors through riches inspires and cherishes industriousness, a thing extremely wanting in this kind of government."[25]

Montesquieu was aware of both the potentialities and the limitations of economic growth in an aristocratic society. Historically, an economy of luxuries is an advanced development, as comparison with primitive egalitarianism well attests. A purely agricultural economy cannot shatter the bonds of subsistence. "Each individual would live from the land and would derive from it just exactly what he needed to keep from dying of hunger."[26] Without a circulation of wealth, without arts and sciences, misery is the common lot. In contrast to primitive agrarianism, which is static and stagnant, the economy of modern monarchy has a kind of inherent dynamic. To be sure, the economy is still primarily agricultural, but aristocratic demands for luxuries foster the growth of a class of merchants, craftsmen, and artisans. The middle class produces more than it consumes and sells the surplus on the market which has replaced the infrequent trade and barter of a subsistence economy. Of the two kinds of riches, land and "movable effects,"[27] primitive agrarianism enjoys only the former. Monarchical commerce enjoys both, and therefore its stock of wealth is not fixed once and for all in the dismal mire of subsistence.

Although capable of enrichment, the economy of modern monarchy cannot achieve self-sustained growth. The trade of luxuries proves to be more an economy of consumption than production, and with rather low consumption at that. Consumption is basically the prerogative of the upper crust in an aristocratic society; mass production and the consumer's society are unknown. Nor were Colbert's mercantilist directives suitable to his hopes of maximizing production. Hostile though he was to the aristocracy, Colbert remained convinced that the quality of marketable commodities was more important than their quantity. Not having experienced the coarse but vigorous spirit of democratic society, he could not imagine that filthy British coal was a better route to economic progress than delicate French tapestries.

Other difficulties of equal magnitude were endemic to the economics of monarchy. When society is aristocratic, superabundance and destitution are found coexisting within the same nation. As one wit quipped, "In France nine-tenths of the population die of hunger and one-tenth of indigestion."[28] It is only at first that luxury appears to serve the interests of all social classes and not just that of the privileged Initially, luxury is useful to the poor because it leads the nobility to disgorge the glut of wealth it has accumulated through class domination. "The augmentation of private wealth is owing to [the privileged] having deprived one part of the citizens of their necessary support; this must therefore be restored to them." The greater the inequality of wealth, the greater the amount of luxury there should be — otherwise the little people will be crushed. And that is why, in a properly functioning monarchy, "luxury ought continually to increase, and to grow more extensive as it rises from the laborer to the artificer, to the merchant, to the magistrate, to the nobility, to the great officers of state, up to the very prince."[29]

But at the same time that the trade of luxuries palliates the harsh contrast between affluence and destitution, it brings about a new form of misery. Cities, the capital especially, are all life and vitality. Their booming, buzzing confusion is the healthy sound of industry. By contrast, the provinces are depleted and lethargic, and their ill-fortune is directly linked to the good fortune of the cities: for the flush of urban life derives from a parasitical withdrawal of resources from the countryside. Trade of luxuries circulates wealth within cities with the result that the bourgeoisie absorbs riches discharged by the obese aristocracy. The provinces, however, remain backwaters drained of human resources by the flow of population to the cities. The city-country gap is great and necessarily widening, because of the inexorable logic of economic forces. Overcrowded cities versus depopulated countryside, centers of ostentatious affluence versus rural squalor — such is the nature of monarchical centralization.[30]

Equally damning, monarchical centralization has placed irresponsible political power in the hands of the prince. Though not yet arbitrary and despotic, the prince of Montesquieu's model is already dangerously absolute. No matter how flourishing the intermediary bodies, the throne is still the seat and source of all power.[31] It makes all the difference in the world that the group politics of monarchy is located at court. All interests must approach the throne, all must bow to royalty. Consequently, the study of monarchical politics is largely the study of the changing moods and whims of the most spoiled person in France.

To explain centralization in the disastrous form of personalized rule, Montesquieu adduced four factors: economics, charisma of office, class stalemate, and centralization of honor. Enough has already been said about the economy of luxuries; we have noted that revolutions of fashion come from the pinnacle of French society, the king. Religious in origin, charismatic kingship is quite another matter. Peasants believe in the divinely inspired nature of kingly office: this Montesquieu proved by pointing to the widespread belief in magical powers that adhere to kingship, especially the conviction that the king's touch can cure disease.[32] Another factor sponsoring arbitrary political authority is the stalemate of class tensions. In its value structure French society is wrought in the mold of aristocratic honor, but in terms of brute social power neither the aristocracy nor the bourgeoisie predominates. The nobility has its privileges and lofty social status;

the bourgeoisie, economic wealth. As long as class stalemate continues, the political realm will remain free from social obstruction.[33]

Finally, the centralization of honor in the prince contributed its share to the cult of the leader. Once a direct emanation from the dispersed nobility, honor in the modern monarchy is naturalized at court.[34] The eighteenth-century nobility still luxuriates in the code of honor but its radiance comes second hand, originating in and mediated by the prince. Feudal rebellions are no more, and eighteenth-century aristocrats know of no more exemplary act than death in defense of the crown. Both the code of honor and the weight of historical precedent stand behind aristocratic deference to royalty.

> The English nobility buried themselves with Charles the First under the ruins of the throne; and before that time, when Philip II endeavored to tempt the French with the allurement of liberty, the crown was constantly supported by a nobility who think it an honor to obey a king, but consider it the lowest disgrace to share power with the people.[35]

No one wants to grant the prince arbitrary power, but everyone — peasantry, bourgeoisie, and nobility — is trapped into furthering the cult of the individual.

Given that monarchy is one-man rule, it was inevitable that Montesquieu should take great interest in the nature of leadership. He never doubted that examples disseminated from on high have a profound impact on overall social psychology. One reason, he believed, for the alienation of monarchy from the public-spirited character of ancient republics lies in the sycophantic, grasping, selfish behavior of courtiers.[36] Now if the courtiers' influence on the populace is of such magnitude, how much greater must be that of the prince. "The manners of a prince contribute as much as the laws themselves to liberty; like these he may transform men into brutes and brutes into men."[37] Even more important than the force of example, the monarch is fully responsible for leadership in policymaking and execution, since his powers encompass both the executive and legislative functions.[38] When he does not rule, the state staggers from crisis to crisis, drifting aimlessly.

Yet the prince does not possess the Olympian remoteness which might make one-man rule less chaotic. As much as everyone else, or even more so, the prince's perceptions are shaped by and contained within the social psychology of honor. Not even Louis XIV, architect of the transformation of honor from anarchistic feudal passion into politically innocuous court etiquette, questioned the social pre-eminence of the nobility. The king was not outside honor but rather its culminating point. Much to Colbert's chagrin, it was easier to convince Louis to update the army than to gain his support for naval construction. And why? Because the navy was overrun with the scum of the earth, and warfare on the seas did not entail heroic individual combat.[39] Honor sensitizes the king to perception of some facts and blinds him to others. It distorts information and saturates the decision-making premises of the king. Whether policy will be based on rational calculation is problematic because honor is a passion; and even when the king does rationally calculate, the end maximized will frequently be that dictated by honor — the quest for *gloire*.

With honor and absolute power centralized in the prince, politics is reduced to the pettiness of court jealousies and intrigues. Early in his career, Montesquieu voiced his awareness of the unremitting struggle of ministers, priests, women, and courtiers for the mind of the absolute prince, and the passing years did not diminish his concern. "If [the prince] commits some evil act, it is practically always one that was suggested to him. . . . A prince has passions; the minister stirs them up."[40] All too frequently a minister advances schemes confounding his power with the prince's glory.

Rica, one of Montesquieu's Persians, remarks that "the character of Western kings cannot be known until they have passed through the two great tests of mistress and religious advisor."[41] The Jesuits were everywhere. Rather than launching a frontal assault on the courts of monarchs, they acclimated themselves to courtly pleasures but never forgot their true mission — subversion of worldliness from within. Ultramontanism became a kind of penance, a necessary condition for the absolution of royal sins in the confessional. Mistresses, too, were important political figures. They made or broke ministers even when they knew nothing about political issues. The Countess du Barry was one such influential paragon of ignorance. "At councils of state," one historian notes, "she would sit on the arm of the royal chair, making faces at the ministers, and interfering in national affairs with the irresponsibility of a pet monkey."[42] And yet her pouting could lead to the elevation of a Maupeou or the dismissal of a Choiseul.

The other contestant for the role of authoritative advice-giver was the nobility. Courtiers were a permanent noble group near the throne, and they did not hesitate to induce the king in favor of one policy or against another. Nothing good could come from the influence of these leeches who shared in "the natural ignorance of the nobility" and were in every respect contemptible.

> Ambition in idleness; meanness mixed with pride; a desire of riches without industry; aversion to truth; flattery, perfidy, violation of engagements, contempt of civil duties, fear of the prince's virtue, hope from his weakness, but above all, a perpetual ridicule cast upon virtue are, I think, the characteristics by which most courtiers in all ages have been distinguished."[43]

Vanity of women, fanaticism of priests, stupidity of courtiers, and ambition of ministers are hardly the stuff out of which rational policies are made and executed. Actually it hardly matters. So deep and systemic were the disabilities of monarchy that even the best advisors could not serve more than a stopgap function, temporarily compensating for permanent deficiences. The only plea that can be entered on behalf of Occidental absolutism is that it was less despicable than the absolutism of the Orient, an examination of which will be our next order of business. Once the veil is torn from Orientalism, the more plausible future for France, should she continue to abide with absolutism, will be offered by recounting Montesquieu's analysis of Spain, the pattern country for the disease of Western absolutism in its advanced stages. Then it will be clear that the only remedy for systemic ills is a systemic change, the entrance into a post-absolutist, post-aristocratic, post-*ancien régime* phase of history, such as England represented.

3. Omnipotence and Impotence

A sociological exposé of absolute power was sorely needed, and Montesquieu busily set about the task. An empirical sociologist, he was as adverse to models of evil that are "nowhere" as he was to the "nowhere" world of utopias. For all the instances of despotism in history, it was only in the Orient, he held, that despotic power was "in some measure naturalized." Allowing for a certain bending of labels, it can be argued that during the sixteenth and seventeenth centuries, the leading nations of the East, as well as of the West, were governed by royal absolutisms. And being educated in the classics, Montesquieu knew that some two millenia into the past Aristotle had already remarked on the spirit of Asian servility. How easy to believe that despotism had always been, was now, and presumably always would be the lot of the Orient. Only in the Orient was the destructive fury of arbitrary government fully discharged. Only in the Orient were the archetypical features of despotism so glaringly transparent that the sociologist could construct an ideal-type of human misery as a system of governance and a way of life.

What is the anatomy of a despotic social system, its "principle" in Montesquieu's terminology? If ancient republics had their civic virtue, and modern monarchies their honor, then despotism is moved by fear. In republics men are citizens, in monarchies they are subjects, in despotisms slaves. Of necessity honor is excluded from despotisms, for whence could its spirit spring? Despotism is totally inimical to the existence of the noble caste, the carrier of honor. Some men, it is true, must be appointed to perform essential political or military functions. But their position is precarious and subject to immediate reversal. "A man who has public esteem on his side is never sure he will not be dishonored on the morrow. Today, here he is, general of the army; perhaps tomorrow the prince will make him a cook."[44] Consequently, a privileged social class cannot emerge, and since despotism is a mass rather than a class society, "no one person can prefer himself to another."[45] No nobility, no honor.

As fear is the motor of despotism, society is atomized and man isolated from man.[46] Life in a republic, spent in the public forum, consists of a continuous exchange of sentiments and opinions; communication is integral to a way of life. Under monarchies political participation is restricted, class exclusiveness abides, and communication correspondingly declines. In despotic states, where alone all traces of liberty are absent, communication is virtually nonexistent.

Unremittingly pernicious, despotism dehumanizes and emasculates, causing society to stagnate in all its aspects. "Man's portion here, like that of the beasts, is instinct, compliance, and punishment."[47] Montesquieu's description of education in a despotic polity is fittingly brief. "Unquestioning obedience supposes ignorance in the person that obeys"; progress in education would be an anomaly in a socio-political system wherein "learning proves dangerous, emulation fatal."[48] Economic progress is just as unlikely. Often the prince declares himself sole proprietor of all lands in his empire, and heir to

all his subjects. The frequency of confiscations and the lack of assurance that riches can be handed from father to son stifle initiative.
Should the spirit of industry survive such blows, it will surely succumb
to exorbitant interest rates. "Poverty and the precariousness of property in a despotic state render usury natural, each person raising the
value of his money in proportion to the danger he sees in lending it."
Under such circumstances, merchant trade may indeed persist but
only as a small-scale operation.[49]

"Silence" and "the desert" are the words most evocative of the
spirit of despotic society. About the despotic wasteland it may be said
that

> in such a condition, there is no place for industry; because the fruit
> thereof is uncertain: and consequently no culture of the earth; no
> navigation, nor use of the commodities that may be imported by sea;
> no commodious building . . . ; no knowledge of the face of the earth;
> no account of time; no arts; no letters; no society; and which is worst
> of all, continual fear, and danger of violent death; and the life of man,
> solitary, poor, nasty, brutish and short.

Hobbes' state of nature is Montesquieu's Leviathan; Hobbes' Leviathan creates the unbearable state of nature and war of all against all
that it was designed to suppress. As for the silence of despotism, "this
tranquility cannot be called a peace: no, it is only the silence of those
towns which the enemy is ready to invade."[50] It is in republics that
speech is most audible. Sovereignty in republics is democratized, and
the universality of political participation inflates each man's feeling of
power. Anyone doubting this need only consult Roman history.
When the republic fell, men were traumatized by their awareness of
personal impotence, and they longed for a leader: their broken spirits
cried out for someone to whom they could submit.[51] History silenced
Rome, but in the despotisms of the East political speech has never
been heard; "there reigns in Asia a servile spirit . . . and it is impossible to find in all the histories of that region a single passage which
evinces a freedom of spirit."[52]

A despotic society is like a man wasting away of consumption.
Economics is typical of the way the organs of the body politic atrophy
and die. "Under this sort of government nothing is repaired or im-
proved . . . everything is drawn from, but nothing restored to, the
earth; the ground lies untilled, and the whole country becomes a

desert."[53] Like an ignorant savage who cuts down a tree to gather its fruit, despotism can consume and destroy but cannot produce or construct.[54] Worse, it is self-destructive and self-consuming and leaves behind a desert on which are strewn the bones of the enemy which is its own self. The sociologist can discuss the conditions under which civic virtue or honor are corrupted, but when he comes to despotism he confronts a unique phenomenon. Despotism is corrupt by its very nature, disintegration is intrinsic to its innermost essence.[55]

What kind of political system is it that inflicts such deep and crippling damage upon society? To answer this question Montesquieu had to divest himself of the entire conglomerate of ideas associated with "enlightened despotism." Eastern monarchies are not rationalized states or efficient bureaucratic machines. Quite the contrary. Instead of an impersonal government, the state is absorbed into a single person. *"L'état, c'est moi,"* a hyperbole in France, is accurate in reference to Asian monarchs.[56] Ubiquitous personalism prevents the development of the division of labor in the bureaucratic apparatus; indeed, the compartmentalization of duties and functions is so retarded that it is the simplicity of despotic government that is striking rather than the alleged grandeur and complexity of bureaucratic empires. Sir John Chardin reports that Persia does not even have a council of state. In ages long past, administration was separated from the household of Western monarchs, unlike the perpetual personalized rule of Asia where slaves and eunuchs attached to the monarch's family may be political officials of the highest rank.

Policy in a personalized polity is only as rational and informed as is the prince, but hopes of his enlightenment are without foundation. For if blind obedience supposes ignorance on the part of the subject, "the same it supposes in him that commands. He has no occasion to deliberate, to doubt, to reason; he has only to will."[57] Skillful advice-givers could, perhaps, save the ruler from his ignorance; their historical appearance, however, is limited to Western monarchies. The wisest of Occidental princes appoint advisors on the basis of merit,[58] unlike the Orient in which slaves and eunuchs monopolize the advice-giving function: miserable, debased, and wretched creatures, their attention is directed less toward dispassionate rules or rational policy than to a seething desire to externalize their resentment at the expense of helpless souls.[59] Again, it is vile eunuchs who "educate" princes, such education as transpires "in a prison where eunuchs corrupt their hearts and debase their understandings." An absentee monarch like Louis XV is exceptional in the West but characteristic of the East, where the prince is totally taken up by the passion that flows unrestrained in the seraglio. Both monarch and subjects in a despotic state are overcome by passion: the prince by the pleasure principle, the subjects by fear. Languishing in the seraglio, ignorant of affairs of state, and unconcerned about public well-being, the absentee despotic prince transfers the whole of his absolute power to a vizier: one despot begets another.[60]

The problems bedeviling despotic administration multiply as one passes from the prince and vizier to the lower level functionaries. At each level of the hierarchy, the relevant official is charged with a magnitude of power that makes him a petty despot. Just as absolute power devolves absolutely upon the vizier, so also is power communicated to the lower officialdom whole and entire, with no differentiating or limiting factors intervening. "The vizier himself is the despotic prince; and each particular officer is the vizier."[61] An administrator is endowed with too much and too little power: too much because he is rendered despotic, too little because the prince or vizier may annihilate him. Strictly speaking, despotic bureaucracy is not hierarchical or pyramidal. Naturally, some men are on top and others on the bottom, but they are not conjoined by a transmission of authority or communication, nor by a stringent subordination of office to office. Analysts of despotism must disabuse themselves of preconceived notions of government as a pyramidal structure whose apex is the prince. Hierarchy of some variety does exist but a void of discontinuity severs any given office from both the next lower and the next higher.

If one substitutes a horizontal for a vertical perspective, the discontinuity of offices is easily accounted for. Officials in any two provinces are not linked in a hierarchical relation of superiority and subordination; as a matter of fact, they do not engage in association of any kind. What matters is the tie between sovereign and local functionary, a relationship unmediated by higher layers of officialdom. All of this underscores once more how unrationalized despotic administration really is, how little impersonal its workings, and how frustrated the advance of the division of labor. Not even the generalized form in which orders are sent down from above can be considered an aspect of rational bureaucracy. A despotic sovereign necessarily states his orders universally because, in his unrelieved ignorance of everything

important, he differs from the ideal Western monarch, who is informed of the particularity of customs and problems within each province.[62] Moreover, it is not a rational rule that the despot applies
indiscriminately, but rather an act of will and passion. The contrast is
not between the general and rational versus the particular and irrational; no, that cannot be, for in a despotic government it is irrationality and ignorance that are the parents of generality.

The most well-meaning of bureaucrats will find it difficult to ex-
ecute the prince's dictates. Regulations are in constant flux in a
government in which mercurial will prevails rather than regularities of
law.[63] Primitivism of communications in a backward society further
negates the efforts of the provincial functionary to decipher the royal
will. Administrative policy degenerates into an uncoordinated chaos
in which the administrator tries to guess what course of action the
prince may happen to favor: "How can the magistrate follow a will he
does not know? He must certainly follow his own."[64] Of course, no
bureaucracy eliminates discretion, but what havoc must result when
each bureaucrat has total discretion in his bailiwick.

Not least among the evils that plague despotic administration is
chronic political corruption. The root of the problem is not difficult to
find. Economic retardation, especially severe among despotic nations,
makes regular salary payments impossible. Neither the ancient republic nor the modern monarchy has a dynamic economy, but each
supplements pay scales with satisfying nonmaterial incentives. In a
republic "the recompenses of the state consist only of public attesta-
tions of [civic] virtue"; in a monarchy "the prince's rewards would
consist only of marks of distinction, if the distinctions established by
honor were not attended with luxury: . . . the prince, therefore, is
obliged to confer such honors as lead to wealth." But in despotic
governments "the prince who confers rewards has nothing to bestow
but money."[65] Since the despot cannot supply the bureaucrat with
sufficient pay or compensatory nonmaterial incentives, the nominal
servants of society become its worst enemies. Soon administrators are
seen despoiling the countryside: "the great men will be prompted to
use a thousand oppressive methods, imagining they have no other
property than the gold and silver which they are able to seize upon by
violence."[66] Corruption reaches up into the highest ranks of government servants, and embezzlement of public funds is a common
occurrence.[67]

Although corruption is rife and oppression by bureaucrats common, the malpractices of the administrative monster are confined within a circle circumscribed by the prince. He intimidates and controls his officialdom with the fear that is the emblem of despotic government. Have we stated that despotism is rule without law? That statement must now be amended:

> It is necessary that the people should be judged by laws, and the great men by the caprice of the prince, that the lives of the lowest subjects should be safe, and the pasha's head ever in danger.[68]

> It is in the interest of an unjust prince that he who executes royal wishes, however tyrannical they may be, should observe, in the manner of executing them, the most exact justice.[69]

By afflicting the bureaucrats with fear, the despot counteracts corruption and buys off the populace. And he does more. It is worth repeating: he also eliminates the danger of hereditary offices, the danger, in other words, of a privileged social class countervailing his power.

Despite the prince's efforts to divert the bureaucracy from exploitation to just governance of the lower classes, the people are not excepted from the disintegrative effects of fear. Fear in a despotic state pertains not to this or that class, but is an engulfing system that allows no qualifications. Scattered throughout provinces remote from the prince, irregularly paid, and without the consolation of nonmaterial rewards, administrators are never reduced to passive instruments of the royal will. As domination ebbs and flows between prince and office holders, the people are continually buffeted back and forth between alleviation of misery and outright victimhood until uncertainty and anxiety erode the human spirit.

Relentless in his exposure of the chaos of despotism, Montesquieu urges his reader to acknowledge one last defect of despotic politics. Where the king's power is so absolute as to eliminate legality, a law of political succession cannot develop. At the death of the despot, the state is thrown into the horrors of civil war as factions within the deceased prince's family, or even personages with no claim to a blood relationship, battle for the throne.

After examining the political and social systems of despotism, one must agree that, either as a means of governance or as a way of life, the pernicious consequences of arbitrary power are without redemption. And yet

most nations are subject to this very government. This is easily ac-

counted for. To form a moderate government, it is necessary to combine the several powers, to regulate, temper, and set them in motion;
to give, as it were, ballast to one, in order to enable it to counterpoise
the other. This is a masterpiece of legislation, rarely produced by
chance, and seldom attained by prudence. On the contrary, a despotic government . . . is uniform throughout; and as passions only are
requisite to establish it, this is what every capacity may reach.[70]

Not rational planning but mindless emotion paves the way to
bureaucratic empire, which itself spreads irrationality far and wide
across the social universe.

Even the despot will be dissatisfied with the fruits of despotism,
since the irony of absolute power is its inseparability from powerlessness. If despotic society is economically stagnant, then the state is
denied economic power. If administrators are corrupt and locked in
an incessant struggle with the crown, then the state is without governing capability. If society is an amorphous mass permeated by fear
and the prince a symbol of naked power, then the internal weakness of
the nation invites foreign attack. Still more disturbing to the prince,
the politics of despotism imperils the very life of the despot. Asiatic
monarchs, usurpers all to contested thrones, rule de facto rather than
de jure. The fear with which they level society obliterates all traces of
popular affection and charisma of office. As poetic justice would have
it, the victimizer is victimized by popular rebellion or military coup,
and in a flash a new despot sits on the throne. Religion may prolong
the prince's longevity by lending the crown a semblance of authority
and charisma. But surely the impact of the sacred will be insignificant, considering that in Mohammedan countries success in a coup
constitutes proof of its divine sanction.[71]

Not a single individual benefits from the paradoxically systematic
disorder of despotism. Only when society is viewed as something
greater than the sum total of human beings composing it are the functions of despotism visible. For it is a rationally intelligible pattern of
events that mutilates man with fear and irrationality day in and day
out. Conceptual understanding requires that despotism be com-
prehended as a logically coherent social and political structure; the
reality revealed by analytical procedure, however, is a condition of
perpetual destruction of structure and differentiation, the levelling
chaos and illogic of men in panic, an amorphous society that is the
negation of society.

Surveying the terrain he had covered during his examination of Oriental despotism, Montesquieu could take deep satisfaction. He was now armed with two intellectual weapons in his struggle against the Machiavellian architects of royal absolutism in France. First, to utilize Machiavellism, he could argue, was to commit a mistake analogous to what philosophers now call a "category mistake." In a passage originally meant for *The Spirit of the Laws,* Montesquieu charged that "it was the delirium of Machiavelli to have given to princes, for the maintenance of their grandeur, principles which are only necessary under despotism, and which are useless, dangerous, and even impracticable under monarchy."[72] Had not Machiavelli informed the prince that it was better to be feared than loved,[73] that the prince should atomize society by striking down the nobility? Was it not Machiavelli who systematized the application of cruelty into a rational method, even as the few intelligent despots in the East maintain their position by "refining" the art of cruelty — the art, that is, of destroying human ties, ever a threat to the established oppressor?[74] Machiavellism belongs to the despotic, not the monarchical, type.

Second, Montesquieu was out to defeat Machiavellism within the terms of its own language of power. Absolute power and impotence, oppositional terms in matters of logic, are identical in matters of fact. That is the lesson taught by Oriental despotism.

4. Hope and Despair

Montesquieu never tried to predict France's future. He did, however, walk up and down Europe with a lantern, looking for clues as to where royal absolutism might lead. The two countries to which his writings return time and again are England and Spain. England exemplified what France might become were she to follow her island rival in casting off the yoke of absolutism; Spain was a grim reminder of what was in store for a country that continued too long under arbitrary power.

Present British freedom was forged in "the fires of discord and sedition."[75] Institutions, quiet but eloquent witnesses of the past, testify to the former existence of absolutism: even in the eighteenth century the form of absolute monarchy lay superimposed upon a free British government.[76] Henry VII, a typical Renaissance prince, initiated the strategy of absolutism by elevating the commons and chastising the lords.[77] By Henry VIII's reign, absolutism could move into its mature phase because the nobility was powerless and the people had not yet begun to feel their power. "In the interval, the king became a tyrant."[78] Later, religious differences turned large segments of society against the crown. Although the monarchy survived the Puritan revolution, absolutism did not.

Neither in its "nature" nor in its "principle" did England conform to Montesquieu's model of monarchy. Representing something entirely novel, England had to be analyzed separately — its political system in the famous Book XI, chapter 6, its social system in Book XIX, chapter 27. Politically, royal absolutism yielded to constitutional monarchy; socially, aristocratic society yielded to democratic society. What Tocqueville discovered in the nineteenth century by contrasting America with Europe, Montesquieu had discovered within Europe a century earlier by contrasting bourgeois English mores with aristocratic Continental honor.

Commerce was the most outstanding feature of British society, as is proved by the universal mania for entrepreneurial success. Everyone, the nobility included,[79] was out to fatten his purse by peddling wares at the market place. Honor, the "principle" of monarchy, forbad aristocratic participation in economic activity. But England was no longer a monarchy; it could more fittingly be described as "a republic disguised under the form of monarchy."[80] And being a republic it adopted the "commerce of economy" peculiar to republican forms of government and altogether different from monarchy's economy of luxury. The greatest economic feats were reserved for republics because their democratic structure gave rise to a mass demand quite unlike the restricted class demand of an aristocratic economy. In the republican economy of production (as opposed to the monarchical economy of consumption), the entrepreneur "gains little" per sale but "gains incessantly."[81] In brief, a work ethic drives out aristocratic leisure and parasitism. "Commerce is a profession of people who are upon an equality,"[82] and is the indispensable ingredient in explaining England's democratic, anti-aristocratic society.*

As befits a democratic society, wealth and merit preceded birth in determining an Englishman's social prestige. Furthermore, England

---

*By modern standards, England was not a democratic society. But that is irrelevant. Montesquieu was willing to idealize England, if need be, because he wanted to draw the sharpest possible contrast between England and France.

was happily without courtiers and flatterers surrounding the throne, one of the most tangible signs of honor. Other less tangible marks of honor, such as politeness, were also missing: "The English are busy; they haven't time to be polite."[83] Least tangible of all, but practically most important, the social psychology of Englishmen, their *esprit général*, was worlds apart from that of aristocratic honor. "The English get along very well with their inferiors and cannot stomach their superiors. We accommodate ourselves to our superiors and are insufferable towards our inferiors."[84] Democratic society continually pulls the rich and prominent down into the middling condition — hence the blessing bestowed upon satirical writings in England. Moreover, it is essential to realize that the modesty of men in democratic society is not weakness. Taken as a whole the British nation was self-reliant even to the point of insolence,[85] and nothing but contempt was felt for the occasional praise of passive obedience that came from a few Jacobite voices.[86]

At the highest level of abstraction, the British achievement was this: under a viable absolutism the political system dominated the social, but in England the social system dominated the political. What is representative government if not a method of allowing social groups to influence public policy? And what are the effects of British capitalism if not to reverse mercantilism? "Other nations have made the interests of commerce yield to those of politics; the English, on the contrary, have ever made their political interests give way to those of commerce."[87]

Spain recurs so often in Montesquieu's thought because its emaciated ghost stalked his dreams of Europe's future. Down to the last detail, Spain was a reverse image of English vitality. Depleted, barren, and virtually without hope, the Spanish nation was worse than stagnant. Relatively, Spain's power was declining in comparison with the rest of Europe. Once the most powerful of Western peoples, the Spaniards now sit idly by while "the rest of the European nations carry on in their very sight all the commerce of their monarchy."[88] Absolutely, Spanish power was in a state of atrophy and decay. Not yet an Oriental desert, she could be reduced to that eventually because such are the debilitating effects of monarchy in politics and aristocracy in society.

At the height of Spain's grandeur, the seeds of her destruction were already present. The cause of her decline can be traced to the rigor with which she followed the maxims of mercantilism, the political economy of absolutism. More than any other European power, Spain raped the Americas and returned home laden with vast stores of gold. With the assistance of the New World, a prodigious accumulation of bullion, the first objective of mercantilism, was easily attained. Needless to say, it was a castle built in the air. Gold was only a symbol of riches, a poor substitute for economic production, and one which declined in value as the quantity of gold arriving in Europe multiplied. "Spain behaved like the foolish king who desired that everything he touched might be converted into gold, and who was obliged to beg of the gods to put an end to his misery."[89]

Other factors compound the mercantilist fallacy and outlaw the preconditions of economic growth in Spain. The unproductive clergy inherited tremendous quantities of land, and what escaped its grasp belonged to the equally stultifying nobility.[90] Aristocratic honor, disdainful of economic activity, was written large across the face of Spanish society, as could be seen in the daily preoccupations of the "typical" Spaniard. A Spaniard, for instance, was always in love, because chivalry, an intimate of the honorific ethos, would have it no other way. A Spaniard, moreover, was extremely proud and excessively polite — traits which society at large had inherited from the nobility. Again like the nobles, Spanish commoners regarded work as an affront to their dignity. All of this leads, of course, to the conclusion that an acquisitive ethic simply had no chance to develop in a nation with an overdeveloped sense of honor.[91]

What little economic endeavor there was would assume the form of a get-rich-quick fever or of a taste for high adventure, both infinitely distant from a societal work ethic comparable to England's. The rape of the Americas, offering gold, high seas, conquest, and immediate fortunes, was typical of the bogus economic outbursts of aristocratic society. Were Spain blessed with a peculiarly French abuse, the venality of offices conferring noble titles, she could have avoided, perhaps, the disastrous economic consequences of honor. But without venality, there was no way to coax anti-economic honor into posing as a stimulant to thrift and industry.[92]

Spain suffered from the common malady of monarchies: affluence at the center and poverty in the provinces. "The king of Spain . . . is only a rich individual in a state extremely poor."[93] An illustrious capital was surrounded by "ruined farmland and desolate countryside."[94] Englishmen quit the provinces for the capital because they had money to burn; the Spanish capital grew because the provinces were impecunious, dry as dust, just so many wastelands.[95]

Two final contrasts between Spain and England are in order. The Spanish military establishment was inordinately large,[96] an albatross around the neck of the state, and a potential oppressor of the people. Compare England: "Military men are there regarded as belonging to a profession which may be useful but is often dangerous, and as men whose very services are burdensome to the nation; civil qualifications are therefore more esteemed than the military." Second, the church in Spain was part of that country's absolutism, just as in England religion was integrated into the system of liberty. English clergy had no political assembly, estate, or political power of any sort. They sought to convince by persuasion or argumentation, and never resorted to force. Like everyone else, they had been assimilated into England's democratic society.[97] The situation in Spain was altogether different. Wielding a power base through its vast land holdings, and winning triumph after triumph in the courtly battle for the mind of the absolute prince, the Spanish church succeeded in tailoring state policy to fit its designs. Calling down the wrath of God, the Spanish Inquisition despoiled society and added to its glut of land by confiscations.[98] Leviathan in practice bears but faint resemblance to Leviathan in theory; the king, who was in Hobbes' theory regulator of the church, is in fact regulated by the church. As surely as the diatribe against Oriental despotism is directed against Richelieu, just as surely is the diatribe against Spain directed against Bossuet. Long ago the Spanish counterparts to Bossuet had emerged victorious over the Spanish counterparts to Richelieu, long enough ago so that by Montesquieu's period the pernicious consequences of such a political development were conspicuously evident. England's liberty was a "system" thriving from top to bottom of the social scale. Spain's liberty was "the liberty of the clergy and a strange slavery of the people."[99]

Against the backdrop of Spain and England, regarded as imperfect but efficacious measuring rods, it is possible for us to plot roughly the perplexities of Montesquieu's feelings about France. On the positive side of the ledger, there was ample reason to be convinced of the vitality of French power. Politically and economically, France remained a nation of the first rank. Of all the European monarchies, her economy alone was still a competitor with the republican economies of England

and Holland.[100] Internationally, France stumbled from one clumsy situation to another still more awkward, and could not regain the hegemony she had enjoyed throughout the middle of Louis XIV's reign. Still, everyone knew France was a great power, perhaps the greatest in Europe.

On the other hand, there was much that marred French splendor. An aristocratic society was capable of large undertakings in shipping and trade of luxuries, but its long-range potential for economic growth was limited. Consumption and demand were along class rather than mass lines; the reward of honor for entrepreneurial success removed the most industrious members of the Third Estate from the market-place; depleted provinces confirmed that, in part, the economic growth of cities rested on a parasitical withdrawal of resources from the countryside. Moreover, a great deal of land was effectively re-moved from productivity by the simple fact that, as in Spain, it be-longed to monasteries.[101]

Montesquieu was also aware of the chronic chaos of royal finances. As long as absolutism persists, he believed, the Dutch solution of a national bank that supplied reliable credit cannot be followed. An ab-solute monarch will not allow organized private business interests, banking or otherwise, to protrude into political affairs.[102] In Holland and England, wealth is readily convertible into political power; not so in absolute monarchy.

The notorious "system" of John Law failed spectacularly and trig-gered, in Montesquieu's mind, an agonizing set of associations with Spanish history. To finance his credit project, Law floated bonds whose interest was to be paid by returns from the ill-fated Mississippi Company. A wave of feverish speculation rolled across France, en-gulfing noble and *roturier* alike, finally hurling them onto the shoals of disaster in 1720. Spain had mistaken a metal for riches, France a piece of paper. In either case, Montesquieu concluded, "That must be a bad kind of riches which depends on accident, and not on the indus-triousness of a nation."[103]

Montesquieu referred to Regency France as "an amorphous mix-ture of weakness and authority,"[104] a description that could well be extended to the France of his mature years. Save for Cardinal Fleury's competent administration, absolute power was rarely more ridiculous or powerless. All through Montesquieu's lifetime the Jansenist-Jesuit controversy continued, and the king's response was either indecision or else an impolitic identification with one or the other party that kept the cauldron of discontent churning. Often absolutism seemed to be losing its grip and the social system was sent freewheeling. But Montesquieu took no comfort whatsoever in royal impotence. Had he not shown that absolute power and impotence were one and the same? Did not royal weakness merely signify that priests maddened by a persecuting zeal might capture the crown, as they had in Spain?

Despotic silence had not yet descended upon France. Indeed, the pace of social intercourse was so frenetic that if man is a social animal, the Frenchman "is man personified, for he seems to be made only for society."[105] Coffee houses, literary periodicals, columnists, gossips, newsmongers, and salon wits kept tongues wagging. Considered compositely, they added up to the new phenomenon of public opinion, the single most important quality of which was that under its influence the social universe had a reference point that neither emanated from nor terminated in the prince. When the court abandoned Versailles for Paris after Louis XIV's death, the capital was consolidating its subtle osmotic influence over the court rather than the other way around. Court and countryside awaited the latest change in fashion of the leading Parisian ladies, instead of pandering after king and queen as they had in the past. And not having made public opinion in his own image, the king could not avoid a crisis in public confidence such as followed in the aftermath of the John Law scandal. Public opinion might even turn against the crown as it did when the king supported Jesuitical ultramontanism against the popular Gallican liberties of the national church. At its most brazen, public opinion was shaped by *philosophes* into doctrines acting as so many exposés of the *ancien régime*.

Death came too early for Montesquieu to see the coming of age of either the *philosophe* movement or the parlementary reaction. Between the *Lettres persanes* and *L'Esprit des Lois*, the only literary work of major political importance — other than Montesquieu's own *Considérations* — was Voltaire's *Lettres philosophiques*. The first volume of the *Encyclopédie* was not published until 1751, some three years after Montesquieu's masterpiece. This helps to explain why, late in life, Montesquieu could complain that "at present . . . our princes find everywhere the most passive obedience."[106] There was a more important reason behind Montesquieu's pessimism, however. As a political sociologist, he never supposed that the babbling of intellectuals could end the silence of despotism. A political opposition institutionally anchored was the only way power could check power. Sometimes Montesquieu's imagery of the political future was despairing and nearly fatalistic: "The rivers hasten to mingle their waters with the sea, and monarchies lose themselves in despotic power."[107] The only institutional bodies not yet eroded were the *parlements*, bodies which, Montesquieu erroneously believed, were historically declining. Early in his career, he wrote of them as "great bodies [that] have followed the lot of things human. They have bowed before time, which destroys everything, . . . and before supreme authority, which has swept all before it."[108] Much later he referred to the *parlements* as pebbles or seaweed, things insignificant in themselves, but which have a slightly arresting influence on oceanic currents.[109]

Neither did he find reason to believe that the Frenchmen of his day were capable of associating together politically. The seeds of jealousy and class cleavage, originally planted by royal authority, had borne their evil fruit. Since the death of Louis XIV, interclass and intraclass jealousy had actually increased.[110] A Frenchman did not experience the acute isolation and atomization of Asiatic despotism, but his group identifications were coupled with scorn for every other social unit. Church, Sword, and Robe were mutually antagonistic, and every bourgeois subgroup deemed its profession superior to every other.[111] The political beneficiary of social cleavage was, of course, the absolute monarch who circumvented political opposition by playing off social island against social island.

Rica reveals the contents of a letter, written by a Frenchman travelling through Spain, in which the anatomy of Spanish despotism is unfrocked. Then he proceeds to suggest the vengeance a Spanish traveller in France could take. Surely his letter to Madrid would be about madness.[112] As despotism stealthily descended upon France, the body politic was struck with the very insanity which long before had reduced Spain from world power to village idiot of Europe.

CHAPTER III

Feudalism and the Problem of the Past

Why write history? In the opinion of many *philosophes*, the past was a mistake unworthy of serious comment. They did, admittedly, derive inspiration from their studies of the earlier enlightenments which had transpired in the polis, the Roman Empire, and the Renaissance city-state. But few *philosophes* were concerned with historiography proper, and most were especially negligent in dealing with the feudal past.

Yet the history of feudalism needed to be written, and the sooner the better. What *was* weighs heavily on what *is* in a feudal society, so that only through understanding the past could the present gain its freedom. Therefore, Montesquieu felt obliged to unravel the history of feudal laws. Those laws could shatter the ossified fancies which enshrouded the past; they held the key to the French present; they could historicize Montesquieu's model of monarchy and lend it a sense of development from past to future.

1. Traditional Society and the Illusory Past

Ever since the French Revolution, the present and future have conspired against the past. "Democratic nations care but little for what has been, but they are haunted by visions of what will be." So Tocqueville held, and he went on to observe that "In proportion as castes disappear, . . . the image of an ideal but always fugitive perfection presents itself to the human mind." This unlimited expansion of the future is matched by an equally astonishing constriction of the past: "among democratic nations each new generation is a new people."[1]

In pre-revolutionary Europe, by direct contrast, the past was real and immediate — and never more so than during medieval times. For a man or woman of the Middle Ages, the past dominated the everyday present, now in the custom of the manor, again in the putative wisdom of the elders, or in an infinity of other ways. And yet, despite this preoccupation with the past, despite this enslavement to the past, the past was not understood. The uneducated lived the past in the form of unreflective habit; and if the educated were reflective, their reflections did not include historical comprehension. Throughout the Middle Ages, Western civilization suffered from an appalling historical deafness.

There is nothing paradoxical in the paucity of serious historical understanding during medieval times. On the contrary, the stronger the hegemony of the past, the weaker the development of critical historical consciousness. It is only when the past is really past that it can readily become an object of reflection. Not surprisingly, then, the age of mature historiography is often said to have dawned in the nineteenth century — that is, after the French Revolution had drawn a line between traditional and modern Europe.

Everything and nothing, the past in medieval times was ostracized at the very moment of its triumph. For lord and peasant alike, there was no temporal spectrum of past, present, and future. The present devours everything when men must struggle incessantly to sustain their very lives, or when illiteracy shuts out all that has been or might be. Even the educated keepers of historical chronicles were perpetually entrapped mentally within their own feudal society and medieval present. Enraged by its enslavement to the past, the present savored its revenge. The past could only be thought of in terms of the present that had been denied; what was in the medieval present became the standard of what must have always been. In the words of Marc Bloch:

> Men thought of past and present as being so closely bound together that they were unable to perceive the contrasts between them and were unconscious even of the need to do so. How could people who believed that the Roman Empire was still in existence and that the Saxon and Salian princes were the direct successors of Caesar and Augustus resist the temptation to picture the emperors of old Rome as men exactly like the rulers of their own day?[2]

Intellectuals of the Middle Ages, in their abortive attempts to think historically, reflected society rather than reflecting on it. Attached though they might be to the past, medieval men from every walk of life lived without an adequate sense of time. In the absence of instruments of measurement, the crudest rules of thumb were resorted to in order to gauge the time of day and year after Christ. Documents frequently carried no trace of a date, and often records of important events simply were not kept or were grossly inaccurate. Nominally under the sway of custom, society was not always ruled by precedent. Lords and officials often made ad hoc decisions because there was no way to ascertain how similar situations had been handled before. Historical incapacity on the part of the intellectuals was but a projection from a deficiency that was chronic to the everyday operation of society.

No more than their medieval predecessors could the men of the *ancien régime* escape the past by simply forgetting it. Feudal institutions, practices, and mythologies kept the medieval past alive throughout the old regime. The past was omnipresent, and the burden it imposed could not be removed unless what *was* became known rather than adored. Luckily, the means were available. Since the Middle Ages, a subject-object dichotomy had opened between the present and the past. For the first time it was possible to step outside the past, treat it as an external object, and pass critical judgment on it. Men suckled by traditionalism had an invaluable opportunity to disabuse themselves of tradition.

Subject and object had to be balanced as well as differentiated, and the delicate scales were easily upset. All was subject and nothing object in the medieval period because man all too literally was his past and could not reflect upon that which had given him his identity. During the *ancien régime*, the scale tipped too far toward the opposite extreme. The possible benefits to be derived from opening a subject-object dichotomy were lost when the object began to lead a life of its own independent of the subject. The object cheated the subject by obliterating awareness of the interpretive side of historiography, the extent to which history is always a question of perspective. Feigned autonomy on the part of the object led to a kind of essentialism, and essentialism is always dogmatic. History, in the mythology of the *ancien régime*, was "out there," external to man, waiting to reveal exactly the same secrets impartially to whatever age, party, or interest questioned her. A creative act of consciousness, history was here regarded as a "thing."*

---

*The *philosophes* were a partial exception to this generalization. As historical pyrrhonists, they were acutely aware of the interpretive side of history. Their in-

Dressed up in essentialist garb, historical thinking could fancy itself a receptacle of absolute truths. That is why it was possible for the historiography of the *ancien régime* to be so very pretentious even though it was entirely lacking in conceptual sophistication. What is more, this was an absolutism of values as well as of facts, for discoveries and pseudodiscoveries of certain facts, notably those of origins, were immediately hailed as evidence of objective values. All parties agreed that origins proved right; royalists and constitutionalists alike hastened to trace royalism and constitutionalism back into the origins of society in the hope of establishing an indisputable moral claim for the political regime of their choice. Subsequent history was then either the cheerful story of righteousness triumphant or a woeful tale of a just order reversed by usurpers.

Several factors cooperated in fashioning the specious mode of thought that pursued absolute moral truth through the study of history. Historians, we have seen, were guilty of regarding the past as an essence, which was enough to promote the belief that incontrovertible verities were somehow within the reach of historical scholarship. In addition, historical writing was absorbed in partisan quarrels, and nothing is more conducive to unconditional utterances than the heat of ideological controversy. Last but not least, a style of thought that searched for right in the origins of tradition was naturally appealing in a traditional society.

Before the demise of the *ancien régime*, when the past became an object because it was no longer part of the present, the past had become an object in the eyes of the antagonists of the old order. Here was a unique opportunity to rid oneself of the past by the route of understanding, but it was squandered. The endeavor to derive absolute moral values from history, and the related inclination to interpret change as usurpation and corruption, are both antithetical to the evolutionary and skeptical attitudes appropriate to historical research. Nor was the past judged critically; instead, it became the critical standard by which the present was judged. From the moment the subject was forgotten, with the consequence that the object could masquerade as an essence, it was a foregone conclusion that the historian would be seduced by his historiography: history would make judgments on men

---

difference to the past did not stem solely from their conviction that the past was a record of crime and folly. They also believed that the past, as recorded by historians, was a pack of tricks that the living played on the dead. Yet, even the *philosophes* could not completely ward off the mesmerizing influence of the past — as we shall see when we discuss Dubos and Boulainvilliers.

rather than men making judgments on history. "Every past is worth condemning,"[3] Nietzsche insisted, but the historians of the *ancien régime*, far from condemning the past, kneeled down before it and gave thanks that it freed them from the trials of moral judgment.

English historiography in the seventeenth century can serve as a case study illustrating our generalizations. By studying Roman law, the legal humanists of the Renaissance had earlier fashioned a method by which the nature of ancient Roman society could be fathomed. Similarly, by studying common law, English scholars were blessed with a body of evidence, clues, and indicators which might form the basis of an understanding of the origins and development of their society. In actuality, however, the common law had more myths projected upon it than wisdom applied to it. Even as social, economic, and political changes drew Englishmen toward modernity, historical thought kept their minds shackled to the past.

Very few historians came to realize that the common law was first and foremost a law regulating land tenures or that these tenures implied the military and feudal arrangements that had been transplanted by the Normans at the time of the Conquest. Those few who did understand were mostly uninfluential outsiders, while the insiders of English historical thought imagined that the common law of the seventeenth-century present had always existed, that it was but a contemporary expression of an "ancient constitution" dating from "time immemorial."[4] As for the critical historical importance of the Norman Conquest in importing feudal laws, the insiders simply denied that the Conquest was a conquest or that it brought about fundamental changes in the legal system. The obscurantist phrase "time immemorial" was infinitely preferable to the discovery of the foundation of common law in an act of conquest, since few were eager to see the formula "origins prove right" slide into "might makes right."

The royalist rejoinder to the myth of an "ancient constitution" is the best possible proof of its resilience. On the face of it, royalists had every reason to dispel the chimeras of an eternal common law and an unbroken historical continuity. But they were ensnared in the same mental trap as that which held their opponents captive. The royalist argument was nothing if not transparently simple: an extensive royal prerogative can hardly be a negation of the fundamental law since it is sanctioned by that law. Royal prerogative is immemorial.

By Montesquieu's day, England stood outside the *ancien régime* politically and economically. This was the England of Walpole, a new Lockean order that was liberal in its politics and progressive in its economics. Judged by the relative independence of its political thought from historical types of proof, Walpole's England had broken free of the past in its theory as well as in its practice. Originally incredible to Tories and Whigs alike by its indifference to history, Locke's philosophy of individualism and natural rights had in Walpole's age become a pillar of the new order. Apologists for Walpole had little use for history until Bolingbroke and his companions, defenders of the old and dying aristocratic social order, revived the myth of the ancient constitution for the purpose of accusing Walpole of subverting it. An answer cast in historical terms was soon forthcoming. The "ancient constitution" was debunked by invoking the explanatory fecundity of the "feudal law," key to the past. Walpole's ideologues were eager to admit that the Conquest was real and that it entailed a radical change in the legal system, because destruction of the idyllic past emancipated the present of which they were much enamored. Before the Revolution of 1688 there was no liberty, and now that the dream of Locke was established fact, the present was all that counted.[5]

For France in the last century of its *ancien régime,* the claims of custom could not be exactly comparable to those earlier pressed by English ideologues at a similar stage of historical development. As in England, custom was praised as an embodiment of the wisdom of the ages, a cumulative wisdom that dwarfed the reason of the individual, but few regarded custom as immemorial. Presumably, the crucial factor here was the coexistence of the *pays de droit écrit* alongside the *pays de droit coutumier.* Customary law had always been proud that it was an unwritten and therefore "natural" accretion of the ages, forwarded to the present unblemished by human caprice. But in France the laws sanctioned by tradition were both written and unwritten, and written law could not be immemorial.

The existence of traditional written law in France erased both the notion that law was immemorial and also the belief that law, being a natural growth, was independent of human volition. Written law must have been written sometime in the past and by someone. The volitional aspect of law was again brought home forcefully by the legal codifications of the fifteenth century that had been carried out under royal auspices. "Codification", writes J.G.A. Pocock, "was an act of sovereignty, an assertion that the ruler's will and reason were superior even to ancient custom, and consequently it gave rise to the historical claim that custom had never had force but by the king's permission."[6] Constitutionalists were caught in a dilemma because they admitted the desirability of codification. Overlapping layers of customary law were ridiculously entangled and fragmented in France, where there was no "common law," no single body of customary law national in scope, so that even the best friend of custom had to admit that some customs were abuses requiring rectification. Once it was conceded that the codifications were not a matter of arbitrary royal fiat, it followed that laws in some measure were "made" and not simply "discovered," as medieval conceptions had taught.

Thus the question became one of who had the right to make law. Ever since the decline of the Estates, the king was the legislative power; but antiroyalist thinkers condemned that development as a transgression of what manifestly ought to be. Royalists and constitutionalists, defenders of the crown and defenders of the nobility, searched history for evidence to bolster their claims, for Frenchmen were no more free from their past than were the British prior to the demise of their *ancien régime*. Again like their British counterparts, French thinkers sought right in origins, the only difference being that French origins were specific whereas English origins from "time immemorial" were diffuse and nebulous. Proponents of the *thèse royale* were called Romanists because typically they argued for royal absolutism on the historical grounds that the contemporary French monarch was a literal heir to the absolute powers of the Roman emperor, the legislative power included. Advocates of the opposing *thèse nobiliaire* were called Germanists because typically they took a contemporary legal body — the Sword preferred the Estates, the Robe favored the Paris *parlement* — and fantasized that it was an heir to an ancient Germanic institution, often the *Champ de Mars*, the moral being that the king's legislative powers ought to be subject to a check by that particular institution.

We arrive at last at the shape and form of historical debate in Montesquieu's lifetime. Boulainvilliers was the leading virtuoso of the historicized *thèse nobiliaire*, Dubos of the historicized *thèse royale*. Boulainvilliers first, as Franz Neumann has conveniently summarized his position:

Feudality is for him as old as is the Frankish monarchy. When the Franks conquered Gaul, they brought with them from the Teutonic forests, not absolute monarchy, but a feudal monarchy, a kingship limited in its very origin by the original power of the lords. The history of the French monarchy is thus the history of the usurpation of feudal powers by the monarch.

And then Dubos' reply, also summarized by Neumann:

Feudalism for him is a corruption of the monarchy which, in its origin, had inherited and continued to practise the Imperium Romanum. The Frankish kings . . . were officers of the Roman Empire, which, under Justinian, had ceded Gaul to them. The French kings of the eighteenth century were thus the successors of Augustus and the feudal lords were usurpers of the royal powers during the weakness of the monarchy.[7]

From this sad state of affairs Montesquieu toiled to save historiography. "A system is not made after having read history," he lamented, "but one begins with a system and afterwards searches for its proof. And there are so many facts in a long history, . . . origins are ordinarily so obscure, that one can always find enough to satisfy all sorts of sentiments." A failure to think empirically and critically was endemic to all such reasoning, and historical writing was hardly more than a grabbag filled with justifications of every conceivable doctrine. "As for myself, I would prefer not writing history to writing it while following the prejudices and passions of the age."[8] The "passions" Montesquieu opposed were party passions, history as ideology: "The Count de Boulainvilliers and the Abbé Dubos have formed two different systems, one of which seems to be a conspiracy against the commons, and the other against the nobility."[9] And the "prejudices" he attacked in the historical writing of others can be subsumed under the heading of history as mythology, the gross misreadings of the past engendered by the idiocy of traditional society. De-ideologizing and demythologizing the past were two of the primary goals behind Montesquieu's laborious project of writing an objective history of the feudal laws.

Besides the disabilities of mind that were an outgrowth of the traditionalist mentality, Montesquieu had also to eliminate a mental myopia peculiar to lawyers. Law, and especially feudal law, was the key to the history of traditional society, both because it was the most visible body of evidence available for examining the past, and also because legal training outfitted the investigator with unusual opportunities for examining the past. Before Montesquieu, however, legal education was often more a hindrance than an aid in exhuming the past.[10] When the history of traditional society was written by lawyers, the regrettable outcome was that legalism was carried into historiography. A professionally trained incapacity, legalism may be described as the tendency of lawyers to treat law as something sui generis — the tendency, in other words, of lawyers to lose sight of the socio-political context of the laws.[11] All the better, then, should we appreciate Montesquieu's professed goal to "treat not laws but the spirit of the laws."[12] Montesquieu was a lawyer, a member of the Robe, but he was something more, a sociologist. In his deft hands, legal training became a path to history in the form of historical sociology. "In order to properly understand modern times, it is necessary to understand ancient times; it is necessary to follow each law in the spirit of each age,"[13] from its origins to its present reality, for it is through law that the *esprit général* of each period is expressed.

A collusion of legalism and traditionalism was also partly to blame for the absurd belief that origins prove right. As Max Weber remarked, traditionalism encourages a view of political office as private and personal rather than public and impersonal, and so true is this that office may come to be regarded as something owned, a possession, private property. Add to this the teaching of legalism that first possession of an object gives proprietary right, and one has explained the attraction of the formula "origins prove right." The question was one of who "owned" the right of governance, the Crown or the Estates, a question that would be decided as soon as it was determined which party held original claim to rule.

"Origins prove right" was a proposition that could never entice a mind so liberated from traditionalism and legalism as Montesquieu's. He was further emancipated from all such nonsense because his sociology was quite adequate to the task of applying moral tests to history. Whatever historical configuration tended toward despotism was evil, and whatever did not was, if not good, at least not irredeemably vicious. Origins are of historical interest, but morally they are empty. And even from the standpoint of historiography, origins should not become an *idée fixe*, dulling sensitivities to the importance of subsequent evolutionary developments.

Montesquieu's history of feudal law was a work of genius, a labor of agonizing criticism[14] and creative interpretation of historical records, an act, finally, of mature and detached judgment made possible by his resistance to the mythologies and ideologies in which France's past was encrusted. While dispassionate, his analysis of feudal law was not passionless. It was not history for history's sake, but history as a deliverance of feudal society from its past. Not only was Montesquieu immune to the walls of illusion surrounding the past, fortifying it, and saving it from capture by the understanding; he also actively tried to destroy those walls through his scholarship.

2. The Monarchical Model Historicized

All of a piece, Montesquieu's researches into French history were guided by a determined effort to unearth the roots of the monarchy, an objective that could be accomplished only if the French laws were forced to reveal all they knew of the obscure past. What those laws disclosed was a world now commonly known as feudalism. In feudalism, Montesquieu demonstrated, lay the much sought for origins of the *ancien régime*. Monarchy, nobility, clergy, *parlements* and all the rest of the eighteenth-century present were the aging descendants of feudal ancestors. Feudalism, and not the Roman or Germanic past, was the key to the present, and thus both Dubos and Boulainvilliers were radically mistaken.

Not that Dubos and Boulainvilliers were totally without knowledge of feudalism; no, those two antagonists did know something, and it was just enough to bolster their respective prejudices. Boulainvilliers projected feudalism all the way back into the Germanic beginnings of French history, and although Dubos correctly assessed that feudalism did not emerge until much later, his momentary insight was quickly overridden by a malfunctioning of the historical sense hardly less severe than Boulainvilliers'. Dubos did not understand that the advent of feudalism was something more than an act of usurpation on the part of overmighty lords. That feudalism had been steadily growing in Germanic soil, that it was a natural excrescence from Germanic mores, was simply beyond Dubos' comprehension. Montesquieu alone perceived that France's history was one of evolution and not usurpation, that the weakness of the monarchy in the ninth century simply completed a process long congenital to Frankish history. And this he demonstrated with a skill so consummate that he anticipated, in its essentials, the understanding of feudalism which is ours today.

There is another sense in which Montesquieu elevated the debate over France's past to an entirely new plane. For Boulainvilliers everything feudal was good, especially the nobility, while nothing but evil could come from the monarchy. As always, Dubos' position was an exact inversion of Boulainvilliers': the monarchy was the source of everything noble in French history and the nobility the source of everything ignoble. Montesquieu was unique in appreciating both the good and the evil of feudalism. Coming as an alternative to anarchy, the system of class rule instituted by feudalism had its relative merits, while insofar as the hereditary nobility was unrestrained by a vigorous monarchy, its predominance amounted to little more than class despotism. Eventually a less qualified good evolved from the feudal system, a constitutional balance that stretched from the twelfth to the fifteenth centuries, in which crown, nobility, third estate, and peasants each had its place and none was able to oppress the others. Unfortunately, the story of evolutionary development from feudal origins had a less sanguine ending. The final historical configuration to which it gave birth was the royal absolutism and aristocratic society of the old regime.

By writing the history of the feudal laws, Books XXX and XXXI of *The Spirit of the Laws,* Montesquieu was able to trace the origins of the nobility. In so doing he historicized the "nature" and "principle" of monarchy, which is government by one man tempered by class privilege and the honorific ethos. Book XXVIII, on the history of civil and customary law, precedes the discussion of feudal law, as is only proper since it is logically prior. Before discussing the subtypes of feudal law and feudal society, Montesquieu first had to analyze the mastertypes under which they were subsumed: customary law and traditional society.

Rule by custom was of the essence of traditional society. To record the waning of rational law and its replacement by customary law, as Montesquieu did in Book XXVIII, was, therefore, to delineate the origins of traditional France. Law is rational when it is kept in writing, and when individual cases are decided by logical deduction from a general principle or by recorded precedent. Customary law, as referred to here, depends on oral tradition, or on ad hoc procedures sanctioned by the presumption of long practice. Roman compilations, codified barbarian usages, and laws of Frankish assemblies (the Capitularies) were the rational laws whose demise Montesquieu recounted, and in the judicial combats of medieval times he found a primary example of the customary law that was their successor.

Customary law triumphed at the end of the second race (the Carolingian) and the beginning of the third (the Capetian) because of cataclysmic events, but that is not to say it had not existed before civil war, invasion, and disintegration of the state wrecked the structure of rational law. On the contrary, customary and written barbarian law had coexisted as far back as the first race (the Merovingian). Lacunae in the various barbarian legal systems and problems of conflicting jurisdictions were originally responsible for the emergence of a customary law that was later left without a challenger when rational law lay in ruins.

Germanic mores, trial by combat, and the steady extension of regulation through custom were pieces of a puzzle which, when fitted together, composed a picture of traditional society. Many of the barbarian systems of law featured, among other things, "negative proofs" by which an accused person "might clear himself, in most cases, by swearing, in conjunction with a certain number of witnesses, that he had not committed the crime laid to his charge."[15] Because negative proofs made it so easy for an offender to escape justice, the Franks were anxious to fashion an alternative procedure from the givens of their customs. Always a militaristic people, they adopted a militaristic substitute for the written law whose effectiveness was hampered by the flaw of negative proofs. Trial by combat or by ordeal, Montesquieu realized, was shocking to modern sensitivities because such proof "had no manner of connection either with innocence or guilt." Yet it was not an arbitrary procedure, but rather a direct expression of the mores of all Germanic peoples, who as far back as the time of Tacitus were known as tribesmen preoccupied solely with warfare.

> In a military nation, where strength, courage, and prowess are esteemed, crimes really odious are those which arise from fraud, artifice, and cunning, that is, from cowardice. . . . I conclude, therefore, that under the circumstances of time in which trial[s] by combat . . . obtained, there was such an agreement between these laws and the manners of the people, that the laws were rather unjust in themselves than productive of injustice, that the effects were more innocent than the cause, that they were more contrary to equity than prejudicial to rights, more unreasonable than tyrannical.[16]

A brutish, warlike people set no great store in the nuances of written law, since they cared little for procedural subtleties and judged the skills of reading and writing as unworthy of a warrior. "Such a nation had no need of written laws; hence its written laws very easily fell into disuse. If there happened to be any disputes between two parties, they had only to order a single combat."[17]

By unfolding the history of customary law, Montesquieu succeeded in establishing France's identity as a traditional society. Next he had to account for the distinctiveness of the traditionalism of the Middle Ages; he had to trace the origins of an aristocracy whose eventual claim to pre-eminence was based not on ability or wealth but on a legally sanctioned separate status transmissible from generation to generation. In the feudal laws Montesquieu had a key that could unlock this chapter of French history.

When the state fell in the ninth century, a new order emerged which multiplied the inequalities within society a thousandfold. Panic was general during the interval of anarchy between public governance by the Frankish monarchy and private governance by feudatories, and men everywhere sought protection. For most people this meant reduction to serfdom, but for the minority with sufficient means to enter into the system of vassalage, protection by their lord was not paid for by forfeiting freedom. The militaristic life of the freeman, which had always been at the center of Germanic mores, was now a class monopoly. Hence the twofold character of the customary law that followed in the wake of Norman invasions, civil wars, and a succession of kings who were as inept as Charlemagne had been resourceful. The lower class had its law of the manor and the higher class its feudal law pertaining to the fief. Feudal law was preoccupied with the relationships between lord and vassal, and was in every respect the law of an exclusive class. A study of the origins and nature of the feudal laws, therefore, promised to explain the distinctive form of medieval traditionalism as a caste society.

Feudalism was a relatively late development but a barely detectable movement had prepared for its reception throughout the entire sweep of Frankish history, from the time of the Germanic invasions of Roman Gaul down through the classical period of feudalism, the tenth to the thirteenth centuries. One side of the story of growing infeudation can be told as a narration of the prolonged incompetence of the Frankish state. From this perspective, feudalism was possible because there was no central authority sufficiently strong to inhibit the movement of localistic fragmentation. Well in advance of the final dissolution of public authority, reason and power had been seeping out of the structure of the French monarchy, and Germanic mores were largely responsible. Actually, the displacement of rational by customary law, previously referred to, was only a single act in the larger drama of the gradual but inexorable flight of reason and power from the Frankish state.

Unlike many of his contemporaries, Montesquieu knew that the Germanic conquest did not extinguish all those Roman institutions and practices that were so notably superior in rational technique to barbarian devices for organizing social and political life. In municipal institutions of organization and administration lay the Roman legacy to the Germanic world, not in Dubos' invention of an alliance between Romans and Germans, and still less in his indefensible suggestion that such an alliance, had it existed, could demonstrate that the eighteenth-century monarch was therefore heir to the absolute powers of the Roman emperor. Roman municipal civilization did survive the barbarian onslaught,[18] as Montesquieu correctly concluded. But steadily thereafter it was barbarized, not by force but of necessity, for the cities were estranged from the now prevalent Germanic mores, which from their inception had nothing to do with walled inclosures, trade, or administration — the lifeblood of municipal existence. Germanic institutions were "founded in the woods"[19] and in the woods they remained, even as they passed economically from the nomadic habits and herdsmen's ways of earliest times to the closed agrarian economy of feudal society.

In the critical areas of state finance and the national army, the collusion of historical circumstance and Germanic mores proved too much for the Roman and homegrown instruments of rational administration employed by the Frankish monarchy. Collection of revenue, originally not a practice of the Germanic peoples who "followed their chiefs for the sake of booty and not to pay or raise taxes,"[20] became an important matter of state when Frankish kings learned to mimic the Roman system of taxation. But important or not, a rational method of tax gathering was not easily assimilated by the ingenuous Franks and with time it fell into disuse. In addition, the struggle to preserve a modicum of order was so pressing that the Frankish monarchy willingly changed its claim to tax into a claim to exact military service.[21] A state that sacrificed its right to revenue in order to gain an army was in serious trouble, and that was only the beginning. Having bought an army at the highest possible price, the price of foregoing the possibility of ever again buying anything, the king soon discovered that he had purchased a defective product. One segment of the military establishment was drawn from the freemen and directed by a royal official, the count, but another part was outside immediate central control. Even before the age of feudalism proper, there was a chain of feudatories living for the fight and off the fief, men tied together by personal relationships that the king could not touch. The king's count led the army of freemen into battle, and the king himself rode at the head of the body of nobles,[22] a spectacle as magnificent as it was misleading — misleading because increasingly the king was nothing more than a special noble pleading from crisis to crisis for military assistance, instead of being a public authority able to mobilize an army upon demand.

Antithetical to organizational discipline and control, Germanic laws and mores enfeebled the monarchy still more fundamentally by striking at the very roots of political stability. Under the provisions of the Salic Law, which regulated succession to real estate, all the sons of a deceased monarch were entitled to an equal share of the "property" of their father. The kingdom was carved up into kingdoms but that never settled matters. As each son wanted all but could legally claim only a share, civil war was chronic. It was characteristic of the Franks that these internecine conflicts should be fought with the fury of one beast attacking another. "The history of Gregory of Tours exhibits, on the one hand, a fierce and barbarous nation; and on the other, kings remarkable for the same ferocity of temper. Those princes were bloody, iniquitous, and cruel because such was the character of the whole nation."[23] As the Franks inflicted wounds, mutilations, and scars on each other, they did not realize that the real victim of their passions was the state.

Discovering the preconditions of feudalism in the incapacity of the state was only a first step. Montesquieu had next to explain the extension of feudal arrangements in the prefeudal era, and the manner in which feudalism eventually gave rise to a governing class that was a rigid caste. Before doing anything else, he had to dispose of Boulain-villiers, who taught that the Franks brought feudalism with them from the forests of Germany. In truth, as Montesquieu demonstrated, the multiplication of servitudes did not occur until the chaos of the late second race and early third.[24] He would have nothing further to do with Boulainvilliers, whose historical writings were unlimited fancy, serving no other purpose than to disseminate his ludicrous conviction that eighteenth-century nobles were literal heirs of the conquering Franks and commoners the heirs of a subject Gallo-Roman population.

Going back to the original Germanic invaders, one finds feudalism nowhere, for there were no fiefs; but it is possible to ferret out of Tacitus' *Germania* a presentiment of vassalage. A body of "companions" gathered around each German prince and rode with him into battle, seeking booty and opportunity to demonstrate manly valor. Living solely to fight, rape, and pillage, these bands used the tactics of hit-and-run, never bothering to settle down and cultivate conquered territories. The prince, it may be concluded, was assisted by men who were rather like what would later be called vassals, but there were no fiefs and no nobility.[25]

After the Franks founded a monarchy in what had been Roman Gaul, all mention of "companions" disappears, but the "antrustiones," referred to in various documents, appear to be successors to that earliest intimation of vassalage. As with the "companions," moreover, these armed retainers may have been vassals, but they were not feudatories. The fief of a "trusty" man "was regulated rather by the political than the civil law, and was the share that fell to an army, and not the patrimony of a family."[26]

Vassalage and fief were first fused together by unauthorized strong men and not by the king. As instability grew during the Merovingian and Carolingian periods, so did the number of lords and vassals, men united for mutual protection by feudal oath and subinfeudated lands. These feudal relationships became pervasive when the freemen were eliminated, a group that may be defined as "those who on the one had had no benefices or fiefs, and on the other were not subject to the base services of villeinage; the lands they possessed were called allodial estates."[27] Chaos forced the freeman to seek protection by "incorporating himself with the other lords and entering . . . into the feudal monarchy because the political no longer existed."[28] Previously, the freemen were under the king's jurisdiction; now they formed just so many links in a feudal chain over which the king presided but could not rule. "Thus it was that those who formerly were only under the king's power, as freemen under the count, became insensibly vassals of one another."[29]

In the matter of property, fiefs everywhere replaced allodial holdings when the freemen were eliminated; and in the social world, the relationships of lord and vassal and lord and serf absorbed everything once the freemen were gone. Feudalism was a social system and no longer a mere tendency. And it was a system that gave birth to a noble caste when the fiefs slowly but inexorably became hereditary. Always the objective of a fief-holder was to enhance the claim of his son to succeed to the fief, its military duties, and its exploitative possibilities. Since the right of bearing arms was the privilege of an exclusive class, since the tie between lord and vassal was an effective bond between families rather than an impersonal contract between individuals, the lord usually acceded to naming his vassal's son as successor to the fief held by the father. Eventually, this practice received the blessing of tradition and was no longer open to question.

As fiefs became patrimonial and perpetual, the upper stratum of society was elevated from an aristocracy to a nobility — that is, from an aristocracy of power and wealth to an aristocracy distinguished by the hereditary transmission of noble titles. The position of an aristocracy of wealth, service, or power is always precarious, and a family that is socially esteemed in one generation may be socially inconspicuous in the next. A nobility of birth is entirely different; its status is perpetual, it can afford the illusion of immunity to the forces of time and change, and hence the appropriateness of its eventual ideological justification as something ordained by a law of nature.

"Italiam, Italiam," exclaimed Aeneas and his comrades when they sighted the land on which the grand edifice of Roman civilization was to be built. This exclamation reappears at the close the *The Spirit of the Laws* when Montesquieu utters his last words on the heritability of fiefs. Upon the bedrock of hereditary fiefs, France's future was to be erected. Once the fiefs became hereditary, the telos was implanted whose culmination was the *ancien régime*, a society composed of privilege and hereditary status. Montesquieu had discovered the Archimedean point of French history.

Society was feudal and soon politics was also. The greatest single step in the expansion of feudalism from a social to a political principle was taken by the monarchy itself when the Carolingians gambled on increasing their power by means of vassalage. At the local level the growth of vassal ties was so effective in imposing a body of powerful magnates between crown and populace that the number of subjects immediately under the jurisdiction of the king steadily diminished. Partly to acquire an army against external enemies and partly to entice the magnates into royal service, the Carolingians stripped the church of its lands, distributing these holdings to royal vassals, bound to the king by a feudal oath.[30] In this one dramatic gesture, the entire significance of vassalage was transfigured: first, the ad hoc practices of vassalage, which were widespread in society, had found their way into the structure of legality; second, instead of a salary that the depleted economy could not afford, a grant of land, first called a benefice and later a fief, was turned over on a temporary basis to the vassal-official as his pay.

Finally, irrepressible feudalism reached up to the state and destroyed it. From the moment ninth-century chaos eventuated in the extension of the hereditary principle to the fiefs of public officialdom — the counts — all was lost.

> When the kings began to make grants in perpetuity, it was natural they should begin with fiefs rather than counties. For to deprive themselves of some acres of land was no great matter, but to renounce the right of disposing of the great offices was divesting themselves of their very power.[31]

However, the feudal principle could not be held at bay for long, and immediately after Charlemagne the office of count was recognized as hereditary.[32] The state dissolved into insignificance, and the second race, for one magnificent reign an empire-building monarchy, ended with the banishment of public authority. In politics, as in society, feudalism was the fundamental reality.

Perched atop the privileges of the nobility, an honorific ethos expressed the pride of the exploiting class. The material crystallization of interests had its ideal counterpart, the substructure its superstructure. Just as Montesquieu traced the origins of the "nature" of monarchy (kingship modified by intermediary bodies) by discovering whence came the privileges of the nobility, so did he trace the beginnings of its "principle," the aristocratic ethos. If one reconsiders the practice of trial by combat, it is apparent that it fell under the rubric not only of customary but also of feudal law, for it was a means of regulation through "point of honor."

Upon a man's declaring that he would fight he could not afterwards depart from his words . . . Hence this rule ensued, that whenever a person had engaged his word, honor forbad him to recall it.

Gentlemen fought one another on horseback, and armed at all points; villeins fought on foot and with bastons. Hence it followed that the baston was looked upon as the instrument of insults and affronts, because to strike a man with it was treating him like a villein.

None but villeins fought with their faces uncovered, so that none but they could receive a blow on the face. Therefore, a box on the ear became an injury that must be expiated with blood, because the person who received it had been treated like a villein.[33]

Out of this social psychology chivalry grew, which found outlets for its energies in tournaments, contests, and highly ritualized competitions for the affections of noble ladies. "The prevailing spirit at the time of our judicial combats must have been that of gallantry" which is "not love itself but the delicate, the volatile, the perpetual simulation of love,"[34] presumably because the woman beloved by the knight was, as depicted in courtly romances, typically the wife of a higher lord to whom fealty was due. A class that lived leisurely on the proceeds it extracted from the poor had time to cultivate refinement and to engage in an endless succession of playful activities. As a superfluous, unnecessary, and nonutilitarian enterprise, play was a mark of class superiority, an alternative to boredom, and an opportunity to carry the competitive ethic of combat into nearly every aspect of life. Brute passion for blood could be transformed into the pageantry of the tournament, the glitter of courtly splendor, the service of a beautiful lady.

Soon the chivalrous ideal permeated literature.

Knights-errant ever in armor, in a part of the world abounding in castles, forts, and robbers, placed all their glory in punishing injustice, and in protecting weakness. Hence our romances are full of gallantry founded on the idea of love joined to that of strength and protection.

In romances are found knights-errant, necromancers, and fairies, winged or intelligent horses, invisible or invulnerable men, magicians who concerned themselves in the birth and education of great personages, enchanted and disenchanted places, a new world in the midst of the old one, *the usual course of nature being left only to the lower class of mankind.*[35] [Emphasis added.]

Thus Montesquieu solved the vexed problem of origins. An understanding of the origins of customary and feudal law was a mental re-enactment of the birth of monarchy. At times the narrator, himself bored by the study of "all those frigid, dry, insipid, and hard writings,"[36] almost forgot that what he related was high drama. But he was saved from ennui by the satisfaction of knowing that the story he told was true, was told for the first time, and was an enemy of the fabrications of Dubos and Boulainvilliers. The evidence of Germanic mores, as first described by Tacitus[37] and then modified by subsequent history, plus the testimony of the laws, is the stuff out of which the *esprit général* of the past was reconstructed and traced through its transmutations. Embellished by a sociology of law, historical studies enable us to experience not just laws but also their spirit, and this "spirit of the laws" illuminates the past. Doubtless this is what it means to say "History must be illustrated by the laws, and the laws by history."[38]

Writing the history of civil laws (Book XXVIII), Montesquieu advanced chronologically as far as the fifteenth century; writing the history of feudal laws (Books XXX and XXXI) he stopped much earlier, putting down his pen after he had shown how fiefs became hereditary. "I finish my treatise of fiefs at a period when most authors commence theirs" are his closing words.[39] Other authors were concerned with assigning the terms "usurper" and "victim" to crown and nobility or nobility and crown. Boulainvilliers, for instance, had forged ahead at this point because he was eager to reveal those ignominious crimes by which the nobility had been struck down. Montesquieu, however, had killed the search for right in origins, and, in doing so, he also brought an end to the search for the usurper. "We must not imagine that the privileges which the nobility formerly enjoyed, and of which they are now divested, were taken from them as usurpations."[40]

And, finally, it must be emphasized that Montesquieu's history is critical history. The source of his value judgments is not origins; rather, he applies value judgments to origins. If Montesquieu spied despotism in the sovereignty of the eighteenth-century monarchy, he was just as quick to see it in the petty sovereigns of the Middle Ages, the feudal caste. The localistic concentration of civil and military powers in the person of the feudal lord[41] disturbed him because "the despotic and military ruler can be found just as certainly in the little prince of a village as in the master of a vast empire."[42] "Government by nobles, when nobility is hereditary, and not the price of virtue, is as vicious as [absolute] monarchy."[43] Overmighty lords crush down-trodden serfs who are little more than "slaves of the field to which they are attached."[44]

Scanning the past, Montesquieu came across only one period worthy of his approval. Late in the Middle Ages, the peasantry was enfranchised[45] and a bourgeois class came to thrive in newly constructed cities, thus giving birth to a period postdating the absolutism of the lords and predating the absolutism of the king. Montesquieu could wax rhapsodical in recollecting the constitutional balance that existed from approximately the twelfth to the fifteenth centuries:

> At first [Gothic government] was mixed with aristocracy and monarchy — a mixture attended with this inconvenience, that the common people were bondsmen. The custom afterwards succeeded of granting letters of enfranchisement, and was soon followed by so perfect a harmony between the civil liberty of the people, the privileges of the nobility and clergy, and the prince's prerogative, that I really think there was never in the world a government so well tempered as that of each part of Europe, so long as it lasted.[46]

What made this period even more appealing was that, with the codifications of the customs in the fifteenth century, the worst stupidities of tradition were erased by reason. So fragmented had the political world been that every lordship had its own customary law "preserved in the memory of old men." This was changed when

> Charles VII and his successors caused the different local customs throughout the kingdom to be reduced to writing, and prescribed set forms to be observed in their digesting. . . . Thus our customs were characterized in a threefold manner: they were committed to writing, they were made more general, and they received the stamp of royal authority.[47]

In every way the new state of affairs was propitious. Instead of acting simply as a judge, the king had in effect made law, as was necessary to achieve reform; but his actions were not yet informed by Bodin's potentially despotic notions of sovereignty and statutory law. From the standpoint of constitutionalist objectives, the end result was equally fortunate: a balance between corporate interest and the interest of the collectivity, a balance also of localism and centralism, of decentralization and centralization.

Our discussion in chapter II of Montesquieu's monarchical model ended with an account of the struggle between contending interests at court. It is only fitting, therefore, that we conclude this attempt to historicize the model of monarchy by tracing the footsteps of the nobility, priests, and women to the throne. Honor drew the nobles to court, where they claimed a paramount place historically among the advisors of the king, invoking as a precedent that favored their primacy the age-old duty of vassals to advise their lord. Women, too, were brought to court as a natural effect of the evolution of feudal society. Centuries before, chivalry had professed an extravagant adoration for the gentler sex, and during the old regime women were leaving the courts of local lords to reside at the court of the monarch, where they would have an influence to be reckoned with.[48]

Not to be outdone, the priests could justify their place at court on the basis of events dating back to the beginning of the second race. At that time the Carolingians, in alliance with the magnates, had wrestled the crown from the Merovingians, using the administrative position of Mayor of the Palace as a springboard to prominence.[49] When the Carolingian usurpers began to play the role of kings, they were badly in need of symbols of legitimacy, and luckily for them the Pope needed protection against Byzantium and the Lombards.[50] The result for France was the coronation oath that gave the monarchy a deeply religious imprint. Where before the clergy only sat in the assemblies, they now had a place at court, because kingship was profoundly sacerdotal. Doubtless that is why, in the same breath that he castigates the first race as "the history of a barbarous people" and the beginning of the third as "that of a people who lived in a sort of anarchy," Montesquieu denounced the second race as "that of a superstitious people."[51]

Nobles, women, and priests all have something of interest to the king: the noble brings glory, the mistress sexual charms, and the priest repentance for the sins urged upon the monarch by the previous two, sins of pride and of the flesh.

As the antagonists arrive at court and assume their respective battle stances — the woman lying in bed, the priest kneeling in the confessional, and the noble half bent over in a courtly bow — we may take our leave because it is no longer a question of historicizing the model of monarchy, but rather of the functioning of the model itself; and this we have previously analyzed. (See above, chapter II, section 2.)

*   *   *

For Montesquieu, as for most of the *philosophes*, the past was already past, but not for the remainder of the intelligentsia. Boulainvilliers and Dubos, for example, would possess the past so as to dispossess either the royal or the noble party, an intention that exposes them as the puppets of tradition. The past possessed them, not they it.

To free the present, the past had to be removed from everyday life and relocated in the realm of remembrance. Tradition had to be changed into history. Remembering that revolution did this for France at large, we are apt to forget that Montesquieu's historiography did so for the intelligentsia of prerevolutionary France.

CHAPTER IV

Feudalism and the Analysis of the Present

1. Feudalism and Comparative Politics

Feudalism was the key to the past, and it was equally effective in analyzing the present. The feudal factor assisted the analyst of the eighteenth-century present by demarcating royal absolutism in the West from its Eastern counterpart, and by linking together the various Western nations. In other words, feudalism supplied the taxonomy indispensable for initiating a project in comparative politics. *Per genus et differentiam* is the implicit logic of Montesquieu's comparative analysis, and feudalism figured twice in this logic: once as *genus* and once as *differentia*. Oriental despotism was royal absolutism minus feudalism, which means that absolutism was the generic term and feudalism the differential that separated out the Western variety and accentuated its distinctiveness. Within the West, feudalism was what the various nations of Europe shared; it was the generic term of comparative logic, the factor assuring that the units compared were in fact comparable. Several centuries into the past, when feudalism was most pure, the visages of Occidental countries bore striking resemblance to each other, and not even the long passage from feudal childhood to the maturity of the *ancien régime* could hide the feudal factor common to European countries.[1]

As an illustration of the utility of feudalism in contrasting East with West and comparing Western nation with Western nation, consider the example of monarchical succession. Hobbes knew that nothing was more fundamental than an orderly succession to the crown. Without a law of succession, there is the threat of discord and civil war whenever a monarch expires; with such a law, the Leviathan is fortified by a kind of "artificial eternity." Having stated the problem of succession with admirable clarity, Hobbes was hard put to offer a solution. Since the sovereign is above law and the fountainhead of all law, how can a law of succession to the throne be safeguarded from his whim? Should Hobbes have his way, he would instruct the king to name his successor before the approach of death.[2] The obvious retort is that while several Roman emperors used this method with great success, it failed to furnish a permanent solution, and Rome's crises of succession were notorious.

To the example of the Roman Empire Montesquieu added that of Oriental despotism in order to demonstrate that actual Leviathans, far from enjoying artificial eternity, are chronically unstable, in large measure because of the absence of a law of succession. It was the example of the law of succession to fiefs that engendered a similar law of succession to the grand fief of the king in the West;[3] but in the East, fiefs never became hereditary,[4] and a customary law of monarchical succession is in consequence lacking. The presence of the feudal factor in the West and its absence in the East accounts for this critical difference.

As effectively as it delineates Western from Eastern monarchies in the matter of succession, the feudal factor discriminates between the various Western monarchies. It explains why the crown is elective in Germany but hereditary in France, and why women are eligible to reign in England and Spain but not in France or Germany.

> The constitution of several kingdoms of Europe has been directed by the state of feudal tenures at the time when those kingdoms were founded. The women succeeded neither to the crown of France nor to the empire because at the foundation of those two monarchies they were incapable of succeeding to fiefs. But they succeeded in kingdoms whose foundation was posterior to that of the perpetuity of the fiefs, such as those founded by the Normans, those made by the conquests of the Moors, and others.[5]

In a fully developed feudal system, women were no longer debarred from succession to fiefs on the grounds of their unknightly physical weakness; and in those kingdoms whose origins coincided with the maturation of feudalism, women were capable, therefore, of succeeding to the grand fief — the crown. As to the second contrast, that between France's hereditary and Germany's elective monarchy, it is essential to realize that the inheritance of fiefs

obtained much later among the Germans than the French, which was
the reason that the empire, considered as a fief, was elective. By contrast, when the crown of France went from the family of Charlemagne, the fiefs were hereditary in this kingdom, and the crown, as a
great fief, was also hereditary.[6]

After indulging thus in a specific illustration of the uses of feudalism
in comparative analysis, we may proceed to note more generally that
if feudalism was the Western genus, its species, taken politically, were
monarchies, city-state republics, and various types of federal arrangements. Taken socially, the species collected under the feudal genus
were the various class structures and distributions of privilege that
predominated throughout Europe. For Montesquieu's purposes the
language of feudalism was sufficiently elastic to include East European countries, even though technically their histories differed from
those of the major countries of Western Europe. Whatever their
origins, these nations were very similar to those which emerged from
the feudal institutions of the Middle Ages. Countries such as Poland
and Hungary were experiencing their own particular old regimes, as a
comparison of their class structures with the classless societies of the
Orient immediately makes clear. Thus, in principle, the feudal factor
could open up all of Europe to comparative analysis.

"I should like there to be better studies of the legal history of each
country."[7] Much as he had rescued the French past from obscurity
and ignorance, Montesquieu hoped that other scholars would do the
same for their respective countries. Ideally he who undertakes comparative analysis should have at his disposal the history of each country included among his comparisons. Since such information was not
obtainable, Montesquieu's analysis was limited in scope to doing
morphologies. How the many countries of Europe had come to be
what they were was impossible for him to tell, but he could nevertheless describe and compare present regimes, class structures, tax
resources (as an index of state power), and economic well- or ill-being.

Surveying Italy, Montesquieu found less a nation than a territorial
entity splintered into a myriad of city-state republics. Considered as a
whole, Italy was still what she had become during Machiavelli's
lifetime: the plaything of the ambitions of the larger and more powerful territorial monarchies of Europe. "Italy . . . relies on political
finesse to counter accidents in the balance of power: searching for two
masters, for fear of having one, she labors to divide the forces of

Europe, much as they have played off one part of Italy against another."[8] Viewed internally, the condition of the Italian republics was fully as unhappy as was their impotence in international affairs. "Feeble," "divided," and timid, theirs had been a history of factionalism and class struggle. These cities "have made war within the enclosure of their walls" with the result that they were "sometimes the theater of tyranny, and sometimes of liberty."[9] In the eighteenth-century present, patrician oligarchies held power but lacked the moderation necessary to make class domination something less than outright oppression.[10] The whole of Italy could be characterized as follows: "The republics of Italy are nothing more than miserable aristocracies, which subsist only by the pity one accords them, and where the nobles, lacking all sense of grandeur or glory, have no other ambition than to maintain their idleness and their prerogatives."[11] Not even in absolute monarchy is the want of liberty so grave.[12]

References to Venice recur in Montesquieu's writings much more frequently than do those to Florence, Genoa, or any of the other Italian cities. This is hardly surprising, since Venice boasted a longer history than any of the national monarchies; moreover, her reputation for prowess in international trade was unequalled for centuries; and her form of government had often been celebrated, usually as an example of the exceptional durability which accompanies a proper mixture of monarchical, aristocratic, and democratic elements in a single constitution. As early as the Italian Renaissance, possibly earlier, Venice's reputation grew to the proportions of a powerful myth which subsequently circulated throughout Europe, taking up residence in England especially, where the course of seventeenth-century events made republicanism a temporary reality and a lasting political watchword. Harrington, Sydney, and the post-Restoration Commonwealthmen were the heirs of Machiavelli and Guicciardini's cult of Venice. Ironically, that cult was conjured up at the very moment of the "most serene" republic's decline. The opening up of new trade routes in the early modern period was Venice's maritime loss. A shadow was cast over the Venetian economy, and her greatest glory came from without in the mistaken praise projected upon her politics by foreigners. So entrenched was the Venetian myth that very few English Tories dared unearth Venetian reality, the better to expose its grimy underside. Most found it easier to accept and re-interpret the myth than to destroy it, because they, too, believed that Venice said of herself and others said of her. After suitable alterations, the Venice of the Tories was a monarchy with the doge as king.[13]

The Venice described by Montesquieu was radically different from the Venice of storybooks. Montesquieu did not deny that Venice had a doge, senate, and great council, but he was insistent that these bodies, rather than assuring liberty through a skillful combination of governmental forms, were all in reality the servants of an oppressive aristocracy. Legislative, executive, and judicial powers were distributed among different political institutions but they all belonged to the same class, and therefore liberty was nowhere to be found.[14] Greatly aggravating matters, the Venetian oligarchy was hereditary, hence self-perpetuating, beyond control, and exempt from the practical necessity of moderation in the exercise of power.[15]

Several mitigating factors saved Venice from the worst abuses of arbitrary power. First, the number of oligarchs was large, which was desirable because the greater the number of oppressors, the smaller the number of persons left over to fill the ranks of the oppressed.[16] Second, the abstention of Venetian nobles from commerce, however much it rendered them parasitical, had the advantage of muting the extremes of economic inequality. More advantageous still in pulling aristocracy toward equality, Venetian law disallowed "the right of primogeniture among the nobles, to the end that by a continual division of the inheritances their fortunes may always be upon a level."[17] Among constitutional devices, the most significant in limiting the otherwise tyrannical nobility was the Council of Ten, the "state inquisitors." "These are terrible magistrates who violently restore the state to its liberty."[18] A method of informing the authorities of the plots and conspiracies of the nobility had been officially sanctioned, and institutionalized in Venice. Thus, would-be upstarts were exposed before their plans had time to ripen.

Decadence had overtaken the Venetian republic. Once a trading power to be reckoned with, she was in the eighteenth century little more than a tourist trap and a dumping ground where men disgraced in their native nations congregated. Prostitution had become her leading economic product, and liberty was confounded with self-indulgence. "The redoubtable Council of Ten [was] no longer the redoubtable Council of Ten," and the state was deprived of revenue by the refusal of the nobility to pay the taxes it owed. "As for the secret deliberations," those renowned secret deliberations by which the patricians once ruled a commercial empire, "that practice has fallen into such decadence that it appears there is scarcely any longer a secret to guard."[19]

Pertinent observations on the politics and society of other Italian city-states are relatively scarce compared to Montesquieu's prolixity on Venice, but his occasional comments are worth reporting. The Neapolitan nobility had been humbled by Spain and thus was less powerful than its Venetian counterpart. But the nobility in Genoa was more powerful: there the systems of justice and taxation were so biased according to class that the Venetian nobility looked magnanimous by comparison.[20] Travelling to Rome, Montesquieu was afflicted by the sight of priests and nuns whose numbers multiplied as the distance to the eternal city diminished. If Italy, "the paradise of monks,"[21] suffered from a surfeit of clergy, all the more so did Rome, that singular city in which priests and not women set the tone of the social atmosphere.[22] As for the peasantry, its plight varied from region to region. "The peasants are well enough off in the Piedmont: each has a morsel of land which is fertile, and sometimes they are as rich as their seigneurs. In Milan, it is completely different: the nobility has much land and the peasants little."[23] Such was, in sweeping terms, the physiognomy of Italy — a collection of city-states, economically stagnant, overrun with parasitical clergy and oligarchs, vulnerable as a whole to the machinations of the great territorial monarchies.

Shifting focus from Italy to the United Netherlands, one finds a series of cities, each a separate republic surrounded by countryside, much as was the case in Italy. Yet the United Provinces came much closer than Italy to approximating a unity because its seven constituent provinces assembled in a States General.[24] One force making for fragmentation was the requirement of unanimity among the seven provinces before any proposal could be embarked upon.[25] Countervailing this tendency, however, was the primacy of Holland, by far the most powerful member of the federation — a primacy that could be translated into effective pressure by the considerable degree of central control Holland exercised over its eighteen member cities, including disproportionately powerful Amsterdam. For example, while each of the seven provinces of the United Netherlands was free to conduct its separate foreign policy, Holland, by contrast, forbad its member cities autonomy in international affairs. A strong confederate republic of city-states[26] ensconced within the larger but constitutionally weaker federation called the United Netherlands, Holland did not allow any of its cities to conclude a treaty without the consent of the others; and Amsterdam, like the smaller cities, had but one vote in other matters of vital importance.[27] Holland was a confederate republic blessed with political procedures that granted her some of the singlemindedness in action of a nation.

Even without the cooperation of the other six provinces, Holland was a great power. Heiress to once proud Portugal's overseas empire,[28] she had amassed enough wealth in trade to compete with England for the title of the world's greatest economic power.[29] Being a republic, furthermore, she readily allowed business interests to have political representation, and this won her great dividends through the creation of secure instruments of credit, especially a national bank.[30]

Nevertheless, Holland's state debt was enormous, apparently because of past wars when the only way to prevent the other six provinces from declaring a premature peace had been for her to shoulder the brunt of military expenses.[31] Perhaps the resulting tax burden could explain the disgusting behavior of the lower classes, especially their attempts to gouge and connive in every possible way for a few extra coins. The financial oligarchs were equally self-serving, if not more so; during those periods of Holland's history when the House of Orange was not allowed to fill the position of *Stadtholder,* a special executive post, the unchecked village magistrates acted as petty tyrants.[32] A possible exception was Amsterdam's commercial aristocracy, which was of "the most sensible" variety inasmuch as it governed "not by hereditary right but by election."[33]

Neither honor, nor virtue, nor fear predominated in the social psychology of the Dutch. Instead, as in England, a commercial ethos and democratic spirit reigned. An ambassador to Holland would not be successful, Montesquieu warned, unless he learned that it was thrift, and not aristocratic haughtiness, that built reputation.[34] "And one must not believe that the nobility of Switzerland and Holland imagines itself to be very free: because the word 'nobility' entails distinctions real in monarchies but chimerical in republics."[35] Everything was for sale in Holland, everything had its price,[36] which is to say that there was much that was crass, cheap, and vulgar in the accepted lifestyle, but such was the route to economic progress. A frenzied mania for success and a narrow individualism were part and parcel of democratic society and had to be tolerated as a necessary evil. The end result was happy even if the means were obnoxious: Holland was second only to England in liberty.[37]

Next we come to Germany. "The confederate republic of Germany, composed of princes and free towns, subsists by means of a chief, who is, in some respects, the magistrate of the union, in others the monarch." But if Germany may be described as a confederate republic, "experience shows us that it is much more imperfect than that of Holland and Switzerland." Governable confederations were made up of uniformly republican city-state regimes; Germany, however, "consists of [both] free cities and petty states subject to different princes." So different were *"l'esprit monarchique"* and *"l'esprit républicain"* that there was little hope of combining them into a workable system.[38] What emerged from this complicated political structure, constantly at cross-purposes with itself, was something much less than a governable whole. There were Germanies, each an autonomous international actor,[39] but no Germany.

One common characteristic of the German princedoms was their penchant for courtly splendor, a passion with which Louis XIV had infected them. "Versailles has ruined all the German princes. . . . Who would have thought that the Sun King had established the power of France in building Versailles and Marly?"[40] Alike in the glitter and ostentation at the top of society — the princely courts — German societies were similar also at their bottom: each rested on a peasantry that was virtually enslaved.[41] Perhaps the most formidable of the Germanies was Prussia. Her military build-up was taking place at a phenomenal rate,[42] and the king of Prussia was a tyrant.[43]

Always prescient, Montesquieu viewed Russia as "a rising empire."[44] At least since Peter the Great, monarch and nobles had been locked in battle, and the outcome was still in doubt.[45] Although Peter was unnecessarily tyrannical in his means, he did manage to effect a Westernization of mores, and Russia had been shaking off the visage of the East in favor of the more healthy appearance of a Western monarchy. In the past

> the women were shut up, and in some measure slaves; he called them to court; he sent them silks and fine stuffs. . . . This sex immediately relished a manner of life which so greatly flattered their taste, their vanity, and their passions; and by their means it was relished by the men.[46]

Observe how industriously the Russian government endeavors to temper its arbitrary power, which it finds more burdensome than the people themselves. They have broken their numerous guards, mitigated criminal punishments, erected tribunals, entered into a knowledge of the laws, and instructed the people.[47]

Whether the crown or the nobility would win out in Russia was uncertain. What was certain, however, was that her greatest weaknesses lay socially in the absence of a third estate and politically of a law of monarchical succession. Consequently, her economic progress and political stability remained in doubt.[48]

All aristocratic governments are oppressive, Montesquieu believed, and none more oppressive than Poland's. "The most imperfect of all [aristocracies] is that in which the part of the people that obeys is in a state of civil servitude to those who command, such as the aristocracy of Poland, where the peasants are slaves of the nobility."[49] Inequality of wealth was extreme in Poland and the whole was impoverished because its economy, to the extent it could be said to have had an economy, was entirely agricultural.[50] The nobles, unchecked by a strong monarch, met in a national diet, which was unable to govern since each member held a veto power; "the independence of individuals is the end aimed at by the laws of Poland, whence results the oppression of the whole."[51] Each noble carved out a portion of land and ruled it as if he were an absolute monarch. Virtually the same situation persisted in Hungary: a weak monarch, a nobility governing locally and refusing to cooperate nationally, an absence of manufactures, and a peasantry living in servitude.[52]

England and Spain will round out our retracing of Montesquieu's journey across Europe, a journey that did not end after he took the Grand Tour, recording his observations in his *Voyages*. In a figurative sense, his journey was a lifelong voyage, continued with every book and scrap of information he could muster on the countries of Europe. Since we have previously discussed Montesquieu's feelings about Spain and England, here we need only refresh our memories and cite reinforcing evidence. (See above, chapter II, section 4.) The downfall of Spain was that idle nobles owned vast estates, and what did not belong to them belonged to the equally unproductive clergy. Honor, "more easy to acquire than personal merit," had infected all social ranks with a disdain for commerce, and Spain, which desperately needed "entrepreneurial merchants [and] industrious workers," had none. Ostensibly absolute, the king really had remarkably little power because neither the nobility nor the clergy could be taxed.[53] By contrast, England, "one of the freest nations ever seen on the face of the earth,"[54] had wealth to tax and — in the relative absence of privilege — taxable wealth. A republic hiding under the form of a monarchy, England enjoyed all the advantages republics have over monarchies.

> In order to form a monarchical state, one needs a rich nobility which has authority and privileges over a poor people; luxury and expenditures in the nobility, misery in the people. In a republic, where the conditions are equal, each shares or can share in the common riches; each, having an honest subsistence, enjoys the wealth of the nation and seeks to increase it.[55]

Money and personal merit counted for much in Britain, honor for little or nothing.[56] Consequently, "all that is called putting on airs displeases the British. They like to see simplicity and decency."[57] Unpretentious middle-class mores were characteristic of Britain, making for a lifestyle similar to that which prevailed in Holland, but Englishmen, in contradistinction to their Dutch brethren, managed to mix a good deal of gentlemanly behavior with their avarice.

Through comparative analysis, Montesquieu acquainted himself with the diversity of the European present. More was at stake in this endeavor than a desire for better appreciation of the countries analyzed, real though that objective certainly was. Doing comparative politics is also a means by which the investigator deepens his understanding of his own country. What lessons about France did Montesquieu learn from comparative analysis?

Comparison of Western absolutism, French or otherwise, with the absolutism of the Orient taught him that the feudal factors, the intermediary bodies and the aristocratic ethos, were what placed such restraints on the French monarch as existed. Conversely, the example of Spain or of Portugal (whose history closely paralleled Spain's) demonstrated that absolutism was one of the political and social forms that evolved naturally from the feudal factor. Spain proved decisively that the retention of intermediary bodies was hardly sufficient reason for rejoicing. The influence of the nobility and clergy through their land holdings, through the social psychology of honor and of religious fanaticism, and through the nobles and priests at court, where the group politics of absolutism is played out, had resulted in not just stagnation but regression. Senile Spain and Portugal were well on the way to becoming deserts as a natural result of the unfolding of the historical logic of feudalism. A similar curse could befall France.

Comparative analysis within the West was effective also in that it allowed Montesquieu to place France between visible signs of its past and of its possible futures. "We still have in Hungary and Poland an accurate idea of the Europe of bygone times"; "I wanted to see Hungary [while on the Grand Tour] because all the states of Europe have been as Hungary is at present, and I hoped to see the mores of our ancestors."[58] Hungary and Poland with their weak king, huge peasantry, and unruly nobles unable to act in concert were a kind of eighteenth-century simulation of France between the tenth and thirteenth centuries, the era of feudalism proper. And just as Hungary and Poland were images of the French past, Spain and England were images of possible French futures. Spain gave some idea of what might be in store for a country that failed to break out of absolutism, England signified the happier fate of a nation that had left absolutism behind.

While this is a stages-of-development scheme, Montesquieu was not arguing that France had to become either Spain or England. An indefinite number of futures was possible, but these two nations were visible and dramatic incarnations of the general directions which the future might take. Furthermore, Montesquieu was not saying that Hungary and Poland were still in the Middle Ages, at stage one, while England was at, say, stage eight. It would not have surprised him to discover, for example, that cities and middle classes had in the past played a larger role in Polish history. He was only saying that Poland, whatever her personal history, now resembled the France of the Middle Ages. Laws of progress or of a uniform series of developmental stages had no place in Montesquieu's thought; his use of Poland in this context was not meant to increase his knowledge of Poland but to illuminate further the past of France.

The lesson England taught a Frenchman of Montesquieu's vision was radical in its implications. "Abolish the privileges of the lords, the clergy, and cities in a monarchy, and you will soon have a popular state, or else a despotic government." England was such a popular state.

The English, to favor their liberty, have abolished all the intermediate powers of which their monarchy was composed. They have a great deal of reason to be jealous of this liberty; were they ever to be so unhappy as to lose it, they would be one of the most servile nations upon the earth.[59]

It was the centralization of Britain's government that Montesquieu found particularly striking, and not the tradition of gentry rule in the countryside. When the Stuart kings declared themselves sovereign, it was inevitable that parliament should respond by claiming sovereignty for itself. But Montesquieu, the theorist of limited government, was opposed to sovereignty in any form. He laid so much emphasis upon checks and balances in England because the centralization of English politics posed novel threats to freedom. British freedom, it is essential to realize, has feudal roots but is also a postfeudal, post-*ancien régime* phenomenon. England's feudalism dates from the time of the Norman Conquest,[60] but by the eighteenth century, Montesquieu observed, the feudal laws were dead[61] and the intermediary bodies gone. Representative government was feudally and Gemanically bequeathed to England,[62] rather than a legacy of Graeco-Roman direct democracy, but representation was no longer based on medieval estates in a society now democratic instead of aristocratic: for example, the clergy no longer enjoyed the advantage of sitting as a separate body in the political assemblies. Having broken free of the feudal past, England was the first new nation, a national republic as opposed to the city-state republics of Italy or the confederate republic of Holland.

Purging the intermediary bodies from France's absolute monarchy could result in remarkably antithetical alternatives: either something like an Oriental desert or a national system of freedom. England was steering a course in uncharted waters, far beyond the outer boundaries marked by feudal tradition. Before the English experience, republicanism on a national scale was unthinkable, and not until the American and French Revolutions did the popular mind imagine the possibility of declaring an end to feudalism and the birth of a national republic as the successor to the national monarchy.

2. Feudalism and Bureaucratic Theory

Bureaucracy in the *ancien régime* was infeudated bureaucracy. The old feudalism was long reduced to little more than seigneurial dues and a nobility socially prominent but politically impotent. In the meantime, however, a new feudalism had grown up alongside the modern state, or more accurately, within what sometimes purported to be a modern state.

Always in need of money because of an unending succession of wars, a retarded economy, inferior credit institutions, and the First and Second Estates' fiscal immunities, the French monarchy constantly sacrificed future to present needs by selling an astonishing number of public offices. Venality repeatedly rescued the crown from financial crisis, but it also compromised the state's drive toward full governing capability. For its effect was to incorporate the principles of France's traditional society into what was struggling to be a modern state. The natural impulse in a traditional society is for office to be regarded as personal property, useful in furthering the private interests of the officeholder's family, instead of as an impersonal public trust. Since venality made public offices into commodities to be bought and sold as private property, it was a literal, explicit, and massive reinforcement of what otherwise was an implicit logic of personal rule in traditional society. Before long, moreover, offices were not only personal but a noble title enhanced the market value of many; and when such offices became hereditary, a neofeudalism was established. The ranks of the privileged were swollen to unseemly proportions, and these were not disciplined bureaucratic nobles dedicated to state service, but nobles who feudalized even so seemingly powerful a bureaucratic state as the Sun King's.

Venality was of such vast importance that it arrested the attention of almost everyone worth speaking of in eighteenth-century France. Many greeted venality with verbal abuse; a few spoke in its behalf. Some were concerned with the impact of venality on social structure, some with its political consequences, and a few spoke of venality in terms of the overall pattern of relationships it was forging between state and society.

The assault on venality came from all quarters, progressive and conservative alike. Cries against the sale of offices, on their progressive side, were a blending together of the voices of raison d'état advocates and of *philosophe* reformers. Richelieu and Colbert had plans for curtailing and phasing out venality, but financial worries always prevented them from pursuing such designs to their fulfillment. Voltaire, the Marquis d'Argenson, the physiocrats, and a host of *philosophes* seconded the royal ministers in their judgment of venality as a rape of bureaucratic ideals. Conservatives such as Fénelon, Saint-

Simon, and Boulainvilliers also had their reasons for assailing venality. Predictably, their bone of contention was those offices bearing noble titles. The rapid proliferation of the number of persons claiming nobility cheapened the meaning of nobility and insulted the old aristocracies of Sword and Race by inviting wealthy parvenus to assume aristocratic pretensions.

Apologies for venality were fashioned, as might be expected, by those who had not yet arrived in aristocratic society, and — surprisingly — by at least one member of the highest nobility. Those who were not noble, and wished to become so, had cause to defend the sale of offices. For the most part, however, they could adduce no better rationalization than the antiquity of venality. Only in a traditional society can the age of an abuse justify its continued existence, but not even the soporific effect of tradition was enough to save such an argument from rejection as patent absurdity. A more penetrating defense of venality, and one which linked its social and political ramifications, was put forth by Saint-Simon, inveterate warrior for the interests of the peerage. Opposed to venality in general, Saint-Simon eventually came to support one of its consequences: the entrenchment of a legal caste, the Robe, which had become the one corps within a corporate society that had the wherewithal to resist the king. Since the peerage could not stop royalty, it was up to the *arriviste* Robe to do so. For one moment of pure lucidity, Saint-Simon proposed as an alternative to absolute monarchy what we now realize was the historical reality — a monarchy absolute in theory but in fact tempered by venality.[63]

By and large, venality — for all the commentary it stimulated — did not evoke in many minds anything that moved beyond an immediate strategy to a fundamental re-examination of the old order. Usually a royalist lashed out against venality, but that was all. It did not occur to him that the venal phenomenon could be adequately understood only if it were seen within the larger context of the obstacles which France's traditional society had always placed in the way of political institutionalization. Nevertheless, there were a few exceptional minds who saw that venality was giving rise to a new feudalism. Seeing this, they did not merely call for an end to venality, but questioned whether Leviathan could ever be a truly awesome monster so long as French society bore a traditional, feudal, and aristocratic stamp. Saint-Simon, the antiroyalist, was cheered by the weakness of an absolutism tempered by venality, but the royalist Bodin was

saddened by the same. To find guidelines showing what an absolutism freed of feudal interference might look like, Bodin turned to
the supposedly natural home of such a political configuration — the
Orient and especially the Ottoman Empire.

As the one absolutist who had developed a political sociology, and
as a pioneer in the use of the comparative method, Bodin was a
worthy opponent for Montesquieu. At stake when these updated
Aristotles duelled conceptually was a bureaucratic theory, Bodin pro-
posing and Montesquieu disposing. We now turn to the specifics of
their argument.

The words "feudalism" and "bureaucracy" amount to an antino-
my in the twentieth-century mind. Embellishing Mosca's account,
which may be taken as typical, a feudal government is characterized
by small social aggregates, each self-sufficient, the political functions
of which, be they economic, judicial, administrative, or military, are
one and all exercised by the same persons as a matter of proprietary
right. A bureaucratic state is distinguished by specialization of functions, separation of the bureaucrat from ownership of the means of administration, and salaried employees paid by the central authority's
tax resources. In a feudal government, power is localized and local
power is lodged in a few hands. In a bureaucratic state, power is in the
hands of many functionaires but centralized through a political structure that governs the whole of a nation.[64] Feudal and bureaucratic institutions, then, are polar opposites, and modern history is the record
of the displacement of feudal by bureaucratic polities.

Before modern readers can understand the bureaucratic theories of
the *ancien régime*, they must reverse their perspectives so that feudalism-
bureaucracy are no longer considered as thesis-antithesis but as a
factual and conceptual continuum. Factually, feudalism and bureaucracy were bound together in the infeudated bureaucracy of the old
regime. Conceptually, "feudalism" furnished a language, a strange
language to modern ears, by which the theorists of the *ancien régime*
groped toward conceptualization of new administrative possibilities.
The history of political thought is in part a study of various vocabularies, legal, religious, and otherwise, which are torn from their original context and refurbished to meet the challenge of new problems.[65]
Feudalism provided one such vocabulary and the problem it addressed in the *ancien régime* was the building of a bureaucratic theory.

On this score, thinkers as different as Bodin, Dubos, and Montesquieu were in agreement.

As a language of bureaucratic thought, feudalism was not only relevant to the eighteenth-century present but at the very heart of political controversy. The theoreticians of absolutism needed to show the way from royal to bureaucratic absolutism. For if absolutists did so, the constitutionalists would have to drop the charge of institutional feebleness which they had pressed against monarchy. The closer absolutist thought came to a theoretical conceptualization of a bureaucratic regime, the more perfect it was, and vice versa.

Feudal language could assist the development of a bureaucratic theory by taking it away from the court — where Machiavellians had left it stranded — and placing it in the provinces where such thought belonged in a territorial monarchy. The language of feudalism focused thought on the functionary in the provinces and his relationship to the king at court, as was proper and necessary. Machiavellians cannot be charged with shortsightedness because they failed to reach downward, revealing the workings of a pyramidal hierarchy, centrally located. Such a charge would be empty for the simple reason that the bureaucracy of the old regime was basically not of the vertical sort. Machiavellians certainly were deficient, however, in missing the horizontal dimension of relationships between king and provincial administrators, the dimension of critical importance. Feudal language, stretched, adapted, and transformed, was qualified to remedy this shortcoming.

Moreover, it can be argued that provincial functionaries in any number of premodern countries with agrarian economies and large makeshift bureaucracies really were less easily assimilated into the image of Weber's ideal-type bureaucrat than into the feudal language of the *ancien régime*. Such administrative servants often received land (as in Czarist Russia) or a combination of fees, perquisites, and tax exemptions (as was true of French *officiers*), rather than a salary, as payment for services rendered. And a strict differentiation of functions was unfamiliar to such officials. They might, for instance, sit as supreme territorial judges as well as carry on routine administrative activities. In these respects, and in the intendant's habit of concluding his orders with a personal repetition of the king's *"car tel est notre bon plaisir,"* the functionary appears less as a dispassionate advocate of impersonal rules, or as an official whose powers are stringently delimited by a specified function, than as the last heir of the feudal noble, mighty in his bailiwick.

For feudal language to succeed, it would have to go beyond the truths of pure description. The more attentive it was to describing the administrative reality of the *ancien régime* as a modification of ancient feudal patterns, the less successful it would be in its creative mission: a prescriptive theory that could pose as an alternative to the half-feudal, half-bureaucratic administrative regime by cutting out the feudal half and streamlining the bureaucratic remainder. What was needed was not a better description of what was, but of what could be, what could grow from or be imposed upon what was.

Doubtless, the greatest contribution of feudal language to normative bureaucratic theory came through its uses in facilitating a comparative and historical study of bureaucracies. The absolutists Bodin and Dubos preceded Montesquieu in hitting upon the heritability of fiefs as the Archimedean point of French history. Their argument amounted to this: subtract the feudal legacy from monarchy and you will have a powerful absolutism bolstered by an efficient bureaucratic apparatus. Dissolving the hereditary principle, so much a part of the French present, would leave the king in control of his officialdom. As long as offices ("fiefs") did not become hereditary, the officeholders ("feudatories") were directly answerable to the king and thus his good and obedient servants. Both men pointed to Turkey as an absolutism of just this sort and as a model for France to follow. Or, speaking in historical rather than comparative terms, they hoped to recreate the France which existed before fiefs became hereditary. The French past of Charlemagne's period and the Turkish present exemplified the kind of administrative machine that France needed and could have if she reversed the tendency central to her society since the ninth century, the tendency for social ranks to form on the basis of hereditary status, and for political office, following the dominant societal principle, to become likewise an irrevocable hereditary possession. Complaining that "the Abbé Dubos . . . carries us to Turkey to give us an idea of the ancient French nobility,"[66] Montesquieu knew what the absolutists had in mind: a program to follow the example of Oriental despotism.

Using feudal language to do a comparative study of administration was not a good method for adequately understanding Eastern culture, but for the most part it harbored no such pretensions. Foremost among Bodin's concerns in making cross-cultural comparisons was the objective of gaining a better vantage point on the West, and only secondarily did he hope to shed light on the East. He knew very well that he was speaking of the Orient in terms of what was absent (feudalism) and not of what was present. At no point was Bodin guilty of forcibly imposing categories fit for only one culture upon another. Feudal language was a mode of conceptualization applied to East and West alike, but its first lesson was that feudalism was uniquely Western and the Orient something entirely different. Exactly what the Orient *is*, as opposed to what it *is not*, remained veiled in mystery and was destined to continue so until the interests of the investigator changed, more factual data became available, and different conceptual modes were employed. The sooner it is realized that Bodin's style of comparative analysis was deliberately geared to addressing an immediate problem of Western politics, the sooner do its merits gain visibility.

Bodin begins by laying a solid foundation for his bureaucratic conceptions with a statement of the kind of society that could support an administrative machine. Then he proceeds to picture the ideal bureaucrat, the operations of the bureaucratic apparatus, and the controls that would keep the bureaucrat under the domination of the politician.

"It is important," he notes,

> that a clear distinction be made between the form of the state, and the form of the government, which is merely the machinery of policing the state, though no one has yet considered it in that light. To illustrate, a state may be a monarchy, but it is governed democratically if the prince distributes lands, magistracies, offices, and honors indifferently to all. . . . Or a monarchy can be governed aristocratically when the prince confines the distribution of lands and offices to the nobles.[67]

For the most part, Bodin believes, absolute monarchy should be accompanied by democratic government and democratic society,[68] with only such concessions to aristocracy as are suitable to bureaucratic designs. Social stations are to be filled on the criterion of merit rather than birth, and a functional division of labor is to be society's leading principle: "Finance should go to the most honest, arms to the bravest, justice to the most upright, moral discipline to those of greatest integrity, work to the strongest, government to the wisest, priesthood to the most devout."[69]

As for the bureaucrats, whether they serve in the army or else-where, they will be exemplars of disciplined specialization, instead of unruly nobles. "[The] callings of arms, and of justice, and civil ad-ministration" must be "separated" and specialized "for it is very difficult to excel in one profession and quite impossible in many."[70] And at the end of his years of service, the bureaucrat will be provided for by a retirement plan: "one should follow the Turkish practice and reward good officers and men, especially when they grow old, with certain exemptions, privileges, immunities, and benefits."[71]

Service in the king's bureaucracy may be encouraged by "rewards . . . either honorable or profitable." "When we speak of rewards we mean . . . honorable charges, estates, offices, benefices, gifts; or im-munities from all or some particular burdens such as tallages . . . ; or letters . . . of nobility, knighthood, and such like honors." Ad-ministrators will become aristocrats, but Bodin takes precautionary measures to keep them under political control. "It is . . . impossible ever to control the distribution of honors and punishments once the prince has offered offices and benefices for sale."[72] Hence the route to nobility through venality of offices must be barricaded. Equally criti-cal, although nobility may be an important reward for bureaucratic service, provisions will be specified to make this a bureaucratic and not a feudal nobility. Preventing noble status from devolving onto the sons of present functionaires is mandatory if one is to avoid the development of a class of men noble by virtue of birth rather than service.

> [The] well-ordered commonwealth of any type whatsoever . . . should provide itself with an adequate force of trained fighting men. These should be maintained by grants of land . . . but granted for life only, as was originally the practice with fiefs and feudal lands, and is still the practice with the timars and timariots of Turkey. . . . Moreover it must be emphasized that these holdings can no more be made heritable, pledged, or alienated than can benefices.

If this is to mimic Turkey in one regard, in another it is only "to restore the original character of fiefs" such as they were in the French past.[73]

In Bodin, absolutist thought reaches one of its highest points of development. Where the theory of absolutism was weakest, in political sociology and bureaucratic theory, Bodin was at his strongest. He alone among the absolutists drew upon the Aristotelian method of

analyzing class conflicts and of prescribing the prerequisites of stability in a strife-torn age. No one followed up on his effort to adapt
Aristotelian insights to contemporary problems, and to that extent
Bodin's effort is the exception proving the rule that absolutist thought
was devoid of sociological imagination. And yet Bodin's overall
achievement did not follow him to the grave. In the heritability of fiefs,
he discovered the leading obstacle to bureaucratic control, and Dubos
was later to echo his opinion.[74] Once again Turkey was praised as an
absolutism that was powerful bureaucratically because of the absence
of the hereditary principle. And this was to suggest for a second time
that extirpating the hereditary principle in France was the most essential prerequisite to the construction of a bureaucratic machine.

Yet, despite its considerable advances, absolutist thought was
troubled by a deep ambivalence and indecisiveness. Absolutists could
not make up their minds whether an absolute state should be pieced
together from the materials of aristocratic society, or whether aristocratic society had first to be dismantled before a state able to govern
absolutely could become a viable reality. The attitude hostile to
aristocratic society entailed two fundamental dimensions. First, insofar as an aristocratic society was a traditional society, an assault on
customary law was initiated. Statutory law and the definition of law
as the command of the sovereign were the means by which Hobbes
and Bodin overcame the customary law that had protected property
rights but had also obstructed the freedom of the king to act as he
pleased. Second, insofar as aristocratic society was premised on an
hereditary social hierarchy, a general levelling of the social universe —
an end to nobility — was required. The favorable attitude toward
aristocratic society was also composed of two ingredients: first, that
venality be suppressed and, second, classes made functional rather
than eliminated. Nobility could persist, in this view, if it were linked to
service. Whether or not absolutism was to be gained by suppressing or
utilizing the givens of aristocratic society was a passionate issue, and it
not only ignited quarrels within the family of absolutist thinkers but
also caused schizophrenia in some absolutist souls.

Bodin was a man of two minds. Attracted to Oriental absolutism
and explicitly urging imitation of the Turkish example, he nevertheless retained a considerable fondness for the corporate associations of
the *ancien régime*, its guilds, estates, and local communities. When all
is said and done, however, the status of aristocratic society was

precarious within his system of thought. Unlike the family, corporate bodies are created through royal grant,[75] and what the king gives, the king can take away. Things pertaining to the father and his family — property rights and consent to taxation most importantly — have a special sanctity; but where previously customary law was their guarantee, Bodin secured them by their incorporation into the realm of natural law. Such a maneuver was well-meaning but meaningless since the sovereign authority was the interpreter of natural law.

There was, moreover, an excellent reason for assuming that the Bodinian sovereign would one day "discover" that natural law had deserted the society of fathers. Gross inequalities of wealth, Bodin was convinced, were conducive to the revolutionary politics on whose eradication his entire system was bent. Nobles, therefore, no less than commoners, should bear the burden of taxation, and to effect this end, he proposed the imposition of a graduated taxation levy.[76] Unfortunately for aristocracy, an egalitarian overhaul of the taxation system was plainly incompatible with the retention of privileges lodged within the family structure of society. One or the other would be banished, and there could be little doubt which it was to be. Against the demands of political expediency, the claims of privilege are nothing. Apparently, then, the sovereign is fated to dismantle aristocratic society, but Bodin could never quite face up to his own logic. Since the legalistic tradition of the West was dear to him, as to nearly everyone else, his Orientalism remained deeply ambivalent, his writings inconsistent, his final message indecisive.

The unambiguous sympathy of most absolutists for aristocratic society can be seen in the forthright rejection of Orientalism by Bossuet,[77] the royalist, no less adamantly than by Fénelon, the defender of aristocratic liberties. Or, as further proof, what could be more striking than to hear Richelieu, who sent more than one prominent noble to the gallows for duelling, proclaim that "honor should be more dear to [nobles] than life itself," or beseeching the king "to help them enlarge the landed estates which they have inherited?"[78]

The overall viewpoint of the absolutists, and the strategy intended as a reconciliation of their ambivalence, was a proposed subtraction of the hereditary principle from offices while leaving it unmolested in society at large. Hopefully, this was the best of two worlds, European and Asian, and the proper compromise assuring both the retention of aristocratic society and also the objective of a proficient, responsible, and rationalized bureaucratic apparatus. The irony of this conclusion is that, appearances to one side, the entire effort of the absolutists to do comparative politics was for naught. Comparative method had courageously called all of aristocratic society into question; but once it was decided that the old order should be saved, the proposals for reform were such as could be, and were, arrived at without recourse to comparisons. Many a reformer ignorant of comparative method had already suggested, or was later to suggest, the suppression of the hereditary principle in regard to offices while shying away from the thought of doing the same within the larger social fabric.

Montesquieu's rejoinder was direct and addressed itself to the absolutists in both their usual mood of vacillation and in their unusual moments of determination. If aristocratic society is retained, so must the abuse of venality be tolerated. Honor discourages economic activity, but the venality of noble offices promotes bourgeois entrepreneurship. So long as demand comes from class rather than mass, so long as a few are conspicuous consumers without also being producers — so long is venality essential and the good intentions of reformers likely to end in unanticipated consequences of the most unpleasant sort.[79] Furthermore, office must confer nobility because an economy of luxury cannot produce enough wealth for a king to pay his officialdom an adequate salary. Nonmaterial incentives are therefore mandatory, and the chief nonmaterial incentive in an aristocratic society is honor — that is, nobility.[80]

If, however, absolutism is retained but the substructure of aristocratic society demolished through uprooting the hereditary principle, disallowing it altogether and not just for political offices, then despotism ensues, which is the weakest and most poorly governed of all regimes. Turkey, already powerful during Machiavelli's period, was still a colossus when Bodin was writing, but by the eighteenth century it was in drastic decline. Montesquieu's prediction that Turkey would be conquered within two centuries was eventually borne out.[81] Instead of a model to imitate, Turkey was a warning of the debility, self-inflicted suffering, and self-liquidation wrought by unmodified absolutism.

Where the absolutists saw a bureaucratic machine in the Orient, Montesquieu countered with the charge that Oriental despotisms were the most personalized of all polities. Where they saw order, power, and efficiency, he saw chronic instability, impotence, and corruption. Sometimes Montesquieu calls the functionaries of Oriental despotism "intendants," sometimes "governors," and at other times "feudatories."[82] Bodin had reason to refer to the provincial functionaries of the Orient as "feudatories," and all the more did Montesquieu, who regarded them not only as paid by the king with revocable land grants (fiefs),[83] but also as combining the military and civilian powers in their persons, much as did the feudatories of the West in the Middle Ages. In other words, the military ruled in the Orient, so that Oriental despotism was really military despotism; and if the king was sometimes able to control the armies in the provinces, it was only by virtue of the praetorian guard with which he oppressed them.[84] But how could he guard himself against his guardians? He could not, and therefore military coups were as common as changes in the weather. At any rate, the ability to tax was as fundamental as was monopoly over instruments of violence in determining whether a country was ruled by a state; and an Oriental despot had neither. We have already seen his difficulties with the military; as for revenues, there was no wealth to tax and the addition of a tax burden to the already unbearable woes of the populace would spark a revolution.[85]

Through the medium of feudal language, Montesquieu, like Bodin, built a theory of administration set within the context of an historical and comparative analysis. However, his intent in this endeavor was completely condemnatory, whereas Bodin's had been laudatory. If bureaucratic absolutism brought disintegration, then no one, not even an absolutist, could maintain his enthusiasm for the proposed bureaucratic route to modernity. What's more, Montesquieu could complement the negative example of decadent Turkey with the positive example of England, the first new nation. Citing the British counterexample, he struck another deadly blow at those who pursue order and power through bureaucratic absolutism. For what the eighteenth-century observer saw in progressive England was not a burgeoning bureaucracy but its very opposite — Walpole's spoils system[86] — so that political strength apparently had nothing to do with bureaucratization. And even from the standpoint of a statist, England's constitutional government was stronger than either Turkey's complete absolutism or France's modified absolutism. While government in England was bolstered by an affluent tax base,[87] the coffers of Oriental absolutisms were empty, and the French state could neither tax its parasitical nobility and clergy, given their privileges, nor its bourgeoisie beyond a certain point for fear of discouraging its one source of economic productivity.[88] In general, the tax resources of a state are directly proportional to its freedom and inversely proportional to its despotism.

> It is a rule that taxes may be heavier in proportion to the liberty of the subject, and that there is a necessity for reducing them in proportion to the increase of slavery . . . We find it in all parts, — in England, in Holland, and in every state where liberty gradually declines, till we come to Turkey.[89]

The last obstacle to Montesquieu's triumph over the absolutists was China. Turkey was in marked decline in his period, as was India, and China had emerged as the greatest power in Asia. China troubled Montesquieu because its despotism appeared to be working too well and was beginning to attract the admiration of the French absolutists, much as Turkey had in the past. After Montesquieu's death the physiocrats made much of China, but already in his lifetime Voltaire and the Jesuits, unlikely allies, expressed great affection for Chinese ways. J.B. Du Halde, a Jesuit missionary, published a glowing report on China in 1735, and other Jesuits returning from the Chinese emperor's court spread similar tales of Oriental bliss.

Montesquieu was out to destroy the China myth, and his method of attack began with a debunking of the Jesuits as sources of accurate information.

> Our missionaries inform us that the government of the vast Empire of China is admirable, and that it has a proper mixture of fear, honor, and virtue. . . . But I cannot conceive what this honor can be among a people who act only through fear of being beaten. Again, our merchants are far from giving us any such accounts of the virtue so much talked of by the missionaries; we need only consult them in relation to the robberies and extortions of the mandarins.

It was not a conscious lie but a mental myopia congenital to their calling that had misled the Jesuits. "Might not our missionaries have been deceived by an appearance of order? Might not they have been struck with that constant exercise of a single person's will — an exercise by which they themselves are governed, [the rule of their monastic order]?"[90]

As a sociologist of knowledge, Montesquieu was willing to admit that "there is frequently some kind of truth even in errors themselves."

It is true that not all despotic governments are equally despotic; Turkey and China were the extreme poles of a spectrum of despotisms, running from most to least intolerable. But that did not alter the overall judgment of China as "a despotic state, whose principle is fear."[91]

How then did the Chinese prince maintain himself while other Oriental despots had hardly enough time to sit down on the throne before a palace coup or popular revolt ended their reign? Whenever a despotic monarch succeeds in governing, it is usually because he is an excellent Machiavellian.

> [Despotism's] principal method of maintaining itself is to outdo itself in cruelty, to excite its barbarism, and in its thirst and hunger, to cover itself with blood in order not to devour itself. If the despotic states are compared with each other, one will see that those sustain themselves best which, refining, so to speak, their cruelty, discover the secret of rendering it excessive and of giving new foundations to the state in multiplying the injuries they cause human nature.[92]

Either through completely atomizing society with fear, or through the other Machiavellian strategy of buying off the populace by terrorizing the ruling class, the monarch prolonged his despotic rule. Of course, these methods rarely were long continued, since they depended entirely on a single person's rational calculations of applied violence, and could never be institutionalized because they were the contradiction of all institutionalization.

Something of this was to be found in China. In that country accidents of climate caused a prodigious growth of population. Famine was therefore a constant threat; and when it struck, a popular revolt was in the offing, the despot knew, unless he acted as a wise and benevolent prince. Marauding gangs roved across the countryside during periods of famine, their numbers swelling along the road to the capital, and by the time they approached the royal palace, the rowdies had become a revolutionary force. "From the very nature of things a bad administration is here immediately punished." "The emperor of China . . . knows that if his government be not just he will be stripped both of empire and life," whereas in other Asiatic nations the threat of revolution was not so visible and the prince felt free to abandon himself to the pleasures of the harem.[93] Voltaire could naively praise China as "the first nation in the world in ethics and the science of government,"[94] but only because he failed to realize that Chinese political science was the sinister Machiavellism which eliminates morality from politics. Reason, such as it was in China, was not the reason of Enlightenment but the rational calculation of violence and brute power.

Other unique features, one religious and one economic, tempered China's despotism. Most Oriental princes saw little more in religious authority than an annoying but pliable obstacle to absolute power.[95] Hence, the king was apt to make over religion in his own image. And when he did so, the result was that religion lost its integrity and could not sanctify the monarchy which desperately needed sanctification. The Chinese monarch, however, had learned not to tamper with the holy books of his nation, which were notable for preaching paternalism. Chinese religion encouraged the populace to view the king as a patriarch, and therefore — the king knew — it was favorable to a continuation of the leadership.[96] One last factor: because of a population explosion, the problem of subsistence was particularly pressing in China, and to overcome it thrift and industry were politically encouraged. Out of fear of revolution, the prince refrained from interfering with private property; and ownership of land, here as everywhere, was the "mother of all" produce.[97]

Despotism was despotism even if special circumstances made some despotisms less hideous than others. Western monarchs had nothing to learn from China or any other Asiatic country, except for the lesson of what to avoid.*

The odyssey of the *ancien régime* in bureaucratic theory culminated in Montesquieu's destructive efforts. Coupled with the English counterexample, Montesquieu's labors signified a victory for constitutionalism as a political ideal and a defeat for the absolutist alternative. Montesquieu finished what others had begun, and finished it by way of destruction. Down fell the house of cards.

Historically, it was the example of discipline, duty, specialization, and efficiency in the military establishment that engendered the institutionalization of a bureaucratic apparatus, Prussia being the classic example. Even Bodin, however, was born too early to divine the lesson historical retrospect has taught us. When speaking of the

---

*Montesquieu was unable to dispose of China as neatly as he wished. He wanted to attribute all examples of despotic longevity to exceptional evil: violence beyond the already excessive norm. But in China's case, he was forced to concede its good qualities, and then to explain them away as minor aberrations.

military, Bodin does not and could not in his period see in it a conglomerate of traits that could be idealized into a bureaucratic theory.
His point is simply that the military must be defeudalized if the king is
to control it. That much Turkey's standing army — the first standing
army known to modern Europe — had taught him, but nothing more.
Though living later, Montesquieu's vantage point was hardly more
favorable than Bodin's, for Prussia's future was very much an enigma.
Excessive militarism, to Montesquieu's way of thinking, was a
breeding ground of the praetorianism that was in every way the opposite of institutional discipline and control. Thus, neither absolutist
nor constitutionalist derived a conceptualization of rational bureaucracy from the positive example of the military machine. Rather, both
discussed administration through the medium of feudal language; and
if this accounts for their relative successes in constructing a
bureaucratic theory, it also accounts for the deepseated deficiencies
that cost absolutists much more dearly than they did Montesquieu.
He had only to destroy, so far as absolutism was concerned, but for
them it was imperative to build.

   The administrative theory welded together from the recalcitrant
materials of feudal language looks best when most removed from an
isolated view of France. Opening up comparative perspectives, as
feudal language had done, was a bold and exciting move, since the
Turkish model did nothing less than call the whole of aristocratic and
feudal society into question. From today's standpoint, of course, it is
clear that even so imaginative and daring an exercise in political
thought was doomed to failure. At the point where Montesquieu
answered the absolutists with an indictment of Oriental despotism as
the weakest of all governments, we are more likely to reply that
"patrimonialism," and not an "ideal-type" bureaucracy, was the best
that feudal language could possibly muster. Under a patrimonial
government, as described by Weber,[98] administrative offices originating in the king's private household were placed in the provinces where
the official was paid in land or in fees exacted from the governed. After
a while tension between the king and his ostensible servant surfaced.
To the monarch the provincial post was part of his patrimony, but the
official, in defiance of royalty, strove to make it his. For the most part,
this battle between centralization and decentralization was waged in
terms of whether or not the office would be regarded as the private

and hereditary possession of the official. Suggesting, as Bodin did, that provincial officials should hold revocable and nonhereditary fiefs was, then, to plead for patrimonialism in its most royalist and least fragmented form. Bodin outpaced the administrative reality of his pre-intendant day by a wide margin. But his scheme left him far from ideal-type bureaucratic institutions and depended entirely on the energy of one person, the prince, for whatever effectiveness it had.

When the administrative theory contrived by feudal language turns away from comparative analysis to its other point of reference — the French past and especially Charlemagne's empire — the sense of excitement fades altogether and that of embarrassment augments. A return to the Middle Ages in search of a bureaucratic theory now seems absurd, for something entirely new was needed rather than the recovery of the past — and least of all the past of Charlemagne's period. As early as Montesquieu, the utter futility of such a notion stood exposed. In his history of feudal laws, Montesquieu had shown that Charlemagne held things together for a moment by virtue of his personal genius, but not even a succession of able kings could have long staved off the triumph of feudalism and the hereditary principle.[99]

Like all forms of discourse, feudal language was sensitive to some phenomena and insensitive to others, an excellent vehicle for expressing some new ideas and an obstacle to others. On the positive side of the ledger, it took bureaucratic theory away from the court and into the provinces; it described the provincial administrator accurately as an official who received land or fees rather than a salary as compensation; it centered on the hereditary principle as the major obstacle to a bureaucratic officialdom; it placed the study of administration in the context of comparative analysis; and it indicated some of the social prerequisites to bureaucratization. On the negative side, feudal language, which had long consorted with fragmentation and disintegration, stacked the deck against a really successful bureaucratic theory. Outstanding in explaining the nature of old regime society, it was utterly incompetent in depicting strong political institutions. Intrepidly it identified feudalism as the social enemy, but in its proposals for a suitable political remedy it could not see beyond a revamped feudal polity. Feudal language locked the absolutists in a feudal world at the precise moment when they were struggling most valiantly to leave medievalism behind.

For all the blind spots inherent in feudal language as a mode of conceptualizing bureaucratic possibilities, and notwithstanding Montesquieu's success in capitalizing on these shortcomings, there was, nevertheless, an element of good sense in this absolutist adventure in ideas. If we move away from Weber's concepts, where Bodin fares so poorly, the French *politique* has his moment of glory. In French Canada, where absolutism was unimpeded by the intermediary bodies of the mother country, a streak of feudalism successfully reinforced authoritarian government by way of a system of seigneurs who were good and loyal servants of the crown, sworn to royal allegiance by oaths of fealty and homage, but denied titles of nobility or a special legal status. It was as if the ghost of Charlemagne, after many centuries of wandering, had finally settled down in the Canadian wilds.[100]

3. Feudalism and Historical Potentiality

After two chapters on feudalism, it is only fitting that we make a few final remarks on Montesquieu's attitude toward tradition. He regarded the feudal past as highly oppressive, each lord acting as an absolute monarch in his fiefdom, and the feudal present as similarly oppressive. "In absolute states where there is a nobility, slavery grows insensibly as one descends the social scale from prince to the lowest subject."[101] Eventually the exploiters-exploited dichotomy sears every soul. Accordingly, noblesse oblige is to be understood as the condescension of the oppressors, and its counterpart among the oppressed is bitter resentment. "In monarchies and despotic governments, nobody aims at equality; this does not so much as enter their thoughts; they all aspire to superiority. People of the very lowest condition desire to emerge from their obscurity, only to lord it over their fellow-subjects."[102]

Yet there were grounds on which a progressive mind could value Western tradition, for it had been pregnant with liberty as well as oppression. Having read Tacitus, Montesquieu saw in the Germanic invaders not just barbaric passion but also a kind of primitive republicanism, so pure as to remind one of Rome's earliest years. Tribal chiefs were chosen for their valor, and decisions of importance were made by all the warriors in a common assembly. From one angle, the Germans lived in a kind of state of nature and could withdraw to the woods whenever political authority weighed too heavily. From another angle, they were primitive republicans, so that it was almost as if Rome's despotic and corrupt dénouement was killed by the republicanism and moral puritanism of her beginning.[103]

Liberty was reborn from feudal elements in the constitutional balance that stretched from the twelfth to the fifteenth centuries. And the last reign of liberty bequeathed by feudalism was contemporary England with its representative government, which had grown out of Germanic and feudal tradition. England was at once the last of what was good in the feudal past and the negation of feudalism, since the abolition of feudal laws, intermediary bodies, and aristocratic society was the other side of England's system of liberty.

Moreover, even in its worst moments feudalism did not give birth to regimes that reached the extremes of servitude characteristic of the Orient. During the period of feudalism proper, custom sometimes curbed the despotism of the local lord; and during the old regime, custom curbed the despotism of the king.[104]

Rome, under the emperors, and the Orient, now and always, suffered the plague of praetorianism. They could not solve one of the most delicate problems of politics — how the state could save itself from the military monster it created as a safeguard against foreign invasion. But even during the feudal period proper, which was a form of military rule, tradition kept militarism from degenerating into the praetorianism that eliminated the evolutionary possibilities of societies. Montesquieu could never see anything good coming out of militarism, and nothing could be more characteristic than his foreboding about Prussia's future: it was military despotism that he feared would result from Prussia's massive military establishment.[105] The thought that a Spartan military machine in Prussia could set the example for an absolutism run by an efficient bureaucracy was the farthest thing from his mind. To Montesquieu, militarism, other than the special militarism of ancient city-states, meant praetorianism: the praetorianism that destroys all institutions and rips open the womb of tradition that has given birth to so many regimes in the West.

City-state republics stemming from late medievalism, monarchies of various shapes and sizes, and a plethora of federal arrangements are evidence of the evolutionary richness of Western tradition, as are the intermittent periods of liberty that punctuate its history. Civic virtue, in contrast to Germanic and feudal tradition, was a one-possibility thing. After the life of public-spiritedness gave way to individualism, luxury, and inequality, the scenario was played out, never to start again. Oriental despotism had no possibilities at all; a society without tradition has no history. It is always the same, a continuous renewal of the same pattern of misery and oppression. Leviathans roamed the East unrestrained, each one guilty domestically of inducing a Hobbesian state of nature in which there was "no account of time." Past and future were equally devoured by an eternal present that is totally abhorrent. On the Western fork of the world crossroads, a trail started with the repetitions of nature in primitive societies and later led to the human growth called history. On the Eastern fork the trail was circular and led nowhere. Beginning with nature (a hostile climate), the Eastern path remained with nature (the Hobbesian state of nature), never reaching out to history, which alone can substitute growth for repetition.

Oriental despotism consisted of governments that could not govern, perpetual political decay, and praetorianism. And where there is no political system, neither is there a social system, for what is there to hold society together? Oriental societies, torn apart by fear, made it impossible for men to interact. Hence, the associational precondition of formal organization was missing; political institutions could never be built; a Hobbesian state of nature was the unvarying reality. Politics destroys society, and a social void cannot support a polity — a vicious circle. Alongside the eternal recurrence of the Oriental nightmare, Western tradition can be appreciated for its extraordinary evolutionary richness.

CHAPTER V

Fiction as a Surrogate for Natural Law

1. In Search of Nature

The inadequacy of natural law philosophy was recognized long before Hume launched his telling critique. Reformulations and supplementations of the old tradition, along with experiments into the possibility of new modes of moral judgment, were in the making decades and more before the *Treatise of Human Nature* was written. It was not necessary to be a full-time philosopher in order to sense the pressing need for new forms of ethical thought. Montesquieu's case illustrates the waning of natural law and the search for an adequate surrogate.

Natural law had to struggle for bare survival in Montesquieu's thought, where skepticism jeopardized the stature of a rationally demonstrable ethics just as certainly as it signalled antipathy to metaphysics. Less a philosopher than an antiphilosopher, Montesquieu was unsympathetic to the dilemmas of pure reason. Metaphysics is "seductive," he contended, because it "deals exclusively with grandiose matters." The metaphysician "seizes the whole of nature, governs it to his taste, makes and unmakes gods, gives and removes intelligence, puts man in the condition of a beast and removes him from the same."[1] Reason for Montesquieu, as for Locke, is the handmaiden of sense perception, and therefore is by nature a limited and earthbound faculty. "Perception, ideas, memory, it is always the same operation and comes solely from the mind's faculty to sense and feel."[2] Men are epistemologically fated to "judge by what they see that which they do not see," an acceptable state of affairs except for its unfortunate tendency to confirm prejudices.[3]

Modern philosophy is distinctly superior to its ancient counterpart because Descartes taught it to doubt.

The terms beautiful, good, noble, great, and perfect are attributes which are relative to the beings who consider them. It is necessary to keep this principle in mind: it erases the greater part of our prejudices. Ignorance of this principle was the flaw of all ancient philosophy, including the physics of Aristotle and the metaphysics of Plato.[4]

It is only by the study of philosophy that we undeceive ourselves. (I speak of the new philosophy because the ancient only served to reinforce prejudices.)[5]

Montesquieu had nothing but scorn for the revival of metaphysics which Malebranche attempted. The *a priori* notion of infinity which Malebranche adored was to Montesquieu nothing more than a human concept of the vaguest sort: "I do not have an idea of matter or of a being to which nothing can be added, no more than of an endless temporal duration, or of a final number."[6] Descartes' rationalism is dogmatic and epistemologically erroneous; Locke's empiricism is correct but must beware of backsliding into dogmatism, either by the philosophical route of ignoring the subjectivity of universals, or by the common sense fallacy of universalizing from the everyday reality that is a carrier of prejudice.

The chief characteristic of perception is comparison.[7] Only after repeated exposure to an object with four sides does the mind form the concept of a square.[8] All other universals have a similar origin. Indeed, the sensuous and subjective nature of thought is so marked that the addition or subtraction of a sense organ would radically alter the world of humanity.[9] Why, then, the persistence of metaphysical sophistry? To understand, epistemological criticism must give way to psychological explanation:

> It seems to me . . . that we never judge of matters except by a secret reflex we make upon ourselves. I am not surprised that Negroes should paint the devil in blinding white, and their own gods black as coal. . . . It has been well said that if triangles were to create a god, they would give him three sides.[10]

Cultural relativism furthered the skeptical work that epistemological and psychological criticisms had begun.

> It seems to me that the mores and customs of nations which are not contrary to morality cannot be judged as some better than others. For by what rule can one judge? They have no common measure, except that each nation makes the rule of its mores proper, and, by it, judges all the others.[11]

These words, which Montesquieu penned while taking the Grand Tour, do not eliminate all judgments of foreign cultures; he hated despotism too much for that. But a change of emphasis is clearly in the making. Natural law, if it were to survive, would have to cease being archetypical. Rather than an eternal and monolithic paradigm, nature is multiplicity and diversity, and any rules garnered from her must be tentatively stated and specify time and place.

Since nature is variety, plenitude, and fecundity, its endless forms[12] can be known only through constant experimentation. As a young man, Montesquieu conducted experiments on the causes of echo, the functions of the renal glands, the properties of physical bodies, and a variety of other subjects, including natural history. When his interest in politics and history became paramount, the experimental method had to be transplanted. Human history is nature twisted, turned, and mutilated in such an infinity of ways that only through experimentation can those acts which are hostile to nature be distinguished from those which are not.

In the *ancien régime,* literature was an exceptionally promising laboratory for moral experimentation and discovery. Circumventing the censor was a precondition of experimentation, since vested religious interests might tolerate the experimental method in physical science, but were steadfast in their opposition to its extension from physical to human nature. Censors always found literature trying because the author could deny that the morally offensive beliefs of his fictional characters corresponded to his own. By those who had eyes to see, ears to hear, and the determination to shed preconceptions, a lesson could be learned: that which is natural and good assumes many cultural forms. Exactly like cultural relativism, literature could teach the virtues of diversity, and it could do so more boldly: first, because it was less restricted by the censor and, second, because it could go beyond the current range of facts to an imaginative construction of what the inaccessible facts might reveal.

It would seem that Montesquieu bore all this in mind while working in literary genres. For in the brief compass of a few pages he conducted a remarkably daring experiment in (human) nature and made his mythical Persians vehicles for the dissemination of unthinkable thoughts. Using literature as a laboratory, Montesquieu invaded the family, that most intimate inner sanctum of Western culture, which had always found its apology in the natural law tradition. Ibben, writing from Persia to his countryman Usbek, travelling through Europe, relates a story which transfigures incest from the tabooed and stigmatized to the natural and desirable. Members of the Gheber religious minority which took Zoroaster for its law-giver, Apheridon and Astarte, brother and sister, fall in love at a tender age; but their passion is threatened by the inhospitable Mohammedanism, which is the established religion of Persia. Their father wishes them to marry in accordance with the ancient religious customs that see virtue and love in what other faiths call incest and disgrace. However, fearing persecution, he feels compelled to separate "a union already formed by nature"[13] but not yet consummated. The remainder of the story, entertaining though it is, need not detain us. Suffice it to say that, despite severe obstacles, Apheridon and Astarte find each other and enter into a marital bliss unshakable by the most unfavorable reversals of fortune. In *The Spirit of the Laws* Montesquieu contradicts his earlier view, deciding in retrospect that horror against incest is natural.[14] Whether he really changed his mind or instead felt compelled to protect himself by feigning orthodoxy is uncertain. It is also irrelevant. The irrefutable point remains that he was willing to experiment morally where others feared to tread, so as to do justice to all the possibilities of nature.

Skepticism, relativism, and toleration, we have seen, uprooted the side of natural law that sought universally valid norms. And careful examination of those few universal propositions left over in Montesquieu's thought after the completion of this onslaught reveals them to be mostly descriptive and empirical rather than prescriptive and *a priori*. As a physical rather than a social being, a part of nature rather than society, man was everywhere the same. All that was needed, then, in order to speak of mankind in general, was to transpose the language of science from nature to man. Thus we find Montesquieu approaching human nature with a materialistic postulate, by means of which he reduces many mental processes to functions of the bodily "machine."[15] Mechanism was only an analogy, albeit a significant one, but in considering man as an animal, Montesquieu was laying aside metaphors to speak in the most direct language possible. It is to animals, Montesquieu suggested, that we should look if we wish to know the laws of nature.[16] Eating, drinking, and sexual intercourse are representative "laws of nature";[17] and these needs are common to man and animal alike. In his notebooks Montesquieu went even further and pondered the possibility that man descended from the apes.[18]

Reviewing the well-worn notion of a "state of nature," Montesquieu discovered that some of its precepts were worthless. But in certain other usages it was a fruitful concept, the only concept that could encompass an occasional statement at once universal and yet applicable to man as a social and not merely as a physical being. For Montesquieu, who regarded association as natural, the habit some natural law thinkers had of conducting searches into social origins was plainly "ridiculous."[19] Nevertheless, sociological awareness did not necessitate the conclusion that discussions of "the state of nature" should be indiscriminately terminated. As a logical construct, the "state of nature" was a means of divesting man of social determination, a way of peeling off successive layers of socialization, a method of arriving at unconditioned human nature. The effort is rewarded if something remains after the reductional process has been completed, if man, that is to say, is more than the ensemble of his social relations. Something did remain, in Montesquieu's estimation, and it was a matter of no small importance. By nature man is a timid and innocent animal, not in the least cursed with aggressive impulses; he flees his fellows rather than confronting them in a Hobbesian war of all against all. Nothing is so unusual as for members of the same species to slay one another.[20] Aggression, which might have been held explicable by a psychology of basic instincts (the soul corrupted by original sin or an innate destructive drive) is rather a matter for social psychology to examine.

However intensive his labors to bend human applications of natural law in the direction of natural science, Montesquieu did, admittedly, leave behind traces of an *a priori* rationalism. Especially in his talk of an eternal justice, Montesquieu was still entrapped in the philosophical rationalism and modernized natural law of Grotius or Spinoza. Like them he was convinced that by mimicking the geometrical method, pure reason could state a truth of existence even as it ignored temporal anchorage: "To say that there is nothing just or injust but what is commanded or forbidden by positive laws, is the same as saying that before the describing of a circle all the radii were not equal."[21]

There are strong reasons for regarding absolute justice as an anomaly in Montesquieu's thought. "Good," "noble," "great," and "perfect" are all relative terms, Montesquieu had unflinchingly insisted; strangely, he shied away from adding "justice" to the list.[22] Through experimentation he dissolved most of the universal laws formerly derivative from nature, and accepted the few laws that remained only after they passed painstaking tests administered in the name of science. But when Montesquieu came to "justice," his skepticism suddenly failed him. Why did "justice" survive? Two suggestions may be hazarded. First, a priori justice is a residue which Montesquieu, not a philosopher and little hampered by a vestige of natural law thought, felt no compunction to expunge. Second, we know that Montesquieu had in fact ruminated on the possibility that absolute justice is fictional, only to dismiss his insight for reasons having precious little to do with philosophical inquiry. "If justice should depend [solely on convention], this would be a horrible truth that we should have to hide from ourselves."[23] Transcendental justice simply had to exist, Montesquieu believed, because without it "whatever is, is right."

An abstract and shadowy notion of justice was all that was left, then, of the moralizing and interventionist natural law of old. But that did not stop a less philosophical "nature" from engaging in constant polemical warfare. Let us consider a few of the ways in which Montesquieu utilized "nature," not as a law, but — far more typically — as an instrument of criticism.

Nature, in one of its significations alluded to in *The Persian Letters*, is coterminous with simplicity.[24] Society accordingly pales into an artificial, bogus, and cheap role-playing in which a person is always forced to act other than as he is, and appearance becomes more important than reality. A typical tourist, Rica attends the Parisian theater, but in his unfamiliarity with Western art forms he mistakes the audience for the actors.[25] Society is play-acting and the price of admission is bastardization of the innocent, natural self.

Enlisting nature to indict society is one of the areas where Montesquieu's thought touches upon that of his beloved predecessor, Montaigne. Besides their common social and geographic backgrounds,* Montesquieu and Montaigne shared a great deal intellectually. Urbane skepticism, facility in unmasking illusions, subjective empiricism, repugnance for religious fanaticism, and a feeling for the

---

*Both were Gascons, both noble, both held at the baptismal font by paupers.

diversity of human customs and the richness of natural forms — these are a few of the points of intellectual and emotional convergence. On the issue of natural law, Montaigne had already realized the need for reorientation from the universal and archetypical to the particular and manifold; likewise, he accentuated a descriptive approach featuring the belief that man is, more than anything else, a creature of passion and instinct. Already in its pre-Christian origins, the natural law tradition had been dual. Stoic philosophers and Roman lawyers had oscillated between natural law as the instincts that man shares with the animals, and natural law as a possession peculiar to man as a rational being.[26] Christians chose the latter version, Montaigne and Montesquieu the former. Their conception had a particular historical tradition as well as modern science behind it, and in general their outlook was associated with a constellation of overlapping and interlocking influences drawn from skepticism, paganism, and science.

Both Montaigne and Montesquieu were led, as they ridiculed society from the standpoint of nature, to toy with primitivism. Montaigne paints an idyllic portrait of barbarians to show that civilized men "surpass them in every kind of barbarity." Simple savages still ruled by the laws of nature have no taste for wars of conquest, they do not persecute their own kind for religious reasons, and they are ignorant of those advances of civilization responsible for some men being "full and gorged with all sorts of good things" while the rest are "beggars at their doors, emaciated with hunger and poverty."[27] Primitivism in Montesquieu's thought is evident in his sympathy for the German barbarians who practiced euthanasia on a Roman society that was supremely civilized but engulfed in the mire of despotic power.[28] And in *The Persian Letters* Rhedi confesses to Usbek his doubts whether the cultivation of the arts and sciences in the West has been on balance more beneficial than harmful.

> I have heard it said that the invention of mortar shells in itself deprived all the peoples of Europe of their freedom. Princes, no longer able to entrust the protection of fortified cities to burghers . . . , have therefore had an excuse for maintaining regular troops, with which, subsequently, they have oppressed their subjects.

War, moreover, grows increasingly violent and destructive as the art of combat is assisted by a science of mass murder. Similarly, the compass has opened new universes, but "this invention has been ruinous for the countries that have been discovered. Entire nations have been destroyed and men who have escaped death have been reduced to crude servitude."[29] Usbek takes up Rhedi's challenge and scores a number of telling points in behalf of civilization, especially with the argument that the absence of a productive economy in primitive societies is an assurance of unmitigated suffering. Other arguments, however, such as that a breakthrough in military technology "would soon be outlawed by international law, and unanimous agreement among nations bury the discovery" are pitifully unconvincing, just as Montesquieu intended.[30] Neither Rhedi or Usbek emerges as the victor in this encounter; instead a point-counterpoint, a dialectic of civilization and its discontents, has come into view.

Understood as a critical standard, "nature" is a leitmotif in all of Montesquieu's writings. Still, it was never the only path to criticism nor necessarily the best. Aware of the deficiencies of naturalistic judgment, Montesquieu refused to grant it exclusive rights over the expression of his moral passions. Prior to Hume, natural law was uncrippled by the disentangling of empirical and normative statements that threatened to separate them completely; but logical feats of the Humean sort were not requisite to arrive at a nature having, in Hume's words, "no more regard to good above evil than to heat above cold." Lucretius, a favorite of Montesquieu[31] and the *philosophes*, taught that nature was a poorly constructed thing, her processes more rightly characterized as strife[32] than harmony, her attitude toward man indifferent and apathetic. Modern physical science, anti-teleological to the core, lent a new credibility to Lucretius.[33] In a more optimistic vein, Lucretius eulogized generation, and Montesquieu seconded him when he praised nature as a "fond, indulgent parent that has strewed her pleasures with a bounteous hand."[34] But no more than the ancient pagan was Montesquieu willing to indulge in the belief that everything natural is a boon to humanity.

Savage society is a case in point. "Nature and climate rule almost alone over savages,"[35] but primitivism is far from attractive. "The prejudices of superstition . . . have the strongest influence on the human mind. Thus, though the savage nations have naturally no knowledge of despotic tyranny, still they feel the weight of it. They adore the sun."[36] No wonder, then, that Christianity found such pliable souls in the German tribesmen who succeeded the fallen Roman Empire.[37] Worse still than its vulnerability to superstition, savage society vies with despotism in the cruelty that man inflicts on man.[38] Montesquieu does not disagree with Rhedi's strictures on civilization, but the alternative of natural primitivism is fully as hideous as it is impractical.

Least of all could Montesquieu embrace a naturalism that allowed despotism to go scot free. Arbitrary government and a fear-ridden polity were "in some measure naturalized" in the Orient, but Montesquieu was not about to let that excuse despotism. One way out was tried by Rica, who denied that despotism is natural.[39] Yet despotic governments had always been the lot of the Orient, so that refusing the appellation "natural" to such regimes begged more questions than it answered.

Condemnation could not be achieved by excluding the term "natural," and it was equally inaccessible by direct recourse to natural law. Neither in its *a posteriori* nor in its *a priori* guise could natural law solve the problem which Montesquieu faced. *A posteriori* he was in no position to argue, as natural law philosophy had, that every society upholds minimal principles of justice, for in the Orient systemic injustice is an omnipresent reality. The natural reign of justice was not simply imperfectly realized or temporarily overthrown, but permanently excluded. *A priori* Montesquieu was no better off. It was no longer feasible to hold, in natural law fashion, that justice was the precondition of all the rule-governed behavior without which society is supposedly unthinkable and impossible. Regardless how disagreeable despotic societies are, or in what sense they are a negation of society, such societies do exist in the Orient. Men can and do live together, however miserably, despite the total absence of justice.

At this point the story related in *The Persian Letters* becomes all-important. Continually the novel draws us empathically into the Asian world of Usbek, his wives, and his travelling companion, Rica. As we learn more about their world, the world of Oriental despotism, our revulsion grows proportionately, doubt fades, and we know, or rather we feel, the certainty that it is an absolute evil which has disturbed us so. A world constructed from the materials of imagination, a fictional world, is void of reality, a thing "made up," but it is not a lie, nor does its storybook quality override its power to create and reinforce convictions. When moral proof is reduced to feelings that cannot be denied, fiction becomes a foremost means of ethical demonstration.

Near the outset of *The Persian Letters*, Usbek relates the Troglodyte fable. Before the era of their virtue, the Troglodytes were totally indifferent to justice, and soon their wickedness caused their self-destruction. "There are certain truths that it is not enough to impress by rational conviction, truths that must be felt. Such are the verities of ethics."[40] So Usbek insists in prefacing his moralistic tale. Little can he foresee that before his European journey ends, he will act the leading part in another tale of injustice, the story of Oriental despotism. No matter how skeptical the reader, no matter how relativistic, he cannot feel anything other than hatred for despotism after he has finished *The Persian Letters*.

2. The Psychology of Despotism in *The Persian Letters*

Fiction and psychology are fused in *The Persian Letters*. Transplanted from Eastern to Western culture, Usbek and Rica are subject to a wealth of new stimuli and sensations whose effect is most readily explained by Lockean psychology. For Locke's *tabula rasa* Montesquieu substitutes Persian travellers, beings with psyches long written full by Eastern culture. Then he suggests the psychic transformations that would transpire as the Western language of freedom threatens the Eastern language of despotism by writing challenging messages upon the tabula of the mind.

Besides the individual psychologies of Rica and Usbek, *The Persian Letters* focuses on the group and interpersonal psychology of Usbek's family. Since a great many letters are devoted to the relationship between Usbek and his wives, and several others to the conjugal tie in France, we would do well to familiarize ourselves immediately with Montesquieu's view of the family in general and his reasons for presenting the psychology of Usbek's family in particular.

"Of all the powers granted," Montesquieu wrote, the paternal power "is least abused; it is the most sacred of all magistracies — the one which does not depend on conventions, the one that predates conventions."[41] To him the family is a natural unit that is social, a social unit that is natural. Love, he believed, is a covert extension of self-love,[42] and he did not exempt familial love. But there is a qualification: within the family, love of self and of others are so conjoined that man's inevitable ego-ism begets no egotism. Never disinterested, passion can nevertheless overflow the confines of the self, as in proverbial "true love" or the family setting. Inequality between man and wife does exist, since he is biologically stronger, but it is an inequality directed toward the threatening environment. Internally, the family is remarkable for the relative absence of coercion, competition, destructiveness, and punitive measures — those hallmarks of society and government.

The family as a natural unit does not exist now and never has existed, except as an abstraction drawn from the propensities of human nature undefiled by society. That is why the notion of a society of natural families is sociologically untenable, and, if expressed at all, must follow the way of myth and fiction, as is true of the Troglodyte story. Each Troglodyte family is an exemplar of social virtue, and together their virtuous society constitutes a "single family."* Natural as well as familial, Troglodyte society enjoys a reign of virtue that is "not to be considered a painful exercise." All a Troglodyte need do is surrender to his passions and he will be virtuous, so different is his virtue from repressive civic virtue, which flourishes only as long as society successfully denatures man. "Justice to others is like charity to ourselves" — that is, the relationships within the natural family are written large across the whole society. "Simple Nature made herself heard," "The Earth . . . seemed to produce of her own accord," and a society of private families dedicated itself to the public good.[43]

Alas, it cannot be. The Troglodyte fable ends with the imposition of government. Education will henceforth replace natural impulse as the guarantor of public-spirited behavior; and the aged Troglodyte, honored with the crown of leadership, weeps at seeing that natural virtue has dissipated. Sometimes for better, but usually for worse, society and government supplant the natural family with a family that mirrors their being; the real family is a microcosm that replicates the macrocosmic socio-political universe. "Everyone follows the spirit of the government, and adopts in his own family the customs he sees elsewhere established."[44] Paraphrasing Maistre, one may say that the natural family or the family in general are nowhere to be observed; there are only republican, monarchical, and despotic families.

"In despotic states, each house is a separate government."[45] The dearth of social communication concomitant to the reign of fear

---

*Such was the idyllic society which sprang forth from the ashes of the earlier, evil, Troglodyte nation.

splinters society into a congeries of families, each an island unto itself. In *The Persian Letters* the relationships within one such. family are explored. During his sojourn in Europe, Usbek corresponds with his wives Zachi, Zelis, Zephis, and Roxane in his Ispahan seraglio. It is a correspondence to remember because each letter further amplifies the reader's realization of what the interpersonal psychology of a despotic family is like.

In *The Spirit of the Laws* Montesquieu insisted that wives in a despotic society are slaves, or the equivalent of slaves, and he condemned slavery as "neither useful to the master nor to the slave."

> Not to the slave because he can do nothing through a motive of virtue; nor to the master, because by having an unlimited authority over his slaves he insensibly accustoms himself to the want of all moral virtues, and then becomes fierce, hasty, severe, choleric, voluptuous, and cruel.[46]

Sociology can go no farther. After it has stated that fear is the central feature in the social psychology of a despotic polity, that social isolation takes the form of insular families, and that a demeaning master-slave relationship characterizes the despotic family, sociology must then confess that it cannot penetrate the protective walls surrounding the seraglio. "We know better," wrote Montesquieu, "what gives a certain character to a nation than what gives a certain spirit to a particular person, . . . [better] what forms the genius of societies that have embraced a type of life than what forms that of a single person."[47] Hence the relevance of psychology. It, and it alone, can reveal the interpersonal relationships within the family. Likewise, psychology is the only chance we have of entering into the struggle within individual egos. Interpersonal and individual psychology must invade the highly fortified sphere of the despotic family.

Usbek lives in two societies. Attached to the seraglio at home, he is an Oriental despot; travelling through Europe, he experiences Western freedom at first hand. Can socialization be undone? Can cultural accretions be dislodged from the psyche? Of necessity Usbek and his companions, Rica and Rhedi, become "sociologists," whether they want to or not. For them to survive in a strange culture, their initial naive impressions must be superseded by understanding. They come to acknowledge that peculiar Occidental ways have social functions. Soon they find that learning can be expedited if they approach their own culture from the outside, just as they originally reacted to a foreign culture as disinterested outsiders. Analogies abound as the familiar and the new culture are juxtaposed, clumsily at first but increasingly with the sophistication of systematic analysis.

Usbek, by intellectual studies, and Rica, by experience and observation, eventually arrive at the same conclusion: fear predominates in Eastern cultures, freedom still exists in the West. Their discovery opens a question rather than closing the story: is it humanly possible for Usbek and Rica to kill the old despotic self and re-integrate their personalities to live the life of freedom? The "ideas" whose "genesis and development" are the subject of *The Persian Letters*[48] must be understood in their full Lockean sense as the sensation, memory, imagination, and reflection composing the human mind. They are as much the history of personalities as the life of intellect.

An exact replication in miniature of despotic Persia, Usbek's family coheres as a functioning system even though the interrelationship of its parts is that of a war of all against all. In the very first letter to his seraglio, a Westward bound Usbek speaks with the voice of a tyrant. "Make them feel . . . their utter dependence," he writes to the first black eunuch in reference to his wives. A Persian husband is a tyrant; and so is each of the eunuchs who administers the husband's tyranny.

Eunuchs are at the forefront of household management, just as they bear the responsibility of state administration in a despotic polity. "You serve [my wives] like a slave. . . . But, by an exchange of authority, you command as master like myself whenever you fear a weakening of the laws of decency and modesty."[49] Reproducing the prince-vizier relationship of state affairs, the absolute power of the familial master devolves upon the eunuch absolutely instead of being parcelled out in fragments. And this means that the eunuch is as much a despot as is the master whom he serves. Forever at the mercy of his lord, the eunuch grinds the women of the harem under his heel and is second to none in inflicting scars, physical and psychological, upon others.

Despite his ostensible power, the eunuch's position is never secure. Women have their ways of winning the husband-despot to their side; they capitalize on his desire and are never more dangerous than when in bed. "They are in their glory there. Their charms can become terrible for me," laments a eunuch. "How many times has it happened to

me to retire in favor and arise in disgrace!" Wives and eunuchs compete for the attention of the master and the outcome is never decided
with finality. "There exists between us something like an ebb and flow
of domination and submission." As a governor delegated absolute
power, the eunuch is the scourge of women, but one of their sighs is
enough to cause his humiliation. Nor do these ladies waste any opportunities to employ the eunuch in degrading tasks, so ready are they to
remind him of his servility and baseness.[50]

Inherently weak and vulnerable, the eunuch has but one way
of defending himself: cunning, dissimulation, stratagems. An able
eunuch develops "maxims of inflexible government"[51] by which
rulership through fear is elevated to the level of a methodical art. The
imperatives of survival dictate that the eunuch consciously disabuse
himself of moral scruples. "Do not put too much store in overly exact
honesty," the grand eunuch advises his apprentice.

> There are niceties that scarcely befit any save free men. Our calling
> does not allow us the ability to be virtuous. Friendship, faith, oaths,
> respect for virtue, are victims that we must continuously sacrifice.
> Forced to work without ceasing, to preserve our lives and turn punish-
> ment from our heads, any means to an end is justified: finesse, fraud,
> artifice are the only virtues of unfortunate wretches like ourselves.[52]

Eunuchs are the Machiavellians of bedchambers, and each despotic
household knows the reign of fear, which, if expertly conducted, even-
tuates in "a deep silence."[53]

By augmenting the number of wives in the harem, the eunuch also
augments his opportunities for causing divisions among them.[54] Soon
he, though universally despised, has a ring of informers at his disposal;[55] scheming wives police each other better than the eunuch
alone could ever manage. He has only to bide his time and one jealous
wife will reveal the plans of another. A clever eunuch, knowing how
inimical to his interests emotional attachments are, will abet in-
constancy and stop at nothing to prevent a particular woman of outstanding beauty from gaining permanent access to her husband's
bedroom.[56] Jealousy in the master and among wives is the stuff out of
which social isolation is manufactured. The family is an extension of
despotic society and politics, rather than an enclave of civility nestled
pacifically in the midst of a storm of inhumanity. There is no truce,
sanctuary, or respite in the war of all against all.

Even without the eunuch's connivance, Usbek's wives fight and claw, dragging each other into the abyss. Zachi recalls an incident in their unremitting rivalry. "Each of us had made pretense to a superiority in beauty over the others. We all appeared before you after having exhausted our imaginations in finery and ornament." Pleased but unsatisfied, Usbek asked for more. "We had to strip ourselves of that finery which had become an annoyance to you; we had to present ourselves to your view in the simplicity of nature. I gave no thought to decency; I thought only of my vanity." And still more servility: "You made us assume a thousand different positions — ever a new command and ever a new submission." Nostalgia and satisfaction mix as she recollects the moment of her glory. "You took me, you left me, you came back to me, and I learned how to hold your attention. The triumph was all mine, and disappointment the lot of my rivals."[57]

Domination and oppression are a way of life in despotic societies. From supreme imperial prince to lowliest slaves in private households, everyone is equally a despot, even if husbands and prince are more equal than others. Some are despots from strength, others from weakness. Diversity of personality types diminishes in despotic society; at most one gets variations within the single despotic type. Particularly instructive in this regard is the vision a Persian woman offers of the afterlife of her sex: "Virtuous women will go to a place of delights, with divine men assigned to their pleasure. Each of them will have a harem in which the men will be shut up, and eunuchs even more trustworthy than ours to guard them."[58] Completely free in their daydreams to conjure up a society to their liking, Persian women can do no better than invert despotism, taking their revenge on men.

The Persian family is like despotic society at large in that it is pervaded with fear; but it is different in that the husband is seldom, if ever, overthrown by internal revolt, the fate which so frequently befalls despotic princes. How can the permanence of the husband's position be accounted for? Partly it is a matter of power: eunuchs, slaves, and wives are not a miniature counterpart to the army that can always subdue the prince. But the more important reason is this: not a single hand is raised against the patriarch of the household because no one knows he is a tyrant, and no one knows because no one wants to know. Illusion and "false consciousness" gird the prison walls of the seraglio.

Usbek is deluded because he doesn't realize he is a despot. Charging the eunuch with power to subjugate his wives, he imagines he is only assuring that "the laws of the harem"[59] will be executed. What strange laws these are by which the wives are commanded but have no say, laws that can be changed at the caprice of the husband, as if unfettered will and legality were the best of friends. Dealing with sub-human eunuchs Usbek has less need of self-deception:

> What are all of you if not base tools that I can break at my fancy — you, who exist in this world only to live under my laws or to die as soon as I shall order; you, who draw breath only so long as my happiness, my love, and even my jealousy have need of your baseness; . . . [I]f you stray from your duty, I shall consider your life like unto insects under my feet.[60]

In Persia, Usbek's frame of reference, arbitrary patriarchal power is customary, socially sanctioned, and beyond the pale of criticism. Examples of despotic patriarchal rule abide from bottom to top of the social scale; the most humble husband in his seraglio is no different from the prince in his. The testimony of time immemorial likewise appears to confirm the propriety and sanctity of the Persian family. Where Usbek goes wrong is in assuming that Persian "tradition" has something to do with consent or authority. Not so much legitimacy and consensus as sheer coercion and power underlie the "traditional" family, and if it were not for their fear and need of illusion the wives would shout as much. Usbek acts as a good Persian husband, a good Persian husband acts as a despot.

Love is the illusion of the wives. Were it not for the self-imposed delusion of amorous affection, their beings would be stripped much more naked than their bodies were in the contest to win Usbek's attention. If the truth is that they are slaves, then truth is not worth the effort. They prefer to believe that Usbek loves them and that they love Usbek. As an absolute ruler instead of someone ruled absolutely, Usbek is less the dupe of love: "It is not so much that I love them. . . . In this respect, I find myself in a state devoid of feeling, leaving me with no desires at all. . . . But from my very coldness there grows a secret jealousy that devours me."[61] This male avowal of marital weariness should be compared to Fatima's female enthusiasm:

> Even were I permitted to leave this place where I am enclosed by the necessity of my calling, were I capable of eluding the encircling guards, were I able to choose among all the men living in this capital

of nations, Usbek, I swear it, I should choose only you. In all the world, there can only be you worthy of being loved.

Fatima has never been permitted to see another man, and yet she proclaims Usbek the most worthy man in the world. Unwilling to admit her real subjection, she idealizes her existence as that of "a woman free by the good fortune of birth, yet slave by the violence of her love."[62] The distinction between slave and wife, a purely formal and meaningless distinction in despotic society, is to Fatima a consolation of the greatest importance.

Of all the inhabitants of the seraglio, the eunuch alone is beyond the spell of illusion. "My will is his property,"[63] Jaron writes to a fellow eunuch, by way of summarizing his relationship to Usbek. A seraglio, the eunuch knows, is a "fearful prison"[64] in which he is sentenced to a life term. "I have never known that attachment called friendship." "I had only myself for intimate friend"[65] — words of two eunuchs that are representative of the social disability of all. Physical intimacy between wives and patriarchal despot gives the husband the appearance of humanity, but the eunuch lacks even that appearance — as he fully realizes: "What can we do with this vain semblance of an authority that is never entirely communicated?," the chief eunuch asks Usbek. "We represent but weakly half of your own self; we can show them only a hateful severity. As for you, you temper fear with hope, you are more absolute when you caress than when you threaten."[66] So impervious to illusions is the eunuch that he, the household Machiavellian, consciously realizes their utility as a method of social control; "How can a man hope to captivate [the wives'] hearts if his faithful eunuchs have not begun by subjugating their minds?," the black eunuch inquires.[67] By osmosis despotism passes through the seraglio walls, severs human from human, and infiltrates the minds of isolated individuals. Vile eunuchs, because of their singular freedom from illusion, are unique in comprehending the ways of despotism and in transforming their comprehension into self-conscious weapons.

If the eunuch is outside the world of mesmerizing illusion, that is because he is inhuman, not superhuman. Castration, in his words, has separated him forever from himself, and his desexualized perspective cuts through all the falseness built into male-female relations. The first eunuch recalls the agony he suffered after castration: "The effect of passion was snuffed out in me without extinguishing the cause, and far from being comforted, I found myself surrounded by objects that provoked my passion without cease." Eventually the fire of desire subsided, and with dire consequences, he saw women for what they are: "I have detested them ever since the moment I was able to consider them objectively, for my reason has allowed me to see all their weaknesses."[68]

As sexual passion dies, other passions are born or accentuated. Usbek's professed belief in the conservation of matter[69] should be combined with Zelis' report on his attitude toward eunuchs:

> I have heard you say a thousand times that eunuchs find with women a voluptuousness unknown to us, that nature compensates for her losses, that she has resources to make up for the disadvantage of their condition, that one can stop being a man but never cease being sensitive, and that, in such a state, a person is as if in a third sensuality, where, so to speak, he only changes pleasures.[70]

The result of this combination? A law of the conservation of sexual energy. When passion stops being overtly sexual, it finds new means of expression, in the eunuch's case consuming resentment.

"As the crowning stroke to my misery I had ever before my eyes a happy man. During those troubled times, I never led a woman to my master's bed, I never undressed her without returning to my room with rage in my heart and horrible desolation in my soul." Being a slave, the eunuch must avenge himself against the wives rather than the master.

> I return to them all the scorn and torture they have made me suffer. I remember always that I was born to command them, and it seems to me that I become a man again when I can still do so. . . . The pleasure of making myself obeyed gives me a secret joy. When I deprive them of everything, I feel I do so for my own benefit, and indirectly, I always receive great satisfaction. . . . [My] ambition, the sole passion left to me, is satisfied a little. I can see with pleasure that everything turns on me and that I am needed every moment.

The perversity of what passes for moral duty in Persian society is not lost on the eunuch. Socially sanctioned "virtue," so far as he is concerned, constitutes an ideology of resentment.

> I bristle with scruples. There are never any other words in my mouth

save duty, virtue, decency, and modesty. I bring [the women] to despair by talking continually about the weakness of their sex and the authority of the master. I thereupon complain of having to be so severe, and I pretend to want them to understand that I act from no other motive than their own well-being and my great affection for them.

The eunuch is not a despot simply because power devolves absolutely on him, or out of necessity in the struggle for survival. He wants to make others suffer.[71]

As Usbek, Rica, and Rhedi journey in the West, they come into contact with an entirely different culture, a different family structure, a different government and society. In direct proportion to the growth of their knowledge of the West, they are familiarized with the spirit of liberty, and as the spirit of liberty becomes less foreign, their native land should take on a more foreign and hideous aspect. Easier said than done, however; the road to such a radical transformation of consciousness is many times obstructed by illusion and by the old self, which dies hard.

En route to Paris, Usbek stops over briefly in Turkey and is astonished by "the weakness of Osmanli empire." Graphically he describes the insolent military, the barren countryside, the economic void.[72] Vividly descriptive, Usbek's account is a morphology of a particular country rather than an explanation of a general phenomenon. Having recorded the symptoms, he cannot name the disease.

At this early stage of his leave of absence, Usbek's jealousy drives him to language that sounds very much like a frank evaluation of his marriages. To Zachi he writes,

You will perhaps tell me that you have always been faithful. Come now! Could you have been anything else? How could you have deceived the vigilance of those black eunuchs. . . . How could you have broken the bolts and the doors that held you in? You vaunt much a virtue that is not free.

Jealousy, however, is an inept means of tearing away the masks of illusion. So it is hardly surprising to hear him invoke "the laws of the seraglio" again, or eulogize "the sacred place that is a cruel prison for you."[73] To the eunuch "duty" is a conscious ideology of resentment, to Usbek an unconscious ideology of domination in the Persian family. As a beneficiary of established social arrangements, Usbek heeds the entrenched creeds that systematically inscribe the word "justice" on the most unjust practices. Macroscopically (Turkey) and microscopically (his Persian family) Usbek stumbles over despotism, verges on the language of understanding, but knows it not.

Before his arrival in Paris, Usbek writes a letter from Italy that rounds out the series of his earliest perceptions. "Women enjoy great freedom here," he remarks. And more significantly:

> It is a grand spectacle for a Mohammedan to see a Christian city for the first time. I am not talking about the things that strike everyone at first, like differences of architecture, clothing, and prevailing customs. For there exists, even in the most insignificant of details, something singular that I feel and cannot express.[74]

That unarticulated something is freedom.

Next we see the West through the eyes of Rica. His comments on the John Law scandal, venality, and *Unigenitus* are culturally-bound and do not penetrate below the surface. The whole force of his letter stems from its satirical effect. Calling the Pope a "magician," Rica displays ignorance, but his inadvertent hit at Christianity amuses (or infuriates) the French reader. Viewed within the context of Rica's mind, the letter contains only one truly important passage. "Do not expect me to be able just now to talk to you seriously about European usages and customs. I have only a faint idea of them myself and have barely had time to be amazed by them."[75] Instead of committing the tourist's fallacy of hastily passing sentence on everything foreign by its similarity to, or divergence from, native customs, Rica has the good sense to suspend judgment.

There follows a letter from Usbek, now in Paris, contrasting his sluggishness with Rica's facility in appreciating novelty. "His alertness of mind permits him to grasp everything rapidly. As for me, since I think more slowly, I am in no condition to tell you anything."[76] A little later the ostensible reason for Usbek's relative slowness becomes clear. "My body and mind are depressed. I surrender myself to reflections that grow sadder with each day. My health, which grows weaker, turns me toward my own country and makes this country ever more foreign to me."[77] Actually, his only malady is psychic — the jealousy that stalks him day and night. From the depths of depression he extolls the Persian family and repudiates the flower of French femininity. "Women here have lost all reserve. They appear before men with faces uncovered, as if they sought to request their own downfall." "How fortunate you are, Roxane, to be in the gentle country of Persia and not in these poisonous climes where decency and virtue are unknown! . . . You are in a joyful state of happy inability to transgress."[78]

Then comes the breakthrough. Rhedi is first:

> My mind is developing each day. I am ferreting out for myself secrets of commerce; I learn about the motives of princes and the form of their government. I do not even neglect popular European superstitions. I apply myself to medicine, physics, and astronomy, and I am studying the arts. In short, I am beginning to come out from behind the clouds that covered my eyes in the land of my birth.[79]

Usbek, too, learns to see:

> The seraglio is made more for hygiene than for pleasure. It is a uniform existence, without excitement. Everything smells of obedience and duty. Even the pleasures taken there are sober, and the joys severe, and they are practically never relished except as manifestations of authority and subservience. Men in Persia lack the gaiety of Frenchmen. You simply cannot find there the freedom of mind and the relaxed attitude that I see here in every rank and profession.[80]

From these observations Usbek gropes toward the first installment in a theory of Oriental despotism.

> Asiatic sobriety derives from the dearth of intercourse between people. They see each other only when forced to do so by ceremony. Friendship, that sweet bond of hearts which creates a gentleness of existence here, is practically unknown to them. They withdraw to their houses where . . . each family group lives . . . in isolation.[81]

To adapt creatively to a new culture, Usbek finds, is to be reborn. "Everything interests me; everything astonishes me. I am like a child whose still sensitive organs are keenly struck by the most insignificant objects."[82] A tabula rasa he and his companions are not, but little by little they unlearn their Persian past and open themselves to new sensations, ideas, and experiences.

As the old and new wage battle within the minds of the Persians, relapses are frequent and the final outcome anything but predetermined. "Our women belong too strictly to us; . . . such calm possession leaves us nothing to desire or fear." Thus ruminates Rica, and we cheer his great stride forward. He ends his letter, however, with an abrupt about-face, taking refuge in the revealed truths of Moham-medanism. "You can see . . . that I have developed a taste for this country where people like to argue extraordinary opinions and reduce everything to paradox. The Prophet has decided the question and laid down the rights of both sexes."[83]

Despite such temporary setbacks, Rica and Usbek both achieve a fuller appreciation of the relative merits of marriage in France and Persia.

> Frenchmen do not worry much about fidelity. They find it just as ridiculous to swear to a woman that they will always love her as to maintain that they will always be in good health, or always happy.

> Here a husband who loves his wife is a man lacking the attraction to make himself loved by another woman.[84]

These words of Rica are critical but not caustic. Their antagonism to French reality comes from the viewpoint of "true love" rather than from the alternative of the Persian family. On balance Rica's com-ments amount to an affirmation of French mores from a sobriety and worldly wisdom that knows how much — or how little — can be asked for in this less than best of all possible worlds.

Immediately following Rica's letter is a comment by Usbek ex-pressing his disappointment with the relationships of the sexes in Per-sia. "Love among our kind involves no vexation, no rage. It is a languid passion, which leaves our soul in tranquility."[85] It is now possible to surmise why Usbek holds Roxane in special esteem. She alone resisted him; for two months after their marriage she protected her virginity, and having lost it, would not look at her husband for another three months. Even when tolerating intercourse she withheld all she could.[86] In Roxane, Usbek discovered the "vexation" so essen-tial in love, or as Rica expresses it, an insecurity of possession that leaves something to be desired or feared. Love must be renewed con-tinuously and is meaningful only if what is given can also be taken away. Freedom is as essential in love as in politics.

As time passes, Rica, by travel and observation, and Usbek, by an intellectually stimulating existence in Paris, each deepens his un-derstanding of the differences between East and West. During his first stay in Paris, Rica was baffled by a city continually in motion. "I have seen nobody walking. There are no people in the world who get so much out of their carcasses as the French; they run; they fly. The slow carriages of Asia . . . would make them swoon."[87] Returning to Paris two years later, Rica attributes its perpetual motion to a pulsating economy, a thing unknown in Persia. Paris is "a city that is the mother of invention." "A young salesgirl will cajole a man for a whole hour to make him buy a package of toothpicks."[88] Visiting Paris again three years later, Rica easily delineates the logic of the economy of luxuries centered in the capital city.[89]

The Persian seraglio, Rica now believes, is characterized by "servitude of heart and mind" and by perpetual fear. "My mind is slowly losing everything Asiatic that was left in it, and I am adapting painlessly to European customs." And he understands the "why" and "how" of his transformation:

> Dissimulation, that art so practiced and so necessary among us, is unknown here. Everything speaks out; everything is visible; everything is audible.

> I can really say that I have known women only since I've been here. I learned more about them in a month than I would have learned after thirty years in a seraglio.[90]

The negative process of condemning the Persian family is soon accompanied by a positive profession of familial ideals:

> Families are a government unto themselves. The husband has only a shade of authority over his wife; the father, over his children. . . . Justice becomes involved in all their differences of opinion, and you may be sure that it is always against the jealous husband, the sullen father, the importunate master.[91]

Rica is a new man.

Usbek, too, learns to identify evil with Oriental despotism, and in a torrential outburst he works out a theoretical analysis of that wretched socio-political configuration. So thorough is Usbek's analysis of Oriental despotism that it almost equals Montesquieu's account in *The Spirit of the Laws*.[92]

Biding his time in vibrant Paris, and more impressed by social mobility in the capital than by its roots in aristocratic demand, Usbek vaguely senses the spirit of democratic society. "Liberty and equality reign in Paris. Birth, reputation, even military glory, however brilliant they be, will not save a man from the crowd. . . . It is said that the first man of Paris is the one with the best horses for his carriage." Nor does the aristocratic ethos keep any secrets from him. "Preferment," he realizes, "is the great divinity of Frenchmen." "Honor," a thing about which Persians "have absolutely no idea," embodies French social values and behind it stands the noble caste. "In Persia the only great men are those to whom the monarch grants some part in government. Here there are people who are great by birth." Through reading and study, Usbek knows also of the civic virtue of ancient republics. Persuasively he argues that no matter how radically different honor and virtue are, they have one thing in common: an origin in human pride. Now it is precisely the sentiment of self-worth and striving after fame that despotism abhors. "It can be established as a maxim that, in each state, the desire for fame increases with the freedom of subjects and diminishes when freedom diminishes; fame is never a companion of servitude."[93] The genesis and development of Usbek's ideas, it is apparent, include a brilliant conceptualization of both liberty and despotism.

Congruence between beliefs and personality is hardly automatic. To overcome a divided self, a man must live his ideas; he must become as they are. Intellect and emotion, thought and action, must fuse. If, however, the old Persian self still lurks in the psyche, coexisting uneasily with the new beliefs, then sooner or later the despotic personality will re-emerge. Therefore, it is essential to determine whether the rejection of the Persian past has gone beyond an intellectual exercise to a new personality.

A culture never imparts anything more intractably to individuals than religious convictions. Should the impact of living in a foreign culture eventuate in a probing into one's own religious beliefs and finally to their dismissal, that would be a momentous occasion signalling the possible death of the old self and the birth of a new. If further supplemented with evidence of a will to live the new beliefs, then the old despotic self is definitely in retreat. We must recount the history of belief and unbelief in *The Persian Letters*.

"I am in the midst of a profane people," Usbek announces after stepping outside his native Persia. "Allow me to purify myself." But already a gap is opening between emotion and belief: "I have doubts. . . . I feel that my reason is straying; guide it back into the straight path. Come and enlighten me," he beseeches a dervish in his next letter. "It seems to me that objects in themselves are neither pure nor impure. I cannot think of any quality inherent to the subject which could make them such." Nothing if not an astute intellectual, Usbek is professing an epistemological skepticism that threatens, even against his will, to undermine his faith in Islam. How the prophet's attempt to restore his faith affects him we are not told. Of one thing, however, we may rest assured; an appeal to blind faith is an unconvincing way to eradicate doubt. And blind faith is all the prophet has to offer: "When . . . you cannot perceive the reason for the impurity of certain things, it is because . . . you are without the knowledge of what took place between God, the Angels, and men. You do not know the history of eternity."[94]

Rica first broaches religion in a diatribe against the Spanish Inquisition. After deriding the cruelty of Christian priests, he caustically remarks that "to console their grief, they confiscate all the property of these wretches to their own advantage." Attacking the religion of foreigners, Rica has, however, only reinforced his belief in Islam. "Happy the land inhabited by the sons of prophets! These sad spectacles are unknown there. The holy religion brought to that land by the angels is protected by its very truth; it needs none of these violent means to preserve itself."[95]

Usbek's next letter on religion marks a definite change of opinion. Where before he shrank from "profane" Christians, he now holds that

> they do not at all resemble infidels. . . . They are more like those unfortunate people who lived within the shadows of idolatry before the divine light came to illumine the face of our great Prophet. . . . If thou but examine their religion closely, thou canst find there in seed, as it were, our dogmas.

He lists a series of specious similarities between Islam and Christianity, and ends his letter flushed with enthusiasm for the future of Mohammedanism. "I can see Mohammedanism everywhere, although I cannot find Mohammed here at all. Do what you will, Truth will out and ever will pierce the shadows that surround her. The day will come when the Eternal will see upon the face of the Earth only true believers."[96] Usbek has quieted his doubts by becoming an "enlightened" believer, skilled in explaining away foreign faiths as temporary aberrations from his native religion; and through him Montesquieu has made it known that enlightened Christians are as little to his liking as are their blatantly superstitious comrades-in-arms.

Next come two letters that stretch credulity almost to the breaking point. Rica criticizes the Persian family only to fly at the last moment to the truths of revealed religion.[97] His letter is immediately followed by a message from a true believer in Persia, whose defense of orthodoxy does more damage than overt skepticism ever could. "After so many brilliant testimonials . . . a man would have to possess a heart of iron not to believe in God's holy law."[98] ·And what are these testimonials? Birds, clouds, and winds arguing over who can serve God better — fables so puerile as to make a mockery of faith. Thus we are not surprised when Usbek shows a greater interest in natural religion than in revelation. "Under whatever religion one lives, the observance of laws, love for fellow men, and piety toward one's parents are always the first acts of religion. . . . Ceremonies contain no degree of goodness in themselves."[99] With these words the Persian past recedes.

As the novel unfolds, Usbek makes various comments on the practices of established religions, and in the process throws further light on the evolution of his sentiments. Vehemently, he decries the stranglehold of the Catholic Church on the economic life of France. "The dervishes hold almost all the wealth of the state. . . . [Consequently] this great wealth falls . . . into paralysis: no more circulation of money, no more commerce, no more arts, no more manufactures."[100] Then in a series of letters Usbek recites with revulsion a litany of the misdeeds wrought by religious fanaticism. Religious wars, persecution, intolerance, and the madness of proselytizing zeal are extraordinarily shocking but very ordinary in terms of historical occurrence, and all are inspired by dogmatic belief. Usbek's humanitarianism is clearly in evidence, but his letters on religion also indicate an uncertainty of mind. First, he congratulates Christianity on showing signs of disavowing its past intolerance. Then he caps an analysis of Christianity's tendency to rationalize social malpractices by professing his faith in Mohammedanism. Finally, he condemns the historical record of both Christianity and Mohammedanism. In one sense this progression is progressive: Western religion, its good and its evil, is more fully appreciated, and native Mohammedan practice comes under fire. In another sense it signifies possible stagnation: Usbek's earlier conversion to natural religion, we now see, has not been accompanied by exorcism of old religious beliefs. He is still a follower of Ali, even if one purged of fanaticism and critical of Mohammedan practice.

The struggle between belief and unbelief moves to a rapid climax. In his last letters on religion Usbek concentrates on holy scripture, the cornerstone of revealed religion. Reviewing biblical tales, he chooses at first to redeem their idiocy by symbolic interpretation. "Reasonable Christians regard all these stories as a very natural allegory that can help make us aware of the misery of the human lot."[101] But in his final letter on religion Usbek comes down hard on the holy book of his native faith.

> It seems to me that inspired books are only divine ideas couched in human terms. In our Koran, on the contrary, we often find the language of God and the ideas of men, as if by some admirable whimsy, God had dictated the words and man had furnished the ideas.

A dramatic breakthrough? Not at all. Slavishly he betrays his intelligence, pleading for faith by reasons of the heart unknown to the mind. "Thou wilt suppose that this is a fruit of the freedom in which people live in this country. No, heaven be praised! My mind has not corrupted my heart, and as long as I shall live, Ali will be my prophet."[102] Penitent and lost in illusion, Usbek takes his leave of religious controversy.

Meanwhile a revolution is taking place within Rica's mind. He chides a society bearing the imprint of Descartes, who spoke the language of universal doubt while making the sign of the cross. "People here make much of the sciences, but I am not so sure they are very learned. The man who doubts universally as a philosopher dares to deny nothing as a theologian."[103] Later he, like Usbek, regresses and even champions Persian superstition. Defending the astrology that is religiously sanctioned in his mother country, Rica meets with a sharp rebuff. "You are living under a yoke much harsher than the yoke of reason,"[104] he is informed by a Frenchman. And finally the transvaluation; Rica takes his leave but only after having demolished his religious past. "I carry all these [religious] rags about through long habit, in order to conform to general practice," he explains. And more pointedly: "Men are certainly to be pitied! They float continually between false hopes and ridiculous fears, and instead of leaning upon reason, they invent for themselves monsters to terrify them or phantoms to seduce them." Lucretius never reduced religion to fear more eloquently. All magic, all mystification, must be driven from the world and that is the mission of reason.

You will say that certain magic spells have caused a battle to be won. And I shall reply that you must be very blind indeed not to find sufficient reasons for that effect (whose cause you prefer not to know) in the location of the terrain, the number and courage of the soldiers, and the experience of the officers. . . . In order to be sure that an effect, capable of being produced by a hundred thousand causes, is supernatural, one would first have to examine whether any one of these causes had not operated — which is impossible.[105]

So Rica concludes in a reasoning that anticipates Hume's famous skeptical treatise on miracles.

Rica's earlier rejection of the Persian family is, we see, later complemented by his rejection of past religious beliefs. Determined to live as an enlightened man, he accepts and needs no surrogate faiths. Rica is at one with himself, the old self has expired. A further proof of that — he remains in the West, apparently forsaking forever the land of his birth.

In the waning pages of *The Persian Letters*, Usbek decides to return to Persia, despite the danger and unhappiness that await him there and notwithstanding his theories of Oriental despotism. Out of fear for his very life, Usbek had decided to leave Persia. Returning will perhaps mean his undoing, but he no longer cares. "Whatever reason I had for leaving my country — although I owe my life to my withdrawal — still, . . . I can no longer remain in this frightful exile!" Living in a free society, far from the mire of despotism, now seems like exile, so far from his understanding have his passions strayed. His decision is all the more remarkable in that he expects no future happiness within the seraglio. "The embraces of my wives shall relieve me no whit; in my bed, in their arms, I shall find joy only in my anxiety."[106]

When Usbek writes, "I am living in a barbarous climate," he has come full circle, returning to his earliest impression of the West. Nine years of effort to understand a foreign culture are lost. The reason for the success of Rica's new identity and the failure of Usbek's is transparent. Rica as a bachelor has few personal ties to Persia; Usbek, however, carries across Europe the memory of his wives. It is the report from a eunuch of growing disorder in the seraglio that draws Usbek back. Challenge and response in a new culture end happily for Rica in integration of personality; for Usbek the dénouement is personality disintegration. Horror-struck, Usbek witnesses the destruction rampant within his psyche. "It seems to me that I am destroying myself and no longer find my own personality except when a dark jealousy ignites within and gives birth in my soul to fear, suspicion, hate, and regret."[107]

Usbek's psyche reels under the jolt of the despotic self's revenge. Fighting its way back into the center of consciousness, the repressed self not only demolishes Usbek's intellectualized liberalism, but also negates the acts which, long into his past, had testified to his real humanity and compassion. A man of standing in Persian society, he had resided at court and "carried truth to the very steps of the throne." "I dared to be virtuous in those surroundings. So soon as I recognized vice, I withdrew from it, but I came back to unmask it. . . . I brought flattery to confusion, and astonished at once both the worshippers and their idol."[108] To shield himself from the growing storm of criticism, Usbek feigned curiosity about Western science and used that as an excuse for temporarily leaving his country; even at the price of virtual banishment he was heroically virtuous. And there is no reason to suspect him of falsifying his past; while in Europe his actions occasionally bore witness to a genuine compassion. A black slave scheduled for castration pleads to Usbek for mercy and his request is granted.[109] Usbek is not the villain of the novel; the villain of the piece is the despotic society which forces each and every man to act the villain.

As disorder grows in the seraglio, and Usbek's jealousy grows proportionately, the old self regains primacy. Zelis let her veil fall, Zachi was found in bed with one of her women slaves, a young man was seen in the garden of the seraglio. The eunuch asks that arbitrary power be delegated to him, and Usbek wastes no time in replying.

> Receive with this letter unlimited power over the entire seraglio. Command with the same authority as myself. May fear and terror walk with you.
>
> I put my sword in your hand. I entrust to your keeping what is now most precious to me in all the world — my vengeance. . . . I am writing my wives to obey you blindly.[110]

More than ever before, the veil of concealment is torn from the despotic Persian family. Will the reign of terror disabuse the wives of their cherished illusions?

The enslaved wives show signs of a liberation from illusion even as their master falls more and more under its sway. Zachi, it is true, holds on to the illusion of love all the more tightly now that its falsity is so pathetically obvious.

> The tiger dares to tell me that you are the perpetrator of all these cruelties. He would like to deprive me of my love. . . . No! I can no longer tolerate the humiliation into which I have fallen. If I am innocent, come back and love me. Come back, if I am guilty, so that I may die at your feet.

But Zelis refuses to prostrate herself and illusion crumbles: "It is the tyrant who offends me and not the man carrying out his tyranny. . . . My heart has found calm since it is no longer able to love you."[111] As for Usbek, at the time of his departure from Persia he was inevitably unaware of his tyranny, but with the passing of years in Europe his initial deception is increasingly self-deception. Distressed and vexed by the inadequacy of Eastern love and long since exposed to freer Western ways, he blocks all he has learned from consciousness.

Ultimately Usbek's relationship to his wives is a master-slave phenomenology worthy of Hegel. Much earlier in the novel Zelis pointed the way by informing Usbek of his enslavement to his slaves.

> Even in this prison where you hold me, I am freer than you. You could not possibly redouble your concern for guarding me without my drawing pleasure from your worry. Your suspicions, your jealousy, and your heartaches are all so many proofs of your dependence. . . . I dread nothing save your indifference.[112]

Displaying Usbek's psychological chains, Montesquieu vindicates Plato, who had insisted that the tyrant is a slave of passion.

The novel ends with the suicide of Roxane, the one woman for whom Usbek cared. His political sociology informs Usbek that a despotic prince never gets what he wants. As usual, he did not bother to extend his insight to the despotic family, but Roxane did this for him. Rather than submit to Persian definitions of wifely duties, she found freedom, and perhaps love, in adultery. Her final letter completes a symmetrical parallelism between the ending and beginning of the novel. "I spoke there a hitherto unknown language," Usbek had written in an early letter of his days at court. "My language, no doubt, seems new to you,"[113] Roxane writes Usbek in the final letter as she dies. The Troglodyte myth and Roxane's death also bind start and finish in an inner affinity. Before their days of familial virtue, the

Troglodytes lived in a world without justice, a war of all against all, and their mutual destruction ensued. "The Troglodytes perished by reason of their very wickedness and . . . they were victims of their own injustices," Usbek moralized.[114] Roxane's revolt proves the validity of his romance on the self-defeating nature of injustice.

Twice in the novel a woman speaks of natural law. Zelis comments, early on in the novel, that nature has placed women in a position subordinate to men. To her way of thinking — a way obviously shaped by Persian culture — nature is "industriously bent on the welfare of men." Nature reappears in Roxane's suicide note. "I have rewritten your laws after the laws of nature,"[115] she informs Usbek. Nature as male domination, nature as female liberation; nature as oppression, nature as freedom, and there is no way to demonstrate which is more natural. The proof is emotive and the entire novel the method of demonstration.

An emotive proof, of course, is not a proof at all. It is an antidote to doubt. After seeing and feeling the destructiveness of despotism, we can no longer doubt. Description has become condemnation. "There are certain truths that it is not enough to impress by rational conviction, truths that must be felt. Such are the verities of ethics." So Usbek said as a preface to his Troglodyte myth; so Montesquieu said through *The Persian Letters*. Fiction is a surrogate for natural law.

Character formation and destruction, cultural determination of consciousness, and much else can be explained with tools adapted from Locke. Lockean epistemology effaced natural law, but Lockean psychology presented materials from which a surrogate could be fabricated. In forging a symbiotic relationship between psychology and fiction, Montesquieu banished despotism from the realm of the humanly acceptable.

Regarded as an attempt to fashion moral judgment from the emotions, *The Persian Letters* was a project with no sequel. Regarded as an attempt to fashion the same from social science, *The Persian Letters* was no more than a first step in a lifelong project. Not just emotionally but intellectually as well, Montesquieu had demonstrated that despotism is self-destructive and contrary to the interests of everyone. To know the nature of despotism thoroughly, to conceptualize it systematically, as Montesquieu here did for the first time, was to despise it. Later, in both the *Considerations* and the *Spirit of the Laws*, Montesquieu would again use models, types, constructs of social science, as a means of examining both what is and what ought to be.

Reason, as it turns out, does have a place in ethics, and a place of honor at that. Between "is" and "ought" there are vital passageways or bridges. The function of reason is to discover them and to grant safe conducts from the "is" to the "ought" side of what otherwise threatens to be a nontraversible chasm. Natural law philosophy, with its emphasis on a rationally discernible connection between "is" and "ought," is acceptable after the emendation that the "nature" in question is not physical nature but the nature of socio-political systems.

CHAPTER VI

Historiography as a Surrogate for Natural Law

1. History as Ethical Judgment

By psychological analysis, *The Persian Letters* vindicated the Troglodyte story, transforming it from myth to truth. Yet this psychology depended on fictional depiction, so its validity remained indecisive. To objectify still further the lesson that injustice is self-repudiating, Montesquieu turned not to the law of nature but to the nature of a particular sociological "law." His definition of laws as "the necessary relations arising from the nature of things"[1] is well-known. Less widely recognized is his meaning that every socio-political system has a law of survival which sanctions certain actions and outlaws others. What does this have to do with justice? Simply this: if Machiavellism in foreign policy, the deliberate suspension of justice in external affairs, necessarily undermines the internal "principle" of a cherished socio-political system, it follows that the liabilities of Machiavellism outweigh any benefits it can confer.

After the Troglodytes formed an idyllically righteous society, the bountiful fruits of their labors aroused the envy of a neighboring tribe. Spoiling for a fight, this odious people attacked the innocent Troglodytes, and in "the battle of Injustice and Virtue"[2] that ensued, the Troglodytes emerged gloriously victorious. Historically, of course, there never has been a people untarnished with evil, and, except in partisan rhetoric, battles are rarely between paragons of virtue and villainous demons — guilt always being plentiful enough to encompass both sides. Still, it was not difficult for Montesquieu to point to a real people in whose very soul a battle between injustice and virtue was waged throughout the course of their spectacular history. Following Machiavelli's example, Montesquieu held that the ancient Romans were unexampled in internal virtue, except for Sparta, and unexampled in external injustice without exception. That is to say, he and Machiavelli were at one in viewing Rome as an extraordinary example of civic virtue and as a ruthless practitioner of Machiavellism in foreign policy.

On one vital point Montesquieu differs from Machiavelli. The eighteenth-century sociologist was out to demonstrate that the Machiavellian means of Rome defeated Rome's ends, and that in consequence such politics was as far from "realism" as any style of politics can be. Wedding the good of one's country to an infliction of evil upon other countries, creating a system of freedom for one city-state at the expense of the freedom of every other city-state — all of this was at the core of the scheme that Machiavelli partially derived from Roman history and partially projected upon it. By way of a rational use of violence and deceit, the Roman senators managed the glorious feat of conquering the world, Machiavelli insisted. But knowing nothing of the rationality of the whole, Montesquieu added, they did not realize that the unanticipated consequences of their foreign policy would necessarily kill the civic virtue at home which they, and Machiavelli, prized so dearly. Civic virtue in Rome was a system of civic virtue to end all civic virtue, eventually including its own, and this, Montesquieu hoped to prove, followed inexorably from the injustice of her foreign policy, her unquenchable imperialistic thirst.

> If anyone doubts the misfortune a great conquest brings, he has only to read the history of the Romans. The Romans took the world away from the most flourishing condition in which it can be; they destroyed the most beautiful establishments in order to form a single one which they could not sustain; they extinguished the liberty of the universe and following that abused their own; they enfeebled the entire world, as bespoilers and bespoiled, as tyrants and as slaves.[3]

Both the Christian deity and the law of nature were expendable as methods of condemning evil. Of and by itself, historiography was equal to the task of rejecting injustice, if cast by its practitioner in the mold of an historical sociology. *"La nature des choses"* cried out against injustice, but the nature in question was not physical nature. Rather, it was the structure and functions of a socio-political system. Such a thing-like entity was made by man but it was not an artifact, nor was it unmaking a matter of conscious design. Physics explains the old nature, historical sociology the new.

Machiavelli's *Discourses* will be examined first and at considerable length, since his interpretation of Roman history set the terms of a debate between himself, Bossuet, and Montesquieu. In the *Discourse on Universal History*, Bossuet presses a possibly decisive attack against Machiavellized Rome, but eventually betrays his achievement by fleeing to providentialism. Upon incorporating Bossuet's insights and exorcising the bishop's God, Montesquieu had defeated both of his favorite enemies in the *Considerations*.

2. Machiavelli on Roman History

The interpretation of Machiavelli's writings has repeatedly floundered between a false antithesis of *The Prince* versus the *Discourses* and equally specious links drawn between the two. One hears that there are two Machiavelli's, or that only the republican Machiavelli is real (*The Prince* is a satire), or, most common of all, that the two works are to be reconciled by the supposition that the Machiavellian means of *The Prince* were designed to achieve the republican ends of the *Discourses*.[4] These fruitless perspectives must be abandoned, once and for all. Those who have seen in him the demon of power worship, and nothing more, have not realized the full truth. Neither, however, have those revisionists grasped his meaning who interpret his sanctioning of power politics as a reluctant but necessary concession to harsh realities, forced upon him because the Renaissance prince could not restore liberty to corrupt Italian city-states by anything less than Machiavellian methods. True enough, he unequivocally condemned the prince who would use Machiavellian political science for his own private ends and lust for power; true also, Machiavelli's ideal prince could gain no greater glory than in inaugurating or reinstating a reign of republican virtue. But that is not the whole story, and the whole story can come to light only if one understands what it was about republics that Machiavelli admired.

The ideal republic, according to him, was the one in which there are liberty and power, each an end in its own right and a means furthering the other. Power promotes liberty and liberty promotes power. A republic is free only if it has the power to ward off hostile outsiders beyond its walls; and in the ideal republic freedom is enjoyed both for itself and also because of the boon to power made possible by incorporating formerly destitute social classes into the political assemblies. Then, and only then, can power reach its maximum, because the entire citizenry can be armed without threat of revolution. Each and every citizen is willing to fight heroically for the common good in which he participates; and a glorious triumph over all other republics, unlimited aggrandizement of power, may well be attainable — provided, however, that the passion of the demos is rationally directed by a ruling class skilled in the arts of deceit and violence. An impossible and utopian goal, far beyond historical example? Hardly so, for Rome had been exactly that sort of republic, or so Machiavelli was willing and eager to believe.

Weaned on the classics, Machiavelli was merely amplifying in the *Discourses* a theme to which Polybius had already addressed himself: the link between the constitutional development of Rome, the exceptional stability of the republic, and the successful conquest of the other city-states of antiquity. As Machiavelli begins with internal and constitutional development, we shall do the same.

When the early monarchs were eliminated, the Roman republic was launched on its fateful course. At first, the insolent nobles, no longer held in check by a royalty above them, were apt to flaunt their contempt for the people. As the class struggle grew increasingly intense, the people resorted to a series of retaliatory tactics. Always they stopped short of revolution, but finally they hit upon a non-violent means of forcing their way into the political system: they threatened a withdrawal from Rome that would have left the senators in charge of a city-state too weak to be of much use to anyone. Roman politics became democratic when the people won the right to sit in a popular assembly.

Class conflict, in the Roman case, produced the greatest advantages, both for liberty and stability. Aristocracy, in the sense of the domination of the few over the many, was brought to an end. But happily Roman democracy was achieved without resorting to the sort of democratic revolution that in Greece destroyed the nobility and had often given rise to a government that was the domination of the many poor over the rich few — "democracy" in Aristotle's usage of a perversion, the dictatorship of the plebeians. Saved from oligarchy by the demands of the demos, and from mob rule by democratization without revolution, Rome advanced to a system in which class was balanced against class, a system combining the best of both oligarchy and democracy. In a word, Rome had evolved to the status of an Aristotelian "polity," the most stable and least oppressive of all political arrangements, because everyone was inside the system, no class had a material stake in revolution, and political institutions were viewed as embodiments of the public good, rather than as sources of plunder.

Another way of looking at the political system of Rome, and one which Machiavelli cites as evidence of its superiority, is as a fortunate combination of elements drawn from monarchy, aristocracy, and democracy. The popular assembly is the democratic ingredient, the Senate the aristocratic factor, and the consuls, with their various executive powers inherited from bygone days of royalty, constitute the monarchical element. By itself the democratic element signified the incorporation of everyone into the system; the democratic element combined with the aristocratic signified a scheme of checks and balances between classes; and the provision of executive power through aristocratic and monarchical elements was an assurance that the system would not be checked to the point of inertia.

In summary, the legacy of Roman constitutional development was thoroughly auspicious. A political system emerged which was of the most stable and enduring sort, a balanced and mixed government, whose institutions, once born of class strife, enjoyed an autonomous existence above party interests. Despite all the checks and balances, there were always offices and centers of influence — the consuls, the magistrates, the leadership of the Senate — that allowed the system to adapt successfully to new challenges. Here was a political system so strong and energetic that it could never be overthrown as most other political structures are: apparently from without but in fact from within. Machiavelli reiterates the standard Polybian scheme of cyclical history — monarchy degenerates into tyranny, aristocracy into oligarchy, democracy into license — but rarely does the cycle run a complete circle, returning to one-man rule. Usually, during one of its periods of corruption, a city-state falls to an external enemy.[5] From this dire fate, Rome was spared because her political system was of the most durable kind, and long immunized her against the germ of historical decay.

Constitutional developments left Rome with an institutional foundation that acted as an unusually tenacious skeletal structure supporting the weight of the body politic. By itself the skeleton was already striking, and when complemented by the flesh and blood of a life-giving principle, a body politic of extraordinary vitality was the result. Civic virtue was the name of the principle energizing the body politic.

The notion of civic virtue is as full-blown in Machiavelli as it was ever to be, not excepting the excellent writings on this subject of Montesquieu and Rousseau. Frugality, equality, discipline, repression of the self, and total dedication to the public good are its essential qualities. Puritanical through and through, the life of civic virtue demands an incessant self-abnegation, a sacrifice of the self on the altar of the common good. Suppressed in its private aspect, the self in its public dimension is correspondingly enlarged. The common good is not a remote and alien good, but an immediate good; individualism is abolished but the individual is stronger than ever before. A kind of competitive ethic is often part of this brand of puritanism, but instead of being channelled into a race for economic achievement, here it assumes the form of a struggle to see who can perform the greatest deeds for his country.[6] Glory is both collective and individual; the individual is glorified insofar as he contributes to the common glory.

All in all, Machiavelli's partisanship lies with the system of civic virtue, particular parties leaving him cold. And yet he definitely had a special sympathy for the lower class, so that this theorist of elites, by an ironic twist, was a democrat of sorts. Again and again, he compares the people favorably to the nobility, pointing out that the nobles desire to oppress, while the people only want to avoid being oppressed.[7] Again and again, he compares the people favorably to the prince, even though this means taking direct issue with Livy.

> If we compare the faults of a people with those of princes, as well as their respective good qualities, we shall find the people vastly superior in all that is good and glorious.

> The excesses of the people are directed against those whom they suspect of interfering with the public good, while those of princes are against apprehended interference with their individual interests.

> We also see that in the election of their magistrates they make far better choices than princes.[8]

Machiavelli was a democrat, even an ardent democrat, whose Roman demos was "the people" and not "the mass."

At times Machiavelli's enthusiasm for the people and disgust for the aristocrats builds to a crescendo of frenzied emotion. Centuries before Rousseau or Michelet, he cited with approval the saying, "The voice of the people is the voice of God." His stomach turns at the sight of "gentlemen," especially feudal nobles.

> I say that those are called gentlemen who live idly upon the proceeds of their extensive possessions, without devoting themselves to agriculture or any other useful pursuit to gain a living. Such men are pernicious to any country or republic; but more pernicious even than these are such as have . . . castles which they command, and subjects who obey them. This class of men abounds in the kingdom of Naples, in the Roman territory, in the Romagna, and in Lombardy; whence it is that no republic has ever been able to exist in those countries.

A remedy is proposed without hesitation or mincing of words: "If anyone should wish to establish a republic in a country where there are many gentlemen, he will not succeed until he has destroyed them all."[9]

If it is asked whether this proposed purge of the nobility conflicts with the Polybian scheme of class balance, the answer is in the negative. Polybius himself dared to substitute Roman consuls for king as the monarchical element, and for Renaissance Italy the well-to-do class can be substituted for the feudal nobility as the aristocratic element. Indeed, such a procedure can claim a Polybian blessing once it is recalled that the passage of political office from able fathers to indifferent sons by hereditary succession is the purported catalyst of degeneration.[10] Characterized by hereditary status, a feudal nobility is bound to trigger the forces of corruption.

When the existing aristocratic element happens to be hereditary, it would do well to follow the Venetian way, thought Machiavelli. In contemporary Venice the hereditary principle is not absent, but a stable government has been successfully maintained despite it because the aristocratic element is nonfeudal and dedicated to service. As opposed to a feudal nobility, "The gentlemen of Venice are so more in name than in fact; for they have no great revenues from estates, their riches being founded upon commerce and movable property, and moreover none of them have castles or jurisdiction over subjects."[11] Unruly and self-serving feudal nobles are a curse to republics, but the

Venetian aristocratic families, for whom politics is a vocation, trick the hereditary principle into quitting its usual role as driving force of political decay. The mantle of rulership is passed from father to son, but not before the sons have been diligently trained to accept their responsibilities. Commercial aristocrats, moreover, unlike feudal nobles, are able to act in concert as a corporate body and each member watches every other, thus preventing the private self from overtaking the public one.

Admiration of Venice was commonplace during the Renaissance, but Machiavelli was much less enamored of her than was his brilliant acquaintance, Guicciardini. Supposedly the political system of Venice was mixed and balanced government. On this Machiavelli and Guicciardini agreed, and likewise they shared the conviction that Florence's republican experiment from 1494 to 1512 had ended in disaster because of a democratically hamstrung government, institutionally weak and devoid of leadership. In antiquity Athens rushed too rapidly from aristocratic to democratic domination with the result that one perverted form was substituted for another, and in modernity Florence had fallen into a similar trap. Lower class dictatorship and a politics of passion, unrestrained and uneducated by an experienced ruling class, was a sure formula for an unstable and directionless polity.

Machiavelli and Guicciardini spoke with one voice on all the foregoing points.[12] Where the two Florentine diplomat-writers differed was in Guicciardini's consistently aristocratic and antidemocratic outlook and Machiavelli's rather more complicated political commitments. Venice embodied most of what Guicciardini cherished politically, but Machiavelli wanted something more.

Fiercely proud and protective of his family's social position in the aristocracy, Guicciardini was equally insistent on the aristocratic tradition of political service to the republic. By severely restricting citizenship, the Venetian aristocracy, in Guicciardini's view, not only safeguarded its political primacy, but promoted a calculating political style through the agency of an astute ruling class, drawn from aristocratic ranks, impervious to the blows of fortuna, and envied everywhere in Italy. Conversely, the democratic character of Florentine politics signified not only a challenge to the social pre-eminence of the aristocracy but also the death of hope for a rational politics. The addition of democracy to a republic entails the subtraction of the ruling elite that is essential to political welfare. It is at this point that Machiavelli crossed swords with Guicciardini; democracy and leadership, Machiavelli believed, can mutually thrive, they should do so, and once did — in ancient Rome.

Mixed and balanced government, in Guicciardini's pro-Venetian version, was strongly skewed in favor of the aristocracy.[13] The signory was designated as the monarchical element and the Grand Council as the democratic factor, but the aristocratic Senate predominated by serving as key to the balance. This special emphasis on the Senate, combined with a strict limitation on the number of citizens, made for a government mixed and balanced, but mixed and balanced in favor of the aristocracy. Now if, as Polybius had said, the best of balanced government was such that even a native might with equally good reason deem it either an aristocracy or a democracy,[14] then Machiavelli has the better of the disagreement in selecting ancient Rome instead of contemporary Venice as the ideal polity whose example Florence should follow. For in Rome the franchise was democratically spread throughout the ranks of society, and democratization without revolution had left the Senate in aristocratic hands. Given a broadly based citizenship and the powers of the popular assembly, the democratic element in Rome's constitution was truly democratic. At the same time, the Senate did not follow the lot of the aristocratic Council in Greek states; the coming of Roman democracy did not entail stripping the upper body of its powers, nor was that body deluged by the demos so as to make for a government mixed and balanced in theory but a pure and unchecked democracy in practice. In Roman history the aristocratic and democratic elements of mixed government were each highly developed with prejudice to neither aristocracy nor democracy.

Aside from its efficacy in exemplifying the best constitutional balance, or in proving the possibility of combining democracy with strong leadership, the Roman model mesmerized Machiavelli for two additional reasons. For one thing, Roman politics was superior to Venetian politics for the democratic reason that the people were not subject to oppression and could live the elevated life of citizenship. This favoring of Rome for democratic reasons, so evident in Book One of the *Discourses*, is, however, less crucial to Book Two than is a second reflection that had the effect of relegating democracy to the status of a means. What was most enthralling about Rome was her successful imperialism, her subjection of the rest of the world through heroic deeds, the communal heroism of civic virtue. Roman flexibility in extending the citizenship was now admirable, not for its internal democratic consequences; but because the highly coveted status of Roman citizen could be dangled before other city-states as a reward that would be granted to any power willing to support Rome.

Rome's gates were always open, beckoning others to enter and welcoming them with the title of citizen in the greatest of city-states. Venice's gates being closed, she could never gain an Italian land empire similar to her maritime empire of trade. Sparta, constitutionally analagous to Venice, had been the Venetian republic's superior in civic virtue. The absence of walls surrounding Sparta signified not that all the world could come in, but that everyone was all the more obstinately excluded. Valorous men who were joined together by civic virtue did not need walls to unite them with each other and to divide them from the rest of mankind. This was all well and good, in Machiavelli's eyes, but not quite good enough, for one of its consequences was that Sparta was not structured, any more than Venice later, in a way that allowed for unlimited expansion. Sparta's era of empire, like Athens', was noteworthy for its miserable brevity and for its deleterious effects on Sparta herself. Clearly the Roman model is the only one that fits Machiavelli's designs: the Romans alone knew how to combine civic virtue with empire.[15]

Sparta's aristocratic government gave her an excellent ruling class, and civic virtue was never wanting. But the emaciation of the democratic principle meant, first, that many of her own people could not be armed without risking revolution, and, second, that an unwillingness to assimilate foreigners foreclosed the possibility of a lasting empire. The democratic nature of Athenian politics, in contrast, enabled a large number of men to be armed for wars of conquest, but the other side of democracy was the demise of a ruling class. With no checks against it, democracy ran wild; the cycle of degeneration accelerated, and before long civic virtue was a remembrance of things past. Moreover, even during the peak of Athenian patriotism, the absence of a ruling class had telling effects. It made for a pattern of warfare fueled by the passions of the demos, similar to what Machiavelli wanted; but no one understood better than he that passion for expansion undirected by *realpolitik* politicians could not win a durable empire. The Roman model outstripped Sparta, Athens, and Venice, one and all.

By now it should be obvious that the amalgam of democratic and elitist sympathies in Machiavelli's thought is not contradictory. His ideal elitists are members of a political class, a ruling class, and their social origins are less important than their political mission of making democracy great. If the rulers are drawn from the nobility, as in Rome, then he is willing to call a ceasefire to his animus against that social class, but with the understanding that the nobility must constantly prove its worth by political service to the democracy, or else be denounced as a parasitical oligarchy that deserved to be overthrown. Within the Polybian scheme of mixed and balanced government, the Roman nobility occupied the aristocratic position and acted in behalf of Roman democracy by providing an antidote to excessive democratic passions. But the role of the nobles was not confined to so narrow and negative a task; they also were the political educators of the democracy since they set the examples followed by the populace. In one way or another men act on the basis of imitation, Machiavelli maintains, and are particularly apt to look to those above them, to the socially prominent and the political rulers, for examples to mimic. When the Roman populace copied the actions of the nobles and senators, democracy was infused with greatness. To its everlasting glory, the Roman elite was "noble" in the true sense of high-minded, high-spirited, distinguished, strong, and valorous; and the contagion of these values downward through the psychology of imitation raised the demos to new heights. Democracy was real but aristocratic values remained intact and permeated the entire society. The people, too, were noble and capable of heroic deeds. Overall both the democrats and the aristocrats gained from the peculiar democratic-aristocratic cross-breeding of Roman society and politics. The effect of the aristos on the demos was to breathe grandeur into their souls; the effect of the demos on the aristos was to prevent the latter from quarrelling or falling into other forms of degeneration as a political class. With the lower class constantly in the wings and making menacing gestures as though it might storm the stage, the aristocrats could not afford to give other than a flawless performance.

When it comes to imperialism, democracy has obviously been demoted to a means in Machiavelli's thought; but so too does elitism, even more clearly than before, find its place solely within the boundaries of instrumentality. Democracy now connotes massive supplies of people ready and willing to undergo a metamorphosis into cannon fodder. And elitism is to be read as leadership by the aristocracy, whether in the army as generals, or in politics as Machiavellian senators untroubled by humanitarian scruples as they impose servility upon the rest of the world. One of the powers never removed from the Senate by the advent of democracy was direction of foreign policy. Spontaneously from the instincts of their noble natures and deliberately from fear of the demos' class resentment, the senators were led to sponsor and oversee that endless succession of wartime and peacetime aggressions which in its process and fulfillment was the grandeur of Rome.

To uncover the maxims by which the senators managed their spectacular feats is to familiarize oneself with the highest form of Machiavellism in foreign policy. In power politics, nothing succeeds like success, and the Roman senators did succeed with remarkable regularity. What were their Machiavellian strategies and tactics?

In the first place, there was the question of how to conduct wars of conquest with maximum effect; in the second place, the question of how to secure the permanent subjection of the losers. As for the wars, the Roman policy of *Blitzkrieg* won victory after victory by its very audacity. Until the Romans besieged Veii, "all their expeditions were completed in six, ten, or at most twenty days."[16] Suddenly, antiquity's comfortable image of democracies — slow, indecisive, and internally divided — was overthrown by Rome's lightning wars, brilliant in design and execution. Democracies, so the conventional wisdom said, were not able to act with concerted determination, but Rome had given the lie to all complacent generalizations.

From the standpoint of imperialistic objectives, it was vitally important that no defeated power break the Roman chains binding it. Always ready to improvise in deciding upon the shackles most suited to particular circumstances, Rome forged one kind of servility for republics and another for principalities. By their unyielding attachment to self-rule, free cities posed a difficult problem and evoked at once the most violent and the most refined Roman strategems. It was completely different when a city had long endured rule by a prince. Nothing very complicated or especially bloody was necessary to consolidate control over a conquered principality. Destruction of the princely family sufficed to render the inhabitants helpless, since they had never learned how to associate together politically or, what amounts to the same thing, how to be free. "But in republics there is greater life, greater hatred, and more desire for vengeance; they do not and cannot cast aside the memory of their ancient liberty, so that the surest way is either to lay them waste or reside in them."[17]

Actually the alternatives, as a further reading of Machiavelli discloses, are not quite so either/or. Between the extremes of laying waste a republic or residing in it, the Romans often adopted the intermediary course of colonization in recently subdued territory. From the colonies implanted on newly conquered soil, Rome could spy on her latest victim and launch retaliatory attacks, if and when the old spirit of municipal freedom stirred from its forcibly induced slumber. Again, these colonies were invaluable because they afforded Rome an opportunity to play a game of divide-and-rule that secured the dual objectives of protecting conquests already made and of preparing the way for further conquests. Through cultivating the seeds of mutual suspicion, Roman colonies set the as yet unconquered neighboring peoples at odds with one another. This tactic both prevented them from joining together in ousting the Roman usurper and rendered each one isolated and vulnerable to the next Roman thrust. The appearance of a Roman colony outside the walls of a conquered city presaged the end of freedom for every other city-state in the region.[18]

In addition to colonization, there were other ways in which Rome enervated republics without resorting to the extremes of destruction or direct take-over. Whenever social strife threatens to tear apart a foreign city-state, the policy of the imperialist should be "to favor the weaker party so as to keep up the war."[19] Now the Romans, Machiavelli assures us, were not only patient in allowing differences to rigidify, but they were also excellent at extending their influence in a strife-torn republic by posing as arbiters. Relishing his Roman forerunners, Machiavelli quotes Livy: "The Romans conquered as much by their justice as by their arms."[20]

In the case of Greek city-states, Rome sometimes felt compelled to save cities for her empire by destroying them,[21] but the earlier subjection of Italian city-states was conducted with infinitely greater guile and brilliance. Of the two broad Roman patterns of imperialism — control through violence as in much of Greece and control through duplicity as in Italy — Machiavelli shrank from neither, but his sympathies reached out to the latter. With the kind of admiration which only one Machiavellian can feel for another, Machiavelli reconstructed the Roman masterplan.

Having created for herself many associates throughout Italy, she [Rome] granted to them in many respects an almost entire equality, always, however, reserving to herself the seat of empire and the right of command; so that these associates, without being themselves aware of it, devoted their efforts and blood to their own subjugation. For so soon as the Romans began to lead their armies beyond the limits of Italy, they reduced other kingdoms to provinces, and made subjects of those who, having been accustomed to live under kings, were indifferent to becoming subjects of another . . . Thus the associates of Rome found themselves all at once surrounded by Roman subjects, and at the same time pressed by a powerful city like Rome; and when they became aware of the trap into which they had been led, it was too late to remedy the evil.

Rome's erstwhile allies paid with their freedom for the folly of trusting an imperialistically-minded power: "from associates they were degraded to subjects." "This mode of proceeding, . . ." Machiavelli explains, "was practiced only by the Romans; and a republic desirous of aggrandizement should adopt no other plan."[22]

Here, in Rome's devious alliance policy, was Machiavellism in its purest form.

As Rome employed every means . . . to promote her aggrandizement, so she also did not hesitate to employ fraud; nor could she have practiced a greater fraud than by taking the course we have explained above of making other peoples her allies and associates, and under that title making them slaves, as she did with the Latins and other neighboring nations.

From humble beginnings to grandiose finale, the Roman republic single-mindedly applied every sinister device that passed into its hands or into the fertile imagination of the senators, ever ready to test the latest in Machiavellian means.

We see . . . that the Romans in the early beginning of their power already employed fraud, which it has ever been necessary for those to practice who from small beginnings wish to rise to the highest degree of power; and . . . it is the less censurable the more it is concealed, as was that practiced by the Romans.[23]

Since Machiavellian fraud and deceit are praiseworthy in direct proportion to the grandeur and in inverse proportion to the meanness of the end they serve, Roman Machiavellism is especially deserving of eulogy because its object and achievement was universal empire.

Behold the greatness that was Rome: treachery and wars of oppression, bloodstained ground and rotting corpses, death to the liberties of peoples so overflowing with civic virtue "that nothing but the exceeding valor of the Romans could ever have subjugated them."[24] Other peoples' liberty and civic virtue were good, but the Romans' liberty and civic virtue, which ended every other, were better — better because more skilfully and less scrupulously directed. Renaissance princes, Machiavelli wrote in *The Prince*, had to be taught "how not to be good" and taught also the two methods of fighting: like men with laws, like beasts with force.[25] As for the Romans, they never had to be taught and were the greatest of teachers, for they devoured other powers, now with uncompromising animal force, now with the finesse of forensic skill, and always they lived, in foreign affairs, beyond good and evil. Necessity — the battle for sheer survival — was the rationale offered by Machiavelli for the amoralism of the "new" prince. Ostentatious Roman amoralism was exceptionally bold in its goal of universal empire. Its amoralism was uncalled for, unnecessary, but all the more admirable for that very reason.

Drenched in blood, Machiavelli's writings do not fit the contours of an interpretation based on the notion of an "economy of violence."[26] A strict adjustment of means to ends is, indeed, characteristic of Machiavelli's thought, just as it is of the economizer's frame of mind. No more violence is permitted than exactly what is necessary to achieve a given end. But once we realize that Machiavelli's favorite end was unlimited conquest, it is imperative that henceforth all formulas downplaying the sanguinary aspect of his thought be discarded.

In every possible way, Machiavelli diverges from the economizing mentality. More than anything else, the actions stemming from Roman civic virtue, as described by him, are splendid and beautiful, the ultimate in aesthetic delight. Glorious and heroic deeds of generals and soldiers, of senators and populace, are more appreciated for their dramatic quality than for the empire proceeding from them. The same principle applies to the Machiavellian calculations of the senators: it was not the triumph of reason — the perfect suitability, rationally speaking, of the means applied to a given end — that fully aroused Machiavelli's admiration. Rather, it was the aesthetic magnificence of Occam's razor applied to politics which fascinated him — the marvel of means that wasted no motion, the awe of a consistent refusal to apply, say, three strategems in pursuing a conquest when two were sufficient.

Here was an incredible people, completely powerful and completely in control of their powers. As they ruthlessly subdued the rest of humanity, Machiavelli's Romans vented the animal passions of the human creature, but only after first transfiguring those passions into ecstatic emotions wonderfully channelled and exactingly directed. Men were never before or since lifted so far above the beasts in grandeur of soul as were the Romans when they undertook a program of systematic destruction and acted the part of beasts abroad. There was more art and beauty in a single moment of Roman politics than in the whole of Renaissance painting and sculpture.

The economizing frame of mind, in direct contrast, is nonsensational, prudent, deaf to enthusiasm, hostile to aesthetic considerations; above all, the economizing frame of mind is quantitative. Machiavelli and the economizer have little in common. It is the quality of actions and their beauty that concerns the Florentine. And he cares less about whether a goal is fulfilled than about the process of fulfilling it. In the final reduction of Machiavelli's many-sided value system, imperialism is praised not because conquest is useful but because Roman conquests were magnificent in spectacle, pageantry, grandeur, and valorous display. Instrumentalism is outdone by aestheticism and a heroic ethic.

3. Montesquieu on Roman History

Machiavelli had to be refuted, and the more the refutation took the form of destroying his world while remaining faithful to its premises, the more the refutation would be devastating. Concede, for purposes of argumentation, that Rome's foreign policy was Machiavellian, but interject, as Montesquieu did, that this systematic injustice killed Roman virtue, and then the words Machiavelli uttered in disgust against the history of Florence can be uttered against the history of Rome: that hers was a record of "what ought to be avoided and brought to an end."[27]

Agreeing with Machiavelli, Montesquieu wrote that "Rome was made for expansion."[28] And if "it did not prove wiser than all other states for a day but continually," that was because "the senate always acted with the same profundity." "While the armies caused consternation everywhere, it held on to the nations that had already been struck down." The conquering practices of the Romans were "in no sense just particular actions occurring by chance."

> These were ever-constant principles, as may be readily seen from the fact that the maxims they followed against the greatest powers were precisely the ones they had followed, in the beginning, against the small cities around them.

And what were these practices? By and large Montesquieu's descriptions are closely analogous to those outlined by Machiavelli. About the Romans one can generalize that "their constant maxim was to divide," a strategy they employed in a great variety of ways.

> When they allowed a city to remain free, they immediately caused two factions to arise within it. One upheld local laws and liberty, the other maintained that there was no law except the will of the Romans.

> After destroying the armies of a prince, they ruined his finances by excessive taxes or a tribute on the pretext of making him pay the expenses of the war — a new kind of tyranny that forced him to oppress his subjects and lose their love.

> When some prince or people broke away from obedience to a ruler, they were immediately accorded the title of ally of the Roman people ... so that there was no king, however great, who could be sure of his subjects or even of his family for a moment.

> If princes of the same blood were disputing the crown, the Romans sometimes declared them both kings. If one of them was under age, they decided in his favor.[29]

The treachery of the Romans, who knew "not even the justice of brigands," was boundless. "They destroyed Carthage, saying that they had promised to save the people of the city but not the city itself." To the Romans, moreover, treaties were never more than "suspensions of war" allowing them to regroup or lull a victim to sleep. In Rome's alliances, Montesquieu saw what Machiavelli had seen: "The Romans never made a peace treaty with an enemy unless it contained an alliance — that is, they subjugated no people which did not help them in reducing others." And with the same finale: "Allies were used to make war on an enemy, but then the destroyers were at once destroyed."[30]

Imperceptibly the world outside Roman walls was ushered to its degradation.

> It was a slow way of conquering. They vanquished a people and were content to weaken it. They imposed conditions on it which under-mined it insensibly. If it revolted, it was reduced still further, and it became a subject people without anyone being able to say when its subjection began.[31]

Yet, for all his fidelity to Machiavelli's interpretation of the Roman senators, Montesquieu, even at this early stage, had injected a germ of disease into the Machiavellian *Weltanschauung*. Later, when he re-constructed the decline of civic virtue, he was to destroy Machiavelli with the word "necessity." But already here, in the midst of his Machiavelli-like recreation of Rome's triumphs, Montesquieu had wounded his prey with the word "accidental." Even though "Rome was not guided by experience of goods and evils,"[32] and managed her amoralism so very brilliantly, a lucky roll of the dice was what really determined that her grandiose objective of universal empire would end in universal glory rather than in universal ruin. Had it not been for the imbecility of foreign statesmen in failing to play according to the easily mastered rules of balance of power, Rome, which won everything, would have lost everything. The winner in a winner-take-all politics of its own making, Rome could much more easily have lost, and as a loser in such politics would have lost everything. Save for the most unlikely of happenings, Greece would never have fallen, and Roman dreams of universal dominion could be dismissed as absurd utopianism.

> Greece was formidable because of its situation, its strength, the mul-titude of its cities, the number of its soldiers, its public order, its morals, its laws. It loved war, it knew the art of war, and had it been united it would have been invincible.
>
> But Philip [of Macedonia], who at the beginning of his reign won the love and confidence of the greeks by his moderation, suddenly changed. He became a cruel tryant, at a time when policy and ambi-tion should have made him just.[33]

Doubtless the Romans were clever in allying, time after time, with the weaker of two opposing Greek parties.[34] With the help of the weaker, the stronger was defeated, and no sooner was this done than Rome betrayed her ally. But not even the most refined and secretive maxims of conquest could have succeeded, had Greece replied with the well-known precepts of balance of power. Accoridng to the maxims of power balance, a protective alliance is imperative whenever an over-mighty and lustful aggressor is on the prowl. That Greece never adopted this obvious course was not due to Roman calculations but to the meanness and stupidity of Philip. If the Romans had been familiar with Rohan's theory of games (See above, chapter I, section 2), which demanded that the interests and probable actions of one's adversaries be calculated as well as one's own, they would have had every reason to abjure their policies. Rome's success came in spite of her inability to control events. Against the greatest odds, the dice landed in her favor.

By ascribing to accident the success of Rome in her all-or-nothing gamble, Montesquieu disoriented Machiavelli's world. The next step was decisive. By ascribing to necessity Rome's loss of civic virtue, when he proclaimed this sad event an inevitable consequence of her imperialism, he shattered Machiavelli's world beyond repair. Rational as means designed to pursue the end of aggrandizement, the Machiavellian maxims of the senators were irrational as means designed to support the end of civic virtue. As Rome expanded, every aspect of civic virtue was compromised, attenuated, and finally corrupted. From frugality to profligacy, from puritanism to debauchery, from patriotism to self-seeking individualism, from equality to extreme inequality, from the citizens' militia to professional soldiers — such was the total atrophy of civic virtue caused by Roman foreign policy. The farther Rome moved beyond her city walls in quest of empire, the nearer the moment when the death knell would sound for her civic virtue.

Equality, "the very soul of democracy,"[35] must have real substance and work in tandem with frugality or it will be of little use to civic virtue. Early in her history Rome enjoyed an egalitarian distribution of land,[36] and frugality was maintained for as long as her wars were brief hit-and-run affairs. But with campaigns prolonged and the stakes high during her imperialistic phase, the spoils of victory became too great for the good of frugality. "It is not sufficient in a well-regulated democracy that the divisions of land be equal; they ought also to be small."[37] Now after an endless succession of victories too much land was available, holdings grew in size, and Rome was cursed by riches. "With possessions beyond the needs of private life it was difficult to be a good citizen."[38] Material prosperity, in land, was inimical to the prosperity of civic virtue.

And material prosperity, in the form of money, was even less compatible with passion for the public good. Ideally a city-state should be economically primitive, even to the point of having no monetary currency.[39] Where there is no money, people have few wants, their few needs are easily satisfied, and equality is natural.[40] Unfortunately Rome did come to have money and, indeed, basked indolently in the known world's sum total of wealth. Never economically productive, she was nonetheless able to accumulate enormous riches by draining conquered territories of their treasures. The agricultural economy and autarchical policy of early Rome were succeeded by an economy of luxuries which multiplied men's desires a thousandfold. Simplicity, frugality, and puritanism gave way to sophistication, culture, and conspicuous consumption. A way of life fit only for ingenuous peoples, civic virtue could not persist once the pleasures of luxury were known. Beneficial to a feudal monarchy as a way of circulating the wealth of the privileged, luxury was fatal in a city-state republic dependent on civic virtue for its sustenance. Monarchies end in poverty, republics in luxury.[41]

As time passed, the entire moral fabric of Roman society came undone. "Rome was a ship held by two anchors, religion and morality, in the midst of a furious tempest"[42]; but the dissolution of authority proceeded inexorably and in direct proportion to the expansion of the city-state. If democracy suffers from inequality, it is no less true that too much equality, or rather the wrong kind of equality, can likewise drastically reduce its life expectancy. "The true spirit of equality . . . does not imply that everybody should command, or that no one should be commanded, but that we obey or command our equals. It endeavors not to shake off the authority of a master, but that its masters should be none but its equals."[43] In Rome, however, the meaning of equality was perverted by setting it in contradiction to authority. The patriarchal family, long the private basis of stern public authority, fell into abeyance. Youth no longer respected age, adolescents rebelled against their parents, and equality came to signify the right of everyone to self-indulgence.

Similarly, under the rapidly changing definitions of value-laden words, liberty was equated with having no obligations or with doing as one pleased. Very much part of this social transformation was the growth of individualism.[44] When civic virtue was pure, it was impossible to distinguish between "the love of oneself, of one's family, [and] of one's country,"[45] but now the individual stood in opposition to the community. Man had been, but was no more, a political animal. Never again would the individual's good be read in terms of the community's. At long last the individual was for himself and indifferent to the community except insofar as it was useful in securing his private objectives.

Stringent political education was impossible, given contact with alien cultures, the decline of the patriarchal family, and the sheer size of Rome. There were so many private spaces in a large republic that men could easily hide from those forces which in the past had forced them to be free. Whatever the benefits sponsored by the many changes in Roman mores, from the standpoint of civic virtue the situation was one of deep and irreversible losses. And all because of Roman expansion. Time, perhaps, is never on the side of so fragile a flower as civic virtue, but of one thing we may be certain. Imperialism sends the hands spinning around the clock at an insane speed, when what is needed is to hold them in place as long as possible.

Too egalitarian in doing away with veneration for age, the family, and the past, Rome was also plagued by the evil of severe inequalities of material possessions. Booty gained from rape and plunder of external foes came to be inequitably gathered and distributed. Class lines were redrawn and class conflict recommenced, but on a scale hitherto unknown. The knights, members of a middling social rank, lined their pockets when they served as tax farmers in conquered provinces. Unwilling to settle for social prestige divorced from wealth, the aristocrats also claimed an exorbitant share of the spoils; they left the Senate to serve as provincial governors, posts most attractive for the opportunity they offered their occupants to extort money from conquered peoples. With their considerable resources the well-to-do compounded inequality by buying most of the land placed in the public treasury by the sweat and blood of the citizen-soldiers. Nothing offset the accumulation of riches by the upper classes, not even the graduated taxation levy of old, for it was no longer in effect. Rome had suspended internal taxation, deeming it more comfortable to extract revenue from her external subjects.[46]

Thus Rome lost her original social composition which had conformed so well to Aristotle's dicta for democratic well-being: a large middle class to avoid a confrontation of haves and have-nots, and better yet, a large agricultural middle class of small freeholders to ensure that conservative instincts would act as ballast to popular sovereignty.[47] Through the rise of great fortunes gained in fleecing the provinces and the related disappearance of small holdings into large estates, the agrarian middle class died out, and Rome was divided between the very rich and the very poor. Indigence expressed itself through envy, and wealth through extravagance.

The evolution of slavery is illustrative of the overall evolution of Rome. As the empire expanded, so did slavery. Originally the incidence of enslavement was low, and the social distance between master and slave was as small as the political distance between citizen and slave was great. Later the number of slaves multiplied prodigiously and the social distance between master and slave increased while the political distance decreased. From a few servants needed to help in the household and fields during the era of frugality, slavery evolved to a sign of luxury in an age fond of luxuries, so the more numerous his slaves, the more the master was esteemed. As objects now superfluous, slaves were poorly treated domestically, but this was compensated for by manumissions.[48] And since the political realm was no longer considered a matter of importance, exclusion from it did not really matter. It was enough, it was everything, to belong to society. The freedman had arrived because the citizen was no more.

Always eager to relate how Rome subdued other city-states, Machiavelli cared little for the story of how those city-states rebelled and could be held in check only by granting them full Roman citizenship. Not about to lose a chance to embarrass Machiavelli, Montesquieu covered the ground that was conveniently sidestepped in the *Discourses* and went so far as to explain that the watering down of the content of citizenship was one of the primary causes of the republic's ruin. One by-product of Rome's victory over the peoples of Italy was that each of the Italian city-states lost its respective *esprit général*.[49] Having nothing of their own to sustain and something Roman enticing them, the Italians demanded Roman citizenship.

> At first most of these peoples did not care very much about the right of Roman citizenship, and some preferred to keep their own customs. But when this right meant universal sovereignty, and a man was nothing in the world if he was not a Roman citizen and everything if he was, the peoples of Italy resolved to perish or become Romans. . . .

> Forced to fight against those who were . . . the hands with which it enslaved the world, Rome was lost. It was going to be reduced to its walls; it therefore accorded the coveted right of citizenship to the allies . . . and gradually to all.[50]

When citizenship became available to all, it was meaningful to none. The most that could be claimed for the new and diluted citizenship was that it allowed one's material interests to be politically protected. Citizenship as a strenuous but glorious dedication to a public life was gone forever, save as a faint memory and a strong nostalgia in a handful of republican souls.

And then came the demise of Roman civic virtue, which up to that point had been the sole surviving example of civic virtue in antiquity:

> Rome was no longer a city whose people had but a single spirit, a single love of liberty, a single hatred of tyranny. . . . Once the peoples of Italy became its citizens, each city brought to Rome its genius, its particular interests. . . . The distracted city no longer formed a complete whole. And since citizens were such only by a kind of fiction, since they no longer had the same magistrates, the same walls, the same gods, the same temples, and the same graves, they no longer saw Rome with the same eyes, no longer had the same love of country, and Roman sentiments were no more.[51]

The final blow to republicanism came from the army. For as long as warfare was confined to Italy, each soldier was equally a citizen.

> But when the legions crossed the Alps and the sea, the warriors, who had to be left in the countries they were subjugating for the duration of several campaigns, gradually lost their citizen spirit. And the generals, who disposed of armies and kingdoms, sensed their own strength and would obey no longer. The soldiers then began to recognize no one but their general, to base all their hopes on him, and to feel more remote from the city. They were no longer the soldiers of the republic but those of Sulla, Marius, Pompey, and Caesar.[52]

The problem of the army conspired with the problem of class warfare, and together they were more than a match for what remained of the Roman constitution. Generals marched through the previously sacrosanct Roman gates, knowing that as the allies of one or another class — Marius of the common people and Sulla of the aristocrats — they would be forgiven anything except failure.

The portrait of the republic's death agony is done in the bold, sweeping strokes of a vocabulary of necessity.

It is not chance that rules the world.

The mistakes of statesmen are not always voluntary. Often they are the necessary consequences of the situation in which they find themselves.

Since the republic necessarily had to perish, it was only a question of how, and by whom, it was to be overthrown.

If Caesar and Pompey had thought like Cato, others would have thought like Caesar and Pompey.[53]

Mourning is not heard at this wake for republicanism, because it is all too evident that the imperialistic drive of Roman history had always been a death wish. Had not Plato and Aristotle warned long ago that an expansionary city-state would inevitably be a decaying city-state? Fortuna had nothing to do with the republic's demise, nor did any of the other facile explanations that Machiavelli offered: wretched human nature or the assurance that nothing lasts forever. Were human nature as miserable as Machiavelli suggested, glorious civic virtue could never have existed in the first place, much less have been the distinguishing characteristic of antiquity. As for the corruptibility of things human, Rome's greed for empire, by Machiavelli's own admission, divided the life expectancy of civic virtue in half. Abjuring empire, Sparta enjoyed civic virtue for eight hundred years; relishing empire, Rome retained her civic virtue for only four hundred.[54] To one such as Machiavelli, who in common with the classical authors thought nothing easier to come by than instability, halving the years of a political system was unforgivable, and especially so when that system was one of civic virtue, a rare and delicate edifice that should be protected at all costs. Yet, cyclical history, the theme of decline, and images of fortune's wheel — classical themes common in Renaissance political thought — conveniently allowed Machiavelli to escape from the conclusion that, of all ancient city-states, Sparta and not Rome was most deserving of admiration. Likewise the argument centering on vile human nature, though sincere and deeply rooted in ancient thought, was of special service, not as an explanation of corruption, but as rhetoric glossing over the true cause of the Roman republic's decline. Psychological explanation was resorted to when a sociological explanation was appropriate because the latter threatened to reveal too much.

Actually Machiavelli knew better. At one point or another in his writings, he expressed his awareness of every factor Montesquieu was to marshal in correlating imperialism with corruption as a sociological relationship of cause and effect. Decline of puritanism, growth of individualism, ravages of class struggle, soldiers more attentive to their general than to Rome, and an infusion of foreign peoples into the native city figure in Machiavelli's account as in Montesquieu's.[55] Nowhere, however, does Machiavelli bother to integrate them into their common denominator: corruption as the price any republic must pay for imperialism.

For all his insistence that others face up to the unpleasant consequences of a decision, Machiavelli failed to apply his own maxim. As the first pages of the *Discourses* had suggested, the choice was between a republic for "preservation" or for "increase," between Sparta and Rome, between a durable civic virtue without empire and half as durable a civic virtue with empire. Rather than accept the harsh alternatives, Machiavelli sought refuge in spurious arguments suggesting that the Roman way had to be followed. Most forceful in this regard was his argument that a city-state is always the target of external aggressors and must therefore either conquer or be conquered. The free German cities of his own period, which abstained from foreign involvement, were not an obstacle to this view of foreign affairs. They were exempted from the jungle of inter-city-state relations, he explained, because of special circumstances. Resting within the Holy Roman Empire, they were subject to a territorial prince's restrictions and thus a minimal rule of law prevailed in foreign affairs.[56] Clever as this treatment of the German cities was, it did not explain away the case of Sparta. When the wolves are at the door, balance of power can just as well, or even better, be practiced than imperialism. Indeed, the risks are much lower.

Ambivalence troubled Machiavelli's attitude toward Rome. Apparently the glitter of grandeur could not completely hide Rome's dark underside. Glory is always bloodstained, of course, but the blood is not always that of formerly free city-states. Slaughtering republican peoples is especially glorious, but also especially iniquitous. A mound of city-state corpses, once alive with civic virtue, tormented Machiavelli. Making excuses for choosing the Roman model, or pretending there was no choice, was one way by which he alleviated his uneasiness. Another way was through the masochism and self-laceration that is evident in some of his minor works. In one of his poems he lashes out against ambition and greed for power, swearing off empire and waxing nostalgic over Germany where "at the present day each

city lives secure though having less than six miles round about."
Yearning for empire, he wrote, is being like Icarus, who destroyed
himself by flying too near the sun.[57]

Montesquieu's analysis of the fall of the republic contains nothing
Machiavelli would not acknowledge. It was not in knowledge that the
Florentine was wanting, but in the will to realism. For Montesquieu
realism came naturally because facing up to realities was enough to
refute "realist" political thought.

With Machiavelli already defeated, Montesquieu continued to dog
his opponent, settling for nothing less than a complete rout. That
Machiavellism cost Rome her virtue was disastrous not only because
the civic spirit is so very precious, but also because Rome was
henceforth denied the more basic value of stability. Rome rotted from
within for want of something to replace civic virtue. Good republican
that he was, Machiavelli ignored the Principate, save for a few words
of deprecation. An equally good republican, Montesquieu paid attention to the Principate in order to demonstrate how the deleterious
effects of Machiavellism compound themselves.

Despotism and limited monarchy competed for the position of
successor to the republic, so monarchy was the most that Rome could
hope for. Undistinguished compared to republicanism, monarchy was
attractive as an alternative to despotism. Many of the phenomena
which undermined civic virtue could be incorporated into a monarchical system as its sources of vitality. Luxury, a courtly ethic, the
liberation of women, severe inequality, a polyglot population, and a
professional military arm — signs of corruption in a republic — were
either harmless or else signs of genuine health in a monarchy.

Yet even though the poison of republics is the meat of monarchies,
a prince following on the heels of a deceased republican regime is
almost always a despot or well on the way to becoming one.[58] Heir to
the powers of republican magistrates, the new prince speaks in the
name of the "people" so as to wield capriciously the power that was
formerly theirs. Republican sentiments, alive long after the republic is
dead, stand in the way of frank acceptance of the privileges that could
countervail the monarch's power. "In republican governments, men
are all equal; equal they are also in despotic governments: in the
former, because they are everything; in the latter, because they are
nothing."[59] It is the great misfortune of a republican past that it cannot give birth to a legally or traditionally sanctioned inegalitarian

order; hence a transition from all must be to nothing, for there is no half-way house. Hostile to privilege, a republic maintains its egalitarian bias when shipwrecked, redefining it as equal servitude. Monarchy is the excluded middle.

One hallmark after another of arbitrary government surfaced and took its place in an unmistakably despotic version of politics. Overmighty princes initiated a reign of terror. Public accusations, conducive in the republic to purity of morals, were transformed into whispers of informers during the Principate.[60] Originally the prince ruled in ostensible cooperation with the senators, but it was only a matter of time until a brutish emperor, disinclined to humoring the aristocrats, would end all such niceties and pretense. Armed with the power to pass criminal judgments, the emperor had little difficulty in decimating once proud senatorial families.[61] Moreover, as with every despotic government, the Roman prince did as much damage through his impotence as through his omnipotence. The absence of a law of succession and the presence of a ravenous military weakened the monarchy and permanently impaired stability. Praetorianism was chronic because the republican past, via the tradition of the citizen-soldier, bequeathed a fusion of civilian and military functions to the professional army of the Empire. From the first the emperors were generals and to the last the army made and unmade emperors, often with dizzying speed. Under monarchies civilian control of the military is possible; not so with despotism. Nominally the despotism of the prince, the Roman Empire was in reality the despotism of the military.

Dissipated by the military, utterly wanting in integrity and inner strength, the Roman political system was pathetically porous, an indiscriminate receptacle of things alien. "Rome was no longer master of the world, but it received laws from the entire world. Each emperor brought to it something from his country, whether by way of manners, morals, public order, or religion . . . [and] there was no longer anything foreign in the empire."[62] Ruler of the Orient but unable to rule herself, Rome was more and more Orientalized. Despotism hiding under republican forms gradually gave way to something approaching an outright Oriental despotism.

The grandeur of Rome spread over the earth like a pestilence, leaving behind it a wasteland. In time Rome inherited the wind, and was itself a wasteland.

How many wars do we see undertaken in the history of Rome, how

much blood shed, how many people destroyed, how many great actions, how many triumphs, how much statecraft, how much sobriety,
prudence, constancy, and courage! But how did this project end — a
project so well planned, carried out and completed — except by
satiating the happiness of five or six monsters?[63]

Fear succeeded civic virtue and fear can sustain nothing. Machiavelli
made much of stability, civic virtue, and power, but Roman Machiavellism proved contradictory to all three of these objectives.

That Rome should be disemboweled by despotism and violence
was poetically just. For even at the peak of republican vigor, she had
sponsored despotism abroad, in the provinces, and at home, in the
family. Each provincial governor brandished a fusion of legislative, executive, and judicial powers; and in the Roman family the father had
absolute power over wife, children, and slaves. The hypocritical jux-
taposition of freedom and despotism ended when speech was no
longer heard in the public forum, fear having silenced everyone.
Under a despotic government the violence and ferocity of the Roman
temperament, in the past vented on foreign peoples or in gladiatorial
combats, was turned against Rome herself; the terror she inflicted
upon others was now the terrorization of Rome.[64]

The maladies of Rome were so deeply ingrained in her social and
political structure that not even the greatest masterstrokes of statecraft
could save her.

> Soon the wisest laws could not re-establish what a dying republic,
> what a general anarchy, what a rigid empire, what a proud despotic
> power, what a feeble monarchy, what a stupid, weak, and supersti-
> tious court had successively pulled down. It might, indeed, be said
> that they conquered the world only to weaken it, and to deliver it up
> defenseless to barbarians.[65]

Machiavelli was dead if Machiavellism was the cause of the death
of civic virtue and of the birth of the succeeding despotic regime that
collapsed from within. And the disintegrating walls of Rome buried
Richelieu as well. His revised Machiavellian theory had rid itself of
the hoary goddess Fortuna, but he advanced not a step toward an
adequate conceptual treatment of unintended consequences. Abstract
and rationalist, the organizing and gaming mentalities of raison d'état
were fatally divorced from the content of history and society. (See
above, chapter II, section 1.)

Bossuet fared no better. The *Considérations* ends with a whirlwind
review of Byzantium which serves, above all else, to demonstrate the

despicability of a politics in which priests are triumphant at the court of an absolute prince. Religion plunged the laity into "profound ignorance" and "enfeebled the minds of princes."[66] Wave after wave of religious controversy broke over the state, weakening its foundation through endless persecutions carried out as public policy. Beginning as vermin held down by Caesaropapism, the monks eventually came to be arbiters of public affairs. Seemingly polar opposites, a political religion and a religious polity are, in fact, the closest of allies. And from their unholy union springs the most unpleasant of political realities: "The history of the Greek empire . . . is nothing more than a tissue of revolts, seditions, and perfidies."[67] Byzantium was so weak because its Bossuets were so strong.

Montesquieu's strictures on Byzantium were, then, so many blows directed against Bossuet's *Politique tirée des propres paroles de l'écriture sainte*. And the entire argument of the *Considérations* was a refutation of the *Discours sur l'histoire universelle*. Not content with attacking the role of priests at court, Montesquieu went on to question God's reputed role in history.

Reading Bossuet's recollection of Rome, one is immediately struck by his deep sympathy for the republic. "Liberty was to [the Romans] a treasure they preferred to all the riches of the universe,"[68] he wrote with profound admiration, his excitement for republicanism bristling on every page. On point after point, moreover, he reconstructs republican Rome, down to the last detail, in exactly the same light as Machiavelli had done before him and as Montesquieu was to do later. We might as well be reading the *Discorsi* or the *Considérations* when reading the chapters on Roman history in the *Discours*.[69]

Indistinguishable from Machiavelli and Montesquieu thus far, Bossuet charted his distinctive course when he seized upon the unintended consequence of republican imperialism, the loss of civic virtue. The guiding hand of providence, key to the entire historical process, was of special significance in explaining unintended consequences. Just as Augustine's providentialism expelled the fortuna and cycles of Polybius,[70] so the providentialism of Bossuet expelled the fortuna and cycles of Machiavelli. As adamantly as Montesquieu, but for different reasons, Bossuet insisted that chance does not rule the world. Unintended consequences do not simply "happen," nor are they attributable to fortuna, fate, or historical cycles. Such pagan legacies are dispelled by the single-minded conviction that unintended consequences are the product of divine intercession.[71] Where there had been cycles and the treadmill of eternal recurrence, there now was a unilinear unfolding of a providential plan, unknown to finite man. Where there had been the arbitrary wheel of fortune or the typically irrational woman fortuna, there now was the unquestionable reason of an omniscient, albeit inscrutable, deity. Augustine, assuredly, would have understood, even if Polybius and Machiavelli would just as certainly have remained bewildered and dumbfounded.

The disagreement between Machiavelli and Bossuet is, then, total and immediate; the disagreement between Montesquieu and Bossuet, on the other hand, is partial and mediated by several attitudes held in common. Both men, light years apart from Machiavelli, hoped through their Roman histories to dissuade the prince from imperialism; but if Bossuet does so to preach humility, that most Christian of virtues, it is overweening ambition that the unchristian Montesquieu takes to task.[72] According to the Greeks, the gods strike down a man guily of *hubris,* a proposition Montesquieu (in effect) reworded to read "history strikes down a people guilty of *hubris.*"

Similarities and dissimilarities of didactic message are paralleled by a correspondence and divergence of analytical modes. Despite his providentialism, Bossuet goes a long way toward anticipating Montesquieu's historical sociology. For in Bossuet's hands providential history becomes infused with generous doses of naturalism, much as Aquinas' Christian philosophy had incorporated large quantities of Aristotelian naturalism. Opposed to those varieties of providentialism that see the hand of God in every historical event, Bossuet envisaged a God directly responsible for unintended consequences, but for nothing else. And even among unintended consequences the deity was selective, guiding only those few which were responsible for the highest drama, notably the fate of empires. For the rest, and for history in general, except for the history of the chosen people, naturalistic explanations were perfectly adequate, because history, no less than nature, had its own patterns, laws, and regularities.

In Bossuet's estimation "the true science of history is to notice in each age those secret dispositions which prepare great changes," dispositions defined as "the inclinations and mores, or . . . the character, as much of peoples in general, as of princes in particular."[73] This sounds naturalistic and much closer to the sober language of historical sociology than to the mystical lyricism of providential history. Moreover, Bossuet adds noteworthy evidence of his capacity for sociological reasoning when he deals with the decline of the Roman republic. Essentially Bossuet adduced those processes cited by Montesquieu later, in particular the steady decline of the large middle class indispensable in a democracy.[74] Such was the course of decay, and the actual cause of the disease was traced to imperialism, so that Montesquieu and Bossuet diagnosed the same malady and isolated the same destructive germ.

The proximity of Bossuet's Rome to Montesquieu's is closer still. Siding with the historians Polybius and Dionysius of Halicarnassus against Plutarch, Bossuet opted for the interpretation of Roman conquest as a preconceived design, the brain child of the senators, men of Machiavellian genius who hoped to divert the populace by foreign wars. To this, as to all Machiavellism, he was unalterably opposed.

> The more these historians reveal a design in Roman conquests, the more injustice they show us. This vice is inseparable from the desire to dominate, which for this reason is justly condemned by the rules of Scripture. . . . Force is given us to conserve our being, and not to usurp that of others.[75]

Viewed in the light of Rome's Machiavellian misdeeds, justice was served when civic virtue contracted in direct proportion to the expansion of the city-state.

On the face of it, Bossuet has rendered a moral judgment while giving a naturalistic account of the republic's demise. Yet this only seems to be so, for he backs off from his accomplishment when, in a concluding section, he cites unintended consequences, especially the fate of empires, as those occasions in which the deity deigns to intervene in otherwise naturalistic processes. Noting at the close of the *Discours* that rulers always "do more or less than they think they do and their counsels have never been lacking in unforeseen effects," he asserts that not chance but Providence is responsible. Historical sociology has gone by the board because Bossuet has returned to the principle enunciated at the beginning of his analysis: "The revolutions of empires are regulated by Providence and serve to humble princes."[76]

Montesquieu had no trouble refuting Bossuet, but this is not to say that Bossuet was of diminutive intellectual stature. On the contrary, Montesquieu's task was facilitated precisely because Bossuet had advanced so far toward enlightened historiography, his religious commitments notwithstanding. All that was needed was to ignore Bossuet's providential but keep his naturalistic condemnation of Roman Machiavellism. Bossuet had already expunged Machiavelli's pagan fortuna from history, and Montesquieu had only to do the same to Bossuet's Christian deity. Gratuitous and superimposed, Providence was something superadded to an already completed analysis. There was no reason to go beyond secondary causes to a final cause, nothing to gain except inscrutability, mystery, and obscurantism — those offensive materials upon which religion feeds.

The *Considérations* is a slender volume rushing its reader through a millennium and more of history at breakneck speed. Hasty, though, it most certainly is not. A trap had been carefully baited and Machiavelli, Richelieu, and Bossuet were successfully ensnared by an expert huntsman. The Machiavellian and Providential universes were reduced to ashes.

One can well imagine Montesquieu's dismay could he hear a recent objection to his Roman history. His use of sources, it is charged, was uncritical, and does not so much as hint of the expert cross-examiner who in a later history of feudalism wrenched the truth from uncooperative witnesses. He is content to cite a Sallust or Livy at a time when the best of antiquarian research had already started to explore archaeological evidence and other novel sources.[77] All of which is quite beside the point. The *Considérations* is as much about Machiavelli and Bossuet as it is about Rome, and its sources must, therefore, be exactly identical to those cited in the *Discorsi* and *Discours*. Were it otherwise, the gain in factual accuracy would necessarily entail loss in argumentative force. An attack from within, an immanent critique, is the most effective method of defeating an opponent. Knowing this, Montesquieu knew he had to accept the presuppositions and sources of his enemies. In no other way could he gain access to the inside of their conceptual worlds. The blows that harmlessly glance off concepts when delivered from without are deadly from within.

Historical sociology was awesomely destructive, then, in its use as a stage for the performance of an immanent critique. Its constructive use was also considerable and lay in its assumption of the moral burden left by the abdication of natural law. In losing its old philosophical supports, "justice" was endangered, but Montesquieu came to its rescue. For purposes of condemning evil, he proved, there was no need to fall back on a defective and unserviceable natural law philosophy. It was enough to entertain the Machiavellian principle, "whatever is good for my city-state is good," and then judge by the disastrous consequences. Roman history is a lesson in the inherently self-defeating character of systematic injustice. Much wiser than the Romans, the Spartans abjured empire not from altruism but from self-interested motives. "The long duration of the republic of Sparta was owing to her having continued in the same extent of territory after all her wars."[78] After the *Lettres Persanes* had demonstrated that the injustice of a despotic regime condemns it to self-destruction, the *Considérations* followed with proof that a republic, just internally but unjust externally, is also self-devouring. The Troglodyte myth was now a sociological and historical truth.

The act of moral judgment was not radically divorced from the study of "nature" when sociology took over the tasks of moral philosophy. Redefined, "nature" did live on in the center of moral concerns, as is attested by the following contention, in effect a summation of the *Considérations:* "Nature has given states certain limits to mortify the ambition of men."[79] From the ethical law of nature Montesquieu moves to the nature of a socio-political system, whose laws of self-maintenance were necessarily moral imperatives for anyone committed to its survival. "Ought" can indeed be derived from "is," ethical judgment can be rendered naturalistically. Natural law has grown senile and is in danger of death, but what was best in it has already been reborn. Social science is its reincarnation.

CHAPTER VII

A World of Leviathans

1. "Is" and "Ought" in International Relations

By Montesquieu's day, the Leviathans which had arisen at the time of the Reformation were more menacing than ever. "Since Louis XIV," he complained, "there is nothing but great wars: half of Europe against half of Europe,"[1] a view historians have corroborated by referring to the Sun King's final conflicts as "the first world wars."[2] The increased scope of warfare was matched by increased intensity. Destruction burgeoned as warfare became rationalized. Artillery, siege warfare, and the like, were all ways of killing more effectively, and Leviathan utilized them to the maximum. Intensification was also a matter of multiplying the human bodies at the disposal of the war machine, and this took the form of conscripting the peasants and workers, a "new invention" which mobilized the population in ways unheard of in feudal Europe.[3] This, combined with the rise of the standing army, made for a military monster more organized than anything hitherto known this side of antiquity,* and so massive in sheer size as to dwarf the citizens' militia of the polis.[4] Under these circumstances, the fate of the smaller powers was unenviable. "Since the Quadruple Alliance [1718], the great European princes do as the Romans did: they dispose of the small states with a view to their interest, and not according to justice."[5] Leviathan was a predator intent on conquest, and everywhere it spied potential victims. There were other Leviathans it hoped eventually to subdue, and in the meantime it could feast on easier prey. To the Americas and the Orient it raced, knowing full well how very vulnerable those territories were. A great age of imperialism was at hand as the struggles of the European

---

*With the exception of Cromwell's Model Army.

Leviathans overflowed into the remote corners of the earth. Political space had filled up, and now there would be heard weeping and a gnashing of teeth.

Such was Montesquieu's immediate "is" of international relations, the descriptive "is" preceding theoretical explanation and understanding. "Ought" follows quickly on its heels and assumes the form of a total rejection. Always morally outrageous, wars are never legitimate, except when fought in self-defense. A state may not attack until it has been attacked, unless a preventive war is its sole hope of survival. Lest prevention be construed as pretext for attack, Montesquieu spells out its proper implications: "small states have more often a right to declare war than great ones, because they are more often in the situation of being afraid of destruction." Once victorious, the state forced to conquer against its will remains bound by morality and may not fatten itself at the expense of the loser. Success creates no rights of rape and pillage, but the conquering state does incur additional duties. "The right of . . . conquest I define thus: a necessary, lawful, but unhappy power, which leaves the conqueror under a heavy obligation of repairing the injuries done to humanity."[6]

Sometimes a prohibition of gratuitous violence, sometimes a regulation of necessary force, the "ought" of international relations can always be traced back to one value source. "The right . . . of war is derived from necessity and strict *justice*." (Emphasis added.)[7] In international relations, as at every critical juncture, justice emerges as the inexpendable evaluative principle of Montesquieu's thought. But what meaning can justice take on in so forbidding a context?

Book I of the *Lois* ventured an *a priori* notion of justice. An anomaly within Montesquieu's system, this "justice" drained of empirical content was incomprehensible until its function was recognized, namely, to outlaw the kind of empirical ethics that overtly or covertly upholds the formula, "whatever is, is right." (See chapter V, section 1.) Other passages in Montesquieu's works attest to a second notion of justice, again ascending to a high level of generality, but this time without leaving social and political reality behind. Beginning with "particular virtues" founded on sociability, the newly conceived "justice" poses as the one "general virtue" which may sit in judgment of the others. Let Montesquieu speak for himself: "Almost all the virtues are a particular rapport . . . ; for example: friendship, love of country, . . . are particular rapports. But justice is a general rapport. Now, all virtues which destroy this general rapport are not virtues."[8]

A further reading reveals that the problem of international relations is the moving force behind justice thus redefined. "Love of country, throughout history," Montesquieu charged, "has been the source of the greatest crimes, because general virtues have been sacrificed to this particular virtue."[9] Unwilling to allow that love of family entails hatred of countrymen, he was also unwilling to allow that love of countrymen entails hatred of foreigners.[10]

To say that justice is the only general virtue is, then, to interpret it as a rank-ordering device that puts the moral life of the group to the test, granting it everything except the right to victimize outsiders. Within a country, the legal system counteracts the moral liabilities which are inseparable from the moral assets of the group. Whenever familial ties or the bonds of friendship are manifest as an aggressive extended egotism, justice can be asserted through the realm of law. Within international politics, however, lawlessness abides, and each Leviathan is for itself. Hence Montesquieu's concept of justice as a kind of super-value situated above a ladder of particular virtues laden with the content of social and group relationships. Making certain each rung in the ladder gets its due, but no more, is the function of justice.

All we need add, now that the meaning of justice has been determined, is that this norm applies to all times and places. Unlike the Stoics of Hegel's interpretation, Montesquieu was not an advocate of a bogus world citizenship and universal ethics because the genuine citizenship and ethical life of the polis was no more. In Montesquieu's opinion, the true heroism of civic virtue can no more excuse unnecessary killings than can the false heroism of honor.

Nor, however, was Montesquieu's opposition to war the product of cosmopolitan sentimentality. More than the *philosophes*, he knew how unreal "humanity" is, how real a Frenchman or Spaniard is. And he knew as well as Rousseau or Hegel how much the substance of ethical life belongs to the community and not to the world. Montesquieu's membership in the "party of humanity" diverges from the position of the *philosophes* in being entirely negative or remedial. His normative guidelines do no more than indicate what a polity may not do to its fellow polities. They give to the community what is the community's, most of all ethical life and the maximal content of justice, but take from it the sword of doom.

At last both the "is" and the "ought" of international relations are clarified. Destructive Leviathans constitute the "is," and an antidotal concept of justice constitutes the "ought." But instead of a solution, the upshot is a problem grown more acute than ever. How can the "is" be forestalled from shaking off the "ought"? How can "ought" be proven something more than Montesquieu's personal "ought"? A bond had to be formed between empirical and normative so that the "ought" could be solidly grounded in, and follow inescapably from, the "is."

Natural law philosophy, in alliance with the "law of nations" school, was the established genre in which a bridge had been built between "is" and "ought." But Montesquieu bitterly denounced the revitalized natural law/law of nations of Grotius, and for good reason. Norms had indeed been saved from irrelevant transcendence by the author of *The Rights of War and Peace*, but they were plunged so deeply into the empirical world as to be swallowed by it. Interpreters miss the mark, historically speaking, when they dwell on Grotius' belief in an *a priori* natural law.[11] The keenest political minds of the old regime — Montesquieu and Rousseau — were surely correct in concentrating on the *a posteriori* version of Grotian natural law, for it was this which informed everything Grotius had to say about international relations. Rousseau stated the case against Grotius most succinctly: "His constant manner of reasoning is to establish right by fact. A more satisfactory mode might be employed, but none more favorable to tyrants."[12]

At the start of his treatise, Grotius sets out to impose the yoke of legality upon masterless Leviathans, but by the end he has studded his performance with so many rationalizations and apologetics that Leviathan can find excuses for the worst of crimes. How is this possible? Purely intellectual factors provide part of the answer. An *a posteriori* determination of natural law and a prescriptive law of nations can be learned, Grotius argued, from the practices common to most civilized nations. But it was not the practices of contemporary powers to which he was attentive. Accepting the Renaissance penchant for classical pedantry, he turned antiquity upside down and shook examples of foreign politics from it. The momentous consequences of this procedure were not lost on Montesquieu.

> The authors of our public law, guided by ancient histories, . . . have fallen into very great errors. They have adopted tyrannical and arbitrary principles, by supposing the conquerors to be invested with I know not what right to kill: from this they have drawn consequences as terrible as the very principle, and established maxims which the

conquerors themselves, when possessed of the least grain of sense, never presumed to follow.[13]

Machiavelli would have savored the irony of having Grotius, an international lawyer, as his accomplice. "Those cannot be considered wars in which no men are slain, cities plundered, or sovereignties overthrown," wrote the great Florentine who wanted nothing to do with the halfhearted bloodletting of modern times. Christianity was the culprit. Its influence on "the way of life and values of mankind" was evident in the regrettable contrast of the ancient and modern laws of nations. Greeks and Romans, unlike the moderns, were never squeamish in dealing with their victims. "Then, all who were vanquished in battle were either put to death or carried in perpetual slavery into the enemy's country where they spent the remainder of their lives in labor and misery.... But at present, those terrible apprehensions are in great measure dissipated and extinguished." Things had degenerated to such an impasse, the will to power was so enfeebled, that fighting a war was no longer a profitable venture.[14]

The predilection of Grotius and his kind for antiquity could mean but one thing. Thinkers in the law of nations tradition were giving back to Machiavelli everything the modern age had denied him. Rights of conquest, enslavement, and pillage were affirmed.[15] From one perspective *a posteriori* natural law had added "ought" to a preexistent, morally noxious "is"; from another perspective it went further by encouraging the development of an "is" far exceeding the evil already existent. Grotius had set out to subject a Machiavellian international reality to legality; he finished by making legalism an extension of Machiavellism. As Montesquieu insisted, the effect of international law was "to erect injustice into a system."[16]

The influence of royal patronage suggests a second explanation of how the noble intentions of Grotius were diverted into rationalization of the status quo and worse. "Grotius, ... a refugee in France, and desirous of paying his court to Louis XIII, to whom his book is dedicated, spares no pains to rob the people of all their rights and transfers them to kings in the most artful manner."[17] The words are Rousseau's, but they could just as easily be Montesquieu's. And their meaning is indisputable. Ostensibly the bearer of good tidings, the law of nations theory is really little more than another ideology of absolutism. Grotius had taken his place at court beside Richelieu and Bossuet.

Natural law had failed again, so it was inevitable that Montesquieu should look once more to his social science for a substitute. Transformation of the prima facie "is" into an empirical theory might very well be a means of discovering an imperative that would halt the aggressions of Leviathan. A newly conceptualized "is" might imply a new foundation for "ought."

In its revelation of the structural logic of the monarchical system, Montesquieu's political sociology uncovered more than an internally deficient system; it also unearthed an inherently aggrandizing external dynamic. Hence it was that political sociology doubled as a theory of international relations. Five suspects were rounded up by the monarchical model and charged with responsibility for the expansive nature of absolutism. They were honor, dynastic claims, reason of state, mercantilism, and religion.

The entire honorific ethos was permeated with combative passion, as was only natural, since it was born of the feudal nobility, a proud and exclusive military caste. War was the very meaning of life, the chance to display prowess, courage, and nonchalance in times of grave danger. Usually, as with Louis XIV's unending quest for *gloire*, there was no shortage of wars to occupy the nobility, and when a Louis XV reigned, seemingly oblivious to the victories which could do him honor, the courtiers won him over to schemes of foreign adventure.

Dynastic politics raised the specter of universal monarchy. The fondest dream of Louis XIV was that he, or his heir, should inherit the thrones of both Spain and the Holy Roman Empire, thus making France the seat of a supranational regime reminiscent of the Hellenistic age. Such was the nature of dynastic politics that hopes of empire sprang eternal, and the fate of Europe hinged on accidents of birth, death, and marriage. Montesquieu understood the pattern and meaning of dynastic politics, and he despised it in direct proportion to his knowledge.[18]

Reason of state was beginning to free power of traditional and religious restraints. It was a sign of the times when the Sun King courted the infidel Turk in order to further his European designs.[19] As never before, amorality was given a good conscience, so that in international relations there abided "a perpetual and restless desire of power after power, that ceaseth only in death." Yet there remained, due to the prodding of raison d'état, a roseate confidence in the capacity of reason to calculate the interests and to predict the actions of each Leviathan in this state of nature. Never was rationalism in politics to be more deplored than when it encouraged the belief that wars could easily be planned, conducted, and controlled by reason.

Most telling of all, in Montesquieu's opinion, was the fatal absorption of raison d'état into pre-established patterns of thought, feeling, and behavior. Honor was at once the source of the appeal of reason of state and of its corruption. Formally raison d'état rested on a denial of the feudal ethos, but in fact it was an integral feature of the aristocratic lifestyle. Be it noted that honor "allows of cunning and craft when joined with the notion of greatness of soul or importance of affairs, as, for instance, in politics."[20] Far from being a repressive ideology, reason of state fostered a reinvigoration of frivolity and play, as if the issues facing aristocratic ambassadors were not of the utmost seriousness. In the long run, the game theory side of reason of state (see above, chapter I, section 2) was much less pronounced than was the penchant for treating life-and-death matters as games.

Mercantilism was a continuation of war by other means. "My gain is your loss," its fundamental article of faith, made trade synonymous with warfare. Precious metals were regarded as wealth, so the whole point of trade was to accumulate bullion. Fundamentally static, the mercantilist doctrine was predicated on the view that the world's sum total of wealth — identical to its sum total of gold and silver — was fixed once and for all. Since victory over the other European powers was a long-range proposition, a short-cut to hegemony via the other continents was highly attractive. A windfall of precious metals would fall to the power that exploited first and best the Americas and the Orient. Extra-European imperialism seemed the quickest route to the fulfillment of intra-European lusts.

Religion aided and abetted the imperialists by blessing the enslavement of non-Christian peoples.

> This was the notion that encouraged the ravagers of America in their iniquity. Under the influence of this idea they founded their right of enslaving so many nations; for these robbers, who would absolutely be both robbers and Christians, were superlatively devout.

> [Again,] Louis XIII was extremely uneasy at a law by which all the negroes of his colonies were to be made slaves; but it being strongly urged to him as the readiest means for their conversion, he acquiesced without further scruple.[21]

For the native peoples of the Americas, and potentially the Orient, Christianity was damnation. Whatever brutality Christianity removed from the European law of nations reappeared, under Christian aegis, outside Europe.[22] Machiavellian imperialism was never entirely successful in overcoming its Christian conscience, but when Christianity itself sponsored imperialist rape, princes could have their cake and eat it too. "The king of Spain was a good Catholic: that is to say, a member of a religion which accommodated his ambition so well."[23]

To the analysis thus far advanced, an examination of the despotic model can supply a vital additional finding. The predatory instinct of the Western Leviathans was likely to assert itself fully, since its aggressive drives would not come up against something able to rebuff and restrain them. A balance of power situation could, perhaps, force the reality principle upon the monarchical id, but radical asymmetry of power existed between Europe and Asia. Occidental Leviathans, meeting little resistance from their impotent Oriental counterparts, could most assuredly crush them.[24]

The problem went deeper still. Asymmetry persisted not only between West and East, but also between Western and Eastern Europe. Poland and Hungary, with their fragmented and impotent political systems, were in no position to hold their Leviathan neighbors at bay. It was as if the feudal regime of the thirteenth century were asked to defend France against eighteenth-century absolutism. Balance of power existed neither between West and East, nor within the West taken as a whole. To the limited and precarious extent that balance had any being, it was between the great powers.[25] Thus, enjoying the pleasurable security of balance of power, the Leviathans also enjoyed the gluttonous delights of power-aggrandizement. As for the weaker powers, their lot was to be carved and eaten. Not long after Montesquieu's death, Poland was partitioned, fulfilling his unhappy prophecy.

We now may summarize the findings that political sociology advances as it changes a prima facie "is" of international relations into an "is" of empirical theory. The monarchical model links imperialism to the Western Leviathans as the foreign behavior natural to their regimes. The despotic model suggests that Eastern Leviathans are paper tigers, destined to crumble in rapid succession when attacked by the real tigers of the West. The monarchical model historicized further underscores what could be known, and was, without resorting to political sociology: that the countries of Eastern Europe were living on borrowed time.

Proving that monarchical imperialism was self-destructive was the next and absolutely vital step. Without it, the Leviathans would remain unleashed, outside and inside Europe; with it, injustice would suffer a decisive rebuff, and a hypothetical imperative would be enjoined against imperialism. If, kings and Machiavellians, you want to preserve your monarchies, refrain from conquest and empire.

Colonialism is a very different phenomenon in its modern monarchical, compared to its ancient republican, guise. Monarchies use colonialism to expand, republics to retain their original size. To avoid the growth that would undermine their institutions, city-states reproduced themselves. Excess population was shipped to a new area, where a politically independent second city was established.[26] By contrast, a monarchy cannot reproduce itself — kings are not made overnight — nor would it if it could. Monarchical colonialism is intent on the kingdom's growth, and it proceeds by continuing a long-established pattern of political behavior. Newly acquired colonies are provinces added to the realm, just as the outer provinces of the mother country were usually her last acquisitions as she undertook the transition from feudal to territorial monarchy.

Politically, then, Montesquieu sees monarchies as extending their system rather than duplicating it; but socially colonialism does involve a reproductive process. "The Spanish conquests in America have metamorphosed into Spaniards all the peoples of that part of the world."[27] Natives have become Spaniards, and Spanish aristocrats, moreover, have sunk feudal roots into native soil. Younger sons of noble families enjoy the opportunities abroad which primogeniture denies them at home. During the colonization period following conquest, aristocrats hungry for civilian, military, and ecclesiastical posts glut the newly acquired territory.[28]

The consequences of conquest may be expressed by an organic analogy. Colonies thus established are like overgrown branches which derive their nourishment from an increasingly hollow tree trunk.[29] Dropping the metaphor, Montesquieu describes "the necessary state of a conquering monarchy" as follows: "a shocking luxury in the capital, misery in the provinces somewhat distant, and plenty in the most remote."[30] Rural blight, a normal tendency in monarchies (see above, chapter II, section 2), is aggravated imperialism. Victories bring new hardships for the provinces, which so badly need relief. Capital and court expect to enjoy a burgeoning luxury after a successful war, but it cannot come from the spoils of annexation. Transplanted nobles in the conquered territory are already treating themselves to a luxurious lifestyle at the expense of the conquered, so that an augmentation of tribute would surely stir the subdued aliens to revolt. The surplus, therefore, is pumped out of the old provinces of the mother country, the very areas that can least spare it. Slowly but surely a conquering monarchy bleeds itself to the verge of collapse.

Much to his chagrin, a monarch soon learns that newly acquired provinces belong not to him, their ostensible owner, but to the nobles who hold them in his name.

> A monarchical state ought to be of moderate extent. . . . [W]ere it very large, the nobility, possessed of great estates, far from the eye of the prince, with a private court of their own, . . . might throw off their allegiance, having nothing to fear from too slow and too distant a punishment.

The cure for this malady is worse than the disease. "The sudden establishment of unlimited power is a remedy which in those cases may prevent a dissolution: but how dreadful the remedy, which after the enlargement of dominion opens a new scene of misery!"[31] For despotism, and for it alone, empire is natural. Fear can, indeed, govern vast territorial expanses, but no matter in whose name it is deployed, it serves no one but itself.

Everything depends on whether or not the foregoing argument against empire is convincing. In transforming the prima facie "is" into a sociological theory, Montesquieu had discovered that the trends of world politics were even more disturbing than what was apparent at first blush. By their very nature, monarchies are aggrandizing and despotisms defenseless, a confirmation of his worst fears. Should monarchical imperialism be anything less than utterly self-destructive, Montesquieu would be thrown back on his abstract "justice" for "ought."

How successful was he? Doubtless, his observations on the difficulties likely to beset monarchical imperialism are well-taken. Portuguese and Spanish colonies, where the pattern of exploitation was feudal, confirmed the initial hypotheses generated by his model. Regions were divided into fiefs, which their holders sought to convert into hereditary possessions. For a while, the Spanish crown was faced with the none too pleasant prospect of reproducing in the New World the Spain which had existed prior to the centralizing measures of Ferdinand and Isabella. A new world more antiquated in its political structure than the old would most assuredly be a colony refractory to control by the mother country. So far, so good; but later developments were not so kind to Montesquieu's model. Happily for Spain, but unhappily for Montesquieu, the crown managed to reassert itself.[32] The difficulties he pointed to were genuine enough, but not insuperable. Much the same can be said about the connection he drew between imperialism abroad and accelerated rural debilitation at home. Successful in demonstrating that expansion is self-damaging, he was not successful in demonstrating that expansion was self-destructive. Denying that imperialism is worth the price it costs is much weaker than charging it with the destruction of its perpetrator, especially so when monarchy, by its innermost nature, lusts for empire and disdains utilitarian calculations.

Because of its defects — a ramshackle political structure and inferior social bonds — monarchy was ironically spared the either/or choice between self-maintenance and empire which for city-states is inescapable. Indifferent to political education, monarchy need not restrict its size in order to politicize its population or to mold them into one people. A polyglot and privatized conglomerate is as fitting for a monarchy as it is fatal for a republic. Republics demand everything, monarchies nothing. That is why the creaking and groaning Austrian empire, composed of territories and peoples bound together neither by geography nor by nationality, with no other union than their common subjection to the Habsburg dynasty, could live on until 1918.

To a limited degree, Montesquieu was guilty of overestimating his achievement. Feudal language was the material from which he constructed much of his theory of monarchical imperialism, and it served him well in the first instance — explaining the genesis of imperialism and the obstacles to colonial control. But it failed in the second instance — explaining the administrative methods by which modern monarchies had learned to offset feudal fragmentation outside the mother country. That Montesquieu cited Charlemagne as an example of the tendency of monarchy to disintegrate feudally is extremely revealing.[33] Earlier, Bodin's effort to develop a bureaucratic theory for the internal government of monarchy had run aground on the paradigm of reflection provided by feudal language. Projected into the international sphere by Montesquieu, the feudal paradigm was no better suited to provide a theory of colonial administration.

But this is to miss the most vital point of all. Montesquieu was no stranger to the past successes of monarchical imperialism, nor was he at a loss in adducing their explanation. Within his scheme of things, monarchies are better equipped than city-states to govern an empire because they separate civilian and military functions whereas republics unite them. When the differentiation of functions is shipped to a new colony, a monarchy avoids what for a republic is natural: a despotic imperial rule which renders the colony rebellious. So useful to the imperialist was a mechanism of civil-military checks and balances that it was adopted by one Eastern power in defiance of the natural inclination of despotism to oppose all rationalization. Intent on holding a vanquished China in subjection, the ruling Tartars divided provincial military and judicial posts evenly between the Chinese and their own kind. "The want of so wise an institution as this has been the ruin of almost all the conquerors that ever existed."[34]

Alexander the Great's empire is another example of a successful monarchical imperialism which arrested Montesquieu's attention. Brilliant in conducting a policy of conquest, Alexander was no less brilliant in his policy of imperial preservation. Overruling the provincial Greeks, who regarded themselves as natural masters and the Persians as natural slaves, Alexander "thought only of uniting the two nations, and of abolishing the distinctions of a conquering and a conquered people." He assumed the manners of the foreigners, permitted them to retain their customs and civil laws, bowed before their altars, and married the women of their royal families. Checks and balances were assured by placing fellow Macedonians at the head of the troops, while government was administered through natives of the subdued countries. "So well were all the parts of his new empire cemented that after his death, amidst the disturbances and confusion of the most frightful [Grecian] civil wars, . . . not a single province of Persia revolted."[35]

Obviously, then, Montesquieu was aware not only of the brittleness of republics, but also of the plasticity of monarchies. His greatest fear was not that the expansion of monarchies would eventually force them into the despotic mold. This largely artificial notion, resting on importation of an Oriental model to an alien Western context, was more flirted with than seriously pressed. Rather, he was haunted by the nightmare of despotism imposed upon one Western country by another. Rape and pillage, so destructive of institutions and customs, were more "natural" than rationalized means of exploitation, and they portended possible catastrophe. "If from a long abuse of power or the fury of conquest, despotic sway should prevail . . . , then human nature would be exposed . . . , even in this beautiful part of the world, to the insults with which she has been abused in the other three."[36] For the country desolated in a losing war and then colonized by the victorious power, the end result could well be destruction of its political and social structures. Expansion entailed an acute risk of despotism not for both conqueror and conquered, but for the conquered country alone. With this realization, the poetic justice of the Troglodyte story returns to the realm of fiction.

Political sociology had given Montesquieu a closely reasoned "is" of international relations, an empirical theory which matched each increment of knowledge with a corresponding increase of disgust; but it refused to grant him an "ought" to which the perpetrators of evil would be forced to assent in spite of themselves. As a result, moral outrage was denied the immanent supports Montesquieu sought. It was a purer but lesser thing, meaningful but inconsequential.

2. Liberalism in Machiavellian Disguise

Possibly direct advocacy at court can yet save the day for what ought to be. Should Montesquieu follow Richelieu and Bossuet to court, the better to confound them? Infiltration of their conceptual worlds, so as to level an immanent critique against them — the masterplan of the *Considérations* — can be complemented by usurpation of their political roles. Sold as a superior Machiavellism, Montesquieu's advanced social science could ostracize Bossuet from court and beat the Machiavellians at their own game of power politics.

From time to time, Montesquieu worked on a startling rite of passage to the less than enchanted land of court politics: a proposed, though never completed, pamphlet which bore among its various tentative designations that of *Le Prince*.[37] The secret of this document, which has been called "a mystery in the literary activity of Montesquieu,"[38] can be learned by noting its relationship to Machiavelli's

book of the same title and to the still older "mirror of princes" literature. As early as the Hellenistic age and as late as the old regime,
philosophers and clerics penned resumés of the rights and duties inherent in kingly office, and offered their products to the reigning
monarch. Either the "ought" of these brief treatises consisted of vague
and irrelevant moralisms, or it was totally ignored in favor of sycophantic praise. As for "is," the description and analysis of political
practice, the "mirror of princes" literature refused to dirty its hands
with such mundane concerns.

Machiavelli's *Prince* marks a radical departure. It glories in the "is"
of power neglected by its predecessors, and its "ought" is devoted to
the accumulation and efficient use of power. In the traditional genre of
princely literature, policy was sometimes ignored altogether, sometimes alluded to but smothered beneath praises of the king's justice
and magnificence. But for Machiavelli and Machiavellism, policy is
an object of intense and "scientific" concern. Machiavelli and Richelieu sought to develop a political science (See above, chapter I, section
2), which explains how politics is conducted, so that there might be a
policy science, which uses these explanations to suggest how to conduct politics more effectively.

Montesquieu's *Prince* is the fulfillment, negation, and transcendence
of the Machiavellian and mirror of princes traditions. Ostensibly, it
was what Richelieu's *Political Testament* had been, a latter day copy of
Machiavelli's *Prince*, updated to fit the contours of the old regime, but
in actuality the best elements of the mirror of princes tradition had
been admitted through the back door. Amoral in tone, speaking in the
vocabulary of power politics, dedicated to policy science, *Le Prince* was
everything except what it appeared to be. Underneath its Machiavellian form rested a camouflaged moral content. The language of
power and statism was designed to conceal a liberal subversion of the
status quo.

Midway in his career Montesquieu wrote a pamphlet, the *Réflexions
sur la monarchie universelle,* which carried the tone and style of *Le Prince*
into the study of international relations. Written as a sequel to the
Considérations, the *Réflexions* sides against monarchical imperialism
without once taking moral objections into consideration. Success and
power are seemingly its only concerns, the sole ends served by the
policy science means that it contains. Those same means and policies
reappear later in the *Lois,* flying the colors of justice and liberty. As

Machiavelli had done before him, Montesquieu understood liberty
and power as correlates. The more liberty, the more power: a belief
which in Machiavelli's thought ends with power devouring liberty, in
Montesquieu's with liberty devouring power. Treating liberal measures as means to the end of power was all that was needed for
Montesquieu to sound like a Machiavellian.

Double-dealing and deception were less essential in carrying out
this mission than might be expected. That liberty confers power was
for Machiavelli a purely political matter, a question of political regimes, while for Montesquieu it was both that and an economic
matter. "Wealth is power" was already a slogan known and beloved
by absolutism; Montesquieu had only to restate it and replace the
static economics of mercantilism with the liberal economics of growth.
As is often said, economics is a science of means, political science a
study of ends as well as means. But so loaded with a covert liberal
content are Montesquieu's economic means that they will surely compromise the end of power. And that, after all, is as it should be, recall-
ing that Machiavellian means have always sacrificed noble ends to
their welfare. Why should not liberal means do the same to Machiavellian ends?

But it was not to be. Over the long haul, Montesquieu's economic
analysis was significant and his attraction to policy science insignificant. For all he wrote in a policy science vein, nothing was published
and this by his own decision. As we recreate his theories of economic
growth and international trade, and examine the Machiavellian dis-
guises he designed for his findings, we must bear in mind that Montesquieu himself spied a trap in the temptation to play the policy
scientist. Detection of that trap will be our last order of business in this
section.

Some four stages, we may postulate, would be needed if Montesquieu were to implement his policy science strategy: first, a purge of
his potential adversaries at court; second, making certain the prince
was aware of the restraints facing him in the international arena;
third, unveiling the economic route to power through build-up of the
domestic economy; and fourth, economics again, but addressed now
to prospects of wielding power over other states.

Stage one is as hoary as it is inevitable. "The most important talent
of a great prince," Montesquieu writes, as had so many others before

him, "is knowing how to choose men well."[39] For the sake of a better power politics, Richelieu and his kind must be banished from court, notwithstanding their Machiavellian credentials. They mouthed the catch phrase "public interest" so as to indulge their private interests the more fully. The wars Richelieu promoted, Montesquieu charged, were not for the national interest, nor even for Louis XIII; first and foremost, they were fought for the glory of Richelieu.[40] Confessors are also suspect, especially when they use their religious role as a springboard to political influence. Of all the men who approach the throne, confessors must be respected the most and listened to the least.[41]

Whenever religious disputes arise, inside or outside of court, the king should be quick to reiterate the long-established *politique* and Machiavellian maxims. Late in Montesquieu's lifetime the revived papal bull *Unigenitus* threatened for a second time to split French society into two camps and to make of her politics an adjunct of the Papacy's. In response, Montesquieu wrote a policy paper addressed to the king, the *Mémoire sur la constitution*. Its call for a political freeze on such conflicts adroitly sidesteps a head-on clash with the prince's religious sympathies. "Everyone knows that the Catholic religion does not in the least admit *tolérance intérieure*." All that Montesquieu asks of the king is what Bodin and Richelieu had previously begged of him: a *"tolérance extérieure"* necessary for the preservation of the state. In effect, Montesquieu rendered unto God what is God's, inward zeal, and unto Caesar what is Caesar's, outward stability and strength.

Since *Unigenitus* had been on the books for almost forty years, and in deference to the king's religiosity, it had to be nominally accepted but its enforcement procedures dropped. Those who tried to administer its religious test would be treated as enemies of the state, and the Gallicans needed only to pay lip service to the detested bull. "The preservation of the state is the supreme law." Not the clergy, therefore, but the *Conseil d'État* should be the king's *"Conseil de Conscience."* Bossuet and the Jesuits might as well pack their bags, for henceforth political affairs would be handled by politicians.[42]

In general, the superior Machiavellism of stage one seeks to repress both religious politics and the old power politics. And if the new raison d'état has its way, the politics of honor will also be abandoned. Unrestricted passions for *gloire* must be sublimated by reason, the courtiers ignored, the prince informed that moderation, "as the most rare virtue, should [thereafter] constitute heroism."[43]

Hoping to capitalize on that side of Machiavellism which disdains irresponsible adventurism in foreign policy, stage two concentrates on hedging in the prince. Economics is cited as particularly obtrusive in its ways and indifferent to absolute rulers. They must adjust to it, not it to them, as the example of exchange rates illustrates. On the domestic scene the king has a say, but not internationally. "The coin of every state has . . . a relative value as it is compared with the money of other countries. This relative value is established by the exchange. . . . It is fixed by the general opinion of the merchants, never by the decrees of the prince." In past ages princes played havoc with economic affairs; "in the present age, a prince might deceive himself but he could deceive nobody else. The exchange has taught the banker to draw a comparison between all the money in the world, and to establish its just value. The standard of money can no longer be a secret." Similarly, in regard to prices, "the prince or the magistrate can no more ascertain the value of merchandise than he can establish by decree that the relation one has to ten is equal to that of one to twenty."[44]

Acquainting the prince thus with *la nature des choses*, Montesquieu hoped to drag him, yelling and screaming, out of the seductive solipsism which absolute power induces. Personally, the great provincial was exuberant that "the exchange . . . has deprived princes of the opportunity of showing great exertions of authority, or at least has rendered them ineffectual."[45] But as a lamb in wolf's clothing — his guise should he go to court — the same point would doubtless be put forward as a Machiavellian discovery of one more out-of-bounds marker that must be heeded in playing the political game.

Still other obstacles thwart the prince, other walls limit his choices. The conclusion toward which Montesquieu unrelentingly drives is that the barriers to world empire are insuperable in modernity, and princes would be well-advised to settle for less audacious gains. Modern communications and an international network of informants have altered the rules of world politics.[46] Acute antennae detect the danger signals that hostile foreign powers unwillingly but inescapably emit, and in consequence one militarization is quickly matched by another. "Does a state augment its troops, does it introduce a new tax? It is an advertisement for the others to do as much." Things have gone so far that "when Louis XIV borrows from his subjects, the English and Dutch borrow from theirs."[47] None of the old methods of aggrandizement retain their viability when all secrets are open. They merely rebalance power, since each initiative is now immediately followed by an offsetting response. Violence may be resorted to despite the built-in retention of near parity between the great powers, but the financial losses are always excessive and the political gains meager. Given the prolonged and agonized nature of siege warfare by standing armies, it cannot be otherwise. Everyone loses, then, except the neutrals.[48]

Obstacles, we have seen, thwart the prince's ambition whichever way he turns. What completes these restraints is the unfitness of raison d'état for steering the ship of state through precarious channels as the monarch chases after an ever-fleeting hegemony. Pouring direct abuse on raison d'état was not Montesquieu's way of discrediting it.

> It is useless to attack reason of state directly by showing how repugnant it is to morality, to reason, to justice. Such discourses persuade everyone and touch no one . . . . I believe it better to take an indirect route and to seek to disgust the powerful with it by demonstrating how little utility they can derive from it.

Raison d'état always goes astray, he insists, because it is rationalistic in the pejorative sense. Its practitioners project upon everyone their own mentality in which everything is calculated, nothing left to chance. Those actions of mankind guided by tradition, undertaken from passion, or engaged in simply to be doing something — which is to say, almost all actions — are totally misconstrued. A related defect is the failure of *Realpolitik* to predict or to control the consequences of actions that it sanctions — its powerlessness to change history from what it has always been, a record of unanticipated consequences. When Henry VIII took religion into his own hands and following that sold the monasteries, he and everybody else believed the power of the monarch was elevated as never before. In truth, he had triggered a chain-reaction which would eventually topple absolutism in England. Isolated above society, raison d'état never even begins to familiarize itself with the infinitely complex chain of causation whose effect is the *esprit général*, a nation's real governor.[49]

The restraining cage Montesquieu had built around Leviathan was a fragile construction, certain to be shattered should the monster's pent-up frustration incite him to fury. As a pacifier, a new route to power had to be suggested, but one whose projects, unknown to those who effectuate them, would tame international competition and entail the domestic side benefits of moderation, reform, and justice. Until now economics has been viewed as a restraint, but what it took from the prince with one hand was returned by the other. The *Reflections on Universal Monarchy* did not limit itself to proclaiming the futility of the old imperialism. It also directly correlated an increase or decrease of economic vitality with a corresponding increase or decrease of power. If this be so, then the best reason of state is not that which is forced upon society from above; actually, it is a reason in society, the economic rationality which methodically subjects everything to calculability.[50] With this in mind, we may proceed to stages three and four, economics in national and then in international form.

That power resides in invulnerability instead of in expansion was argued by Montesquieu as a corollary to his finding that monarchy is sufficiently elastic to accommodate empire, but destined to be weakened by its success. Too many territories, too widely scattered, are easy prey for enemies and a curse to the rural provinces of the mother country. Therefore, "the real power of a prince does not so much consist in the facility he meets with in making conquests as in the difficulty an enemy finds in attacking him and . . . in the immutability of his condition."[51] Under the sponsorship of economic theory, this argument can be changed from nay-saying to the positive program of stage three. Relinquishing dreams of conquest can be regarded as the beginning of aggrandizement if military build-up is succeeded by economic build-up, arms race by economic race. In antiquity a poor and frugal city-state republic was often more powerful than an imperial monarchy that enjoyed a trade of luxuries; but in modernity the country boasting a burgeoning economy outstrips its economically retarded neighbors, one and all, whatever their political regimes.[52] What counts most is knowledge of the means conducive to economic growth, and mercantilism is not the source of such wisdom. Nor is its physiocratic challenger familiar with the whereabouts of the missing horn of plenty.

Agriculture posed especially difficult problems. Physiocrats would solve them by eulogizing the splendors of bucolic existence, mercantilists by converting the dreaded rural backwater into an extension of the city's commercial vitality. Also preoccupied with rural adversity, Montesquieu takes a unique position. Agricultural output is a necessary but not a sufficient condition for sustained growth. Before the economy can advance to more ambitious endeavors, its agricultural sector must satisfy subsistence needs and supply a surplus. Gains in agricultural productivity beyond the subsistence point make possible the development of a commercial, trading, and manufacturing class.[53] "Movable" effects then supplement "immovable," wealth is circulated, a flow of savings and investments feeds a steadily growing economic offspring. The physiocrats, therefore, are correct in stressing agriculture but wrong to stress it at the expense of commerce and industry. Rehabilitation of the countryside is rather the first step than the end of the journey. It also follows that the commercial bias of the mercantilists is hardly an improvement over the agricultural bias of the physiocrats. Moving industry into the hinterland aggravates the rural blight it is meant to end. The agricultural stage of economic growth can no more be skipped than it can be both first and last stage. Mercantilism is as wrong-headed as physiocracy.

Generosity to agriculture consists of freeing it from the clutches of doctrinaire approaches and rethinking its problems afresh. Different rates of agricultural productivity are attributable partly to peculiarly agricultural factors, partly to the socio-political environment surrounding agriculture. Whether land supports grazing, as in England, viniculture, as in France, or grain crops, as in Poland, makes a difference; but the contrasting English, French, and Polish socio-political systems make a greater difference still. In the absence of the state, aristocratic anarchy reigns in Poland. Enslaved peasants, driven on by the cattle prods of their ignorant noble oppressors, cannot be expected to startle the world with feats of economic prowess.[54] Security is the ally of economic progress, the whip its nemesis; and better yet than security is freedom.

The reductio ad absurdum of monarchical economics may be seen in Spain and Portugal. Of all the ill fates which can befall an economy, the worst is when "in a non-commercial state, such as Spain, the lands belong to a few and the people have none at all."[55] Normally, Montesquieu was opposed to the subdivision of lands into small morsels fit only for subsistence farming, thinking such fragmentation proper for ancient republics but not for modern monarchies.[56] Frugality and equality, so essential to the city-states of antiquity, had been well served by an egalitarian subdivision of lands which ruled out economic development. Old regime monarchies, however, needed economic development as much as ancient republics needed to avoid it. It is, therefore, a measure of Montesquieu's pessimism about the future of Spain and Portugal that in their case he counselled an egalitarian parcelling out of lands into subsistence units. In effect this was to say that, short of revolutionary change, stagnation of the Spanish economy is irreversible, and so long as present conditions continue to prevail, it would be more humane for poverty to be evenly spread than for the privileged at court to die of gluttony while the provincials starve to death.[57]

As is incumbent upon a policy scientist, Montesquieu offers the French state a course of action in agricultural affairs. First, untilled and unowned land should be turned over to impecunious peasant families and equipment given them for its clearing and cultivation. When such neglected lands already belong to lords or clergy, the same policy will be initiated should they fail to take remedial measures within a specified time period.[58] Second, the prince should take advantage of the many devices at his disposal for righting the balance between the capital and the provinces. Decreasing selected taxes in the provinces and increasing them in the capital, returning courtiers to their provincial posts, allowing provincial tribunals to make decisions about provincial problems instead of deciding everything at court — these are only a few of the "thousand means" available to the prince by which he can "[reverse the rural exodus,] return equilibrium, and restore the provincial people."[59]

Notice how readily the foregoing can be translated into the vocabularies of both power and liberty. "If I wish to know the power of a prince," Montesquieu wrote, it is not enough "to enter his palace, to see the beauty of his gardens, the richness of his suites, the baseness of his courtiers. There is nothing so equivocal. The least village teaches me better what his true strengths are."[60] Would not the king of Spain be infinitely greater if he had a great people instead of an illustrious court and a treasury stockpiled with fool's gold?[61] Able through agriculture to pour humane content into the word "power," Montesquieu could also, through that medium, eulogize freedom. "Countries are not cultivated in proportion to their fertility, but to their liberty."[62] The poetic vision of Troglodytes perishing from want of justice deserted Montesquieu when the monarchical model failed to repudiate imperialism. But the idyll of a fecund earth-mother, joyously bestowing her favors upon a people untroubled by arbitrary government, the other side of the tale, comes back to life during Montesquieu's discussions of productivity.

An affluent agricultural sector is only the precondition of growth; it is left for industry and commerce to launch a country into self-sustained development. Contrary to what the mercantilists say, economic produce and not gold is wealth, and for any country that possesses adequate natural resources the riches that can be accumulated by labor and entrepreneurship are in principle open-ended. More laborers, more agricultural workers, more entrepreneurs, better use of oceans and lands, mushrooming industries: all these are already within reach, and with time a great deal more can be accomplished.[63] Visions of abundance should, therefore, replace the miserly "my gain is your loss" outlook of mercantilism. In the terminologies of game theory and economics, Montesquieu supplanted the "zero-sum-game" of the mercantilists with his version of the "multiplier effect": "the sources of . . . riches are commerce and industry, and these sources are of such a nature that one who engages in them cannot enrich himself without enriching many others."[64]

Industry begins with the extraction of mineral and other natural resources, and that is why the *Voyages* is sprinkled with remarks on mines, an interest also evident in the *Lois*.[65] Likewise, the *Voyages* anticipates the *Lois* in its diagrams of machines that Montesquieu came across during his travels; later, in his magnum opus, he was to note the boon that mechanization offered to mankind.[66]

But what he was more attentive to was the outline of a monetary and financial policy that could stimulate commerce and industry. Since a high level of expenditure is essential to fuel the economy, money should be "easy." As for the consequent inflation of prices, it is tolerable in all but stagnant economies.[67] Credit is the open sesame of feverish spending and capital investment, and as a formula of successful promotionalism it has already proven itself in England and Holland. Goaded on by the proper credit mechanisms, reassured by its awakening from an age-old slumber and docility, society will abound in projects, wealth will circulate rapidly, and the day will approach when Europe will witness the birth of mass production and a consumer's society.

Stepping far enough back to gain an overview, we cannot help but observe that the new economy Montesquieu proposed implied a new society as well, a society freed from the tutelage of clerical, aristocratic, and governmental oppression, a liberal and enlightened society. Liberty and productivity, he insisted, go hand in hand. "A nation in slavery labors more to preserve than to acquire; a free nation more to

acquire than to preserve." "Commerce is sometimes destroyed by
conquerors, sometimes cramped by monarchs; it traverses the earth,
flies from places where it is oppressed, and stays where it has liberty to
breathe."[68] Not only that: economic activity is also a positive training
in liberalism. It picks up where the political education of the ancient
republics left off by unconsciously inculcating a crude appreciation of
justice. "The spirit of trade produces in the mind of a man a certain
sense of exact justice, opposite, on the one hand, to robbery, and on
the other to those moral virtues which forbid our adhering rigidly to
private interest."[69] Lackluster and imperfect this social education
most certainly is, but that does not diminish its significance.

Most of all, an affluent society presupposes self-confidence, initiative, imagination, and daring on the part of its members — the very
traits which monarchy had eradicated until now. Those who believed
that treating humans as "mules"[70] was the surest way of increasing
production (Richelieu and the mercantilists) were egregiously mistaken; and those who would protect the human creature with a paternalism rendering him permanently infantile (Bossuet and the
patriarchalists) were little better.[71] Industrious workers and self-
reliant entrepreneurs are the one natural resource that a flourishing
economy cannot dispense with. By a roundabout course, the in-
strumental calculations of economics lead to a hypothetical appreciation of the individual human being, and thereby provide a functional
equivalent for liberal ethics, in which individual personality is
sacrosanct. Economic analysis, in Montesquieu's hands, treats men as
means so that they may eventually be known as ends in themselves.

If economic development dictates the liberalization of society, it is
equally insistent upon the liberalization of the state. Boom or stagnation hinges upon the choice the state makes between two options:
"Shall the state begin with impoverishing the subjects to enrich itself?
Or had it better wait to be enriched by its subjects?"[72] So long as the
state breathes down their necks, entrepreneurs and laborers cannot be
enlightened materialists, more dedicated to multiplying their riches
than to hoarding the little they have.

> The effect of wealth in a country is to inspire every heart with
> ambition: that of poverty is to give birth to despair. . . . But if an ar-
> bitrary prince should attempt to deprive the people of nature's boun-
> ty, they would fall into a disrelish of industry; and then indolence and
> inaction must be their only happiness.[73]

Ever so slowly, the prince is learning that to have power he must have an economically productive society, and to have an economically productive society he must govern justly and govern less. The history of the Jews is particularly informative in this regard. Maimed and tortured for the greater glory of God and the increase of the royal treasury, they invented letters of exchange, "invisible effects" which the prince could not confiscate.

> From this time it became necessary that princes should govern with more prudence than they themselves could ever have imagined; for great exertions of authoritarianism were . . . found to be impolitic; and from experience it is manifest that nothing but the goodness and lenity of a government can make it flourish. We begin to be cured of Machiavellism, and recover from it every day. More moderation has become necessary in the councils of princes. What would formerly have been called a master-stroke in politics would be now . . . the greatest imprudence. Happy is it for men that they are in a situation in which, though their passions prompt them to be wicked, it is, nevertheless, to their interest to be humane and virtuous.[74]

Government will have to mend its ways and limit its scope if it hopes to achieve compatibility with a dynamic economy. Above all, this means an end to meaningless wars for glory, which unfailingly result in a heavy state debt and soaring taxes. According to the sophisms of mercantilism, taxes should always be crushing so as to spark the industriousness necessary to pay them. But in fact an impoverished lower class cannot consume, and, if fallen into despair, will not produce. And the middle class, subject also to a mounting tax burden, will retrench instead of seeking out opportunities for expansion. Ultimately, the state loses from the losses of its subjects.[75]

The restraints that economic considerations place on taxation levels need not compromise the prince. Much of the governmental apparatus is unnecessary, and society, at least in its economic aspect, can largely be left to fend for itself. Huge portions of the bureaucracy can be scrapped and the overgrown military whittled down to size. Not only will the state's need for revenue shrink in consequence, but economic growth will increase the amount of wealth available for taxation.

In the laissez faire economy which Montesquieu envisioned, the role of the state would recede but not fade into insignificance. Obstacles to free trade require removal by political action, and sometimes the free play of economic forces should be modified by the state. Interest rates are a case in point. Demand and supply of money determine the rate of interest — a view which Keynes was later to cite as an anticipation of his doctrine — but the state may be well advised to set a legal ceiling on interest rates. Otherwise the exploitation-minded moneylender of the old regime might ruin the borrower, in that way undermining economic progress.[76]

Least of all does laissez faire spell political inactivity in the sphere of welfare. The road to progress is never smooth and unbroken, for economic advance creates new problems as it solves the old. Machines increase productivity but also throw workers out of jobs.[77] Periodic crises of unemployment and hardship are intrinsic to the perpetually oscillating economic nature of things, and should be assuaged by "the state which owes to every citizen a certain subsistence, a proper nourishment, convenient clothing, and a kind of life not incompatible with health." Whether it be "to prevent the sufferings of the people or to avoid a rebellion," the state "is obliged to lend them a ready assistance."[78] So wrote Montesquieu in a characteristic blend of humanitarian reasons with reasons of state.

Ending the old welfare system and starting a new was an objective Montesquieu hit upon while studying British history.

> Henry VIII, resolving to reform the Church of England, ruined the monks, of themselves a lazy set of people that encouraged laziness in others, because as they practised hospitality, an infinite number of idle persons, gentlemen and citizens, spent their lives in running from convent to convent. He demolished even the hospitals in which the lower people found subsistence as the gentlemen did theirs in the monasteries. Since these changes, the spirit of trade and industry has been established in England.[79]

The great virtue of Montesquieu's British examples, however, is that he knows how to take *and* leave them. Approval of Henry VIII's action does not imply acceptance of Walpole's policies. Across the channel, the new liberal order was beginning to evince the harsh attitude toward the poor and jobless that was to become a hallmark of nineteenth-century laissez faire. Leaving medieval paternalism far behind him, and skipping over the laissez faire of the nineteenth century, Montesquieu embraces Keynes and Keynes returns the greeting by designating Montesquieu as the most prescient and levelheaded of French economists.[80] Welfare statism is for the welfare of the economy's individual victims, for the welfare of the economy itself, and indirectly for the welfare of the state.

Before leaving the topic of the state behind, we would do well to examine one last policy advocated by Montesquieu. Immediately following the Sun King's death, political concern turned to the legacy that Louis' wars had bequeathed to his successor, a stupendous state debt. As the *Chambre de Justice* rounded up the tax farmers and forced them to disgorge their excessive profits, a well-meaning but inadequate move, the Baron de la Brède addressed to the regent a *Mémoire sur les dettes de l'état*. In it a youthful Montesquieu was already plying his sometime trade of packaging anti-absolutist ideas in the protective covering of Machiavellian semblance.

Under the pretext of saving the financially distraught state, he sought a reprieve for those few provincial assemblies not yet defunct, and argued for the establishment of other such assemblies in the intendant-ruled *généralités*. So as to deflect criticism, he asserted that, though the number of provincial assemblies would grow, their functions would not. Such services as the assemblies still performed were basically financial, and Montesquieu's case was accordingly argued in strictly financial terms. First, he called attention to the tax collection record, much more effective in the *pays d'état* than elsewhere, and then he cited a second benefit the provincial bodies can bestow upon royalty. "The king does not have, nor can he have credit any longer, but the estates do and find it easy to borrow."[81] Collection of revenue and the raising of credit, heretofore the domain of the now disgraced tax farmers, could be assumed by the provincial estates. What the memorandum neglected to tell the regent was that control of the purse strings, even if by provincial estates instead of by the Estates General, was incipient constitutionalism.

The strategy of increasing power through economic growth was so rigged that if minimally successful it would chain Leviathan, if maximally it would remove the monster's absolutist fangs.

Fourth and last among the stages by which Montesquieu sought to domesticate the beast was in its international behavior. Turned outward, economic competition would be a welcome substitute for the clash of animals in the jungle. From the supplement to war, which international trade was in mercantilist doctrine, Montesquieu would transform trade into a substitute for war.

"All grandeur, force, and power are relative," he had argued in his comments on balance of power. Therefore, a strong power contiguous to a declining neighbor ought not to precipitate the ruin of the latter since "it seldom happens that by subduing such a state the absolute power of the conqueror is as much increased as the relative is diminished."[82] Of the many advantages accruing to Montesquieu as he restates the foregoing proposition in economic terms, not the least is that he can entice Leviathan from conquest to commerce.

How does this happen? Relativity of power is economically underscored by the perpetual flux and reflux of fortune to which even the most productive countries are liable. Indeed, economic affairs are of such a nature as to "vary continuously and to be relative to a thousand accidents," so much so that the blessing of high productivity breeds a problematic effect which is as historically novel as its cause. Flourishing manufactures inflate prices and wages, everything becomes expensive, and other nations can sell their merchandise at a lower rate. All business is unfinished business, and the power attained through economics is not absolute or fixed for all time. In the long run, the wealth of nations is their most significant source of power, but riches and power never reach completion and are always relative.[83]

Similarly, the argument in favor of a "hands-off" policy toward feeble neighbors is decisively reinforced when economic considerations are brought to bear. Economic self-interest supplies the argument against international banditry which in a better world would be morally derived. "A state which ruins others ruins itself, and if it fails to contribute to the common prosperity, it fails to contribute to its own. The reason why is clear. A ruined state cannot carry on exchange with the others; the others cannot carry on exchanges with it." Because of trade, "all nations are chained together and communicate their evils and their goods to one another."[84]

How radically Montesquieu's view of international trade diverges from the mercantilist position is worth recounting. Whereas mercantilism habitually meddled in the most trivial business dealings, attaching strings and raising tariffs, Montesquieu advocates an opposing policy for free trade.[85] For mercantilism, moreover, trade is an exacerbation of the separation of mankind into distinct national communities, each severed from and suspicious of the rest. At the opposite pole stands Montesquieu's conclusion that "the history of commerce is that of the communication of peoples."[86] That which one nation produces in abundance is a scarce item in another nation and vice versa,[87] so there are mutual benefits to be gained from trade that belie the piratical "my gain is your loss" attitude. To satisfy their needs, countries have entered into reciprocal trade agreements which make them increasingly interdependent. By the eighteenth century the progress of interlocking agreements has advanced so far that the history of people x can be read to illuminate the history of people y.[88]

At first glance, it seems to be material goods alone that are exchanged in the international marketplace. But on a second look the center of selling and buying may be seen as a trysting place where the intellectual and moral goods of Enlightenment are disseminated. "Commerce is a cure for the most destructive prejudices": under its educative tutelage, savage mores have been considerably refined.[89] That is not all. Inventions, means of extracting mineral resources, methods of production: these and other fruits of progress are also enlightenment, and they are transnationally broadcast by the beacon of light with which commerce has dispelled darkness from the spaces between peoples.[90] Most precious of all, international trade holds out to the modern world the hope of peaceful coexistence.

> Peace is the natural effect of trade [because] two nations who traffic with each other become reciprocally dependent.

> A prince believes he will become greater by the ruin of a neighboring state. On the contrary! Things are such in Europe that all states depend on one another. France needs the opulence of Poland and Muscovy, just as Guyenne needs that of Brittany, and Brittany that of Anjou. Europe is a single state composed of several provinces.[91]

Though the break with mercantilism was a full-scale rupture, several of the old opinions reappear in the new economics. Reconsidered and revised, the strands of the old outlook incorporated into the new are no less important than the elements stamped as obsolete. The definition of trade entertained by Montesquieu is enough to make a free trader tremble: "Commerce is the exportation and importation of merchandise with a view to the advantage of the state."[92] When we are told that a sustained imbalance of trade is potentially disastrous, we might again mistake Montesquieu for a mercantilist. And the danger of mistaken identity arises still another time when he repeats the orthodox attitude toward colonies, according to which they were to produce what the metropolis cannot and buy the goods manufactured at home.[93]

The flavor of mercantilism which clings to the laissez faire core of Montesquieu's economic writings is not the upshot of confusion or inconsistency, nor is it a residue. It is nothing less than an integral link in his economic reflections. To understand the sometimes kindly workings of the international division of labor is not to mistake it for a panacea. A magic elixir gives everything and takes nothing, but the debits and credits of world trade are responsible for unhappiness as well as hope. Gains are not evenly distributed and far from mutual in every case. "He who gains least still gains" — the slogan of free traders — is an admission of inequality, but a denial that inequality matters. Adding, as Montesquieu does, that all countries gain but some gain less than they lose is to portray a mercantilist-like world of winners and losers inside an economics of growth totally foreign to mercantilism.

Who were the consistent winners, who the chronic losers, as Montesquieu saw it? "Europe carries on the commerce and navigation of the other parts of the world; as France, England, and Holland do nearly that of Europe." Two republics and one monarchy add up to "the three tyrants of Europe and the world." A prostrate Orient is face-to-face with a "Europe [which] has arrived at so high a degree of power that nothing in history can compare with it."[94] Within Asia variations of commercial prowess are notable, Turkey alone being so steeped in despotic ignorance as to refuse to learn from her rivals. Japan and China, more than the rest of the East, do know the frantic pace of commercialism. Overall, however, no Asian nation or combination of nations, regardless how extensive their inland commerce, can match the international trade carried on by any one of several Occidental countries.[95]

Among Western losers Spain and Portugal top the list. Long ago Holland displaced Portugal in international trade, and each of the leading commercial powers has carved out a chunk of Spanish trade — for some time now carried on by every nation except Spain. Generally a winner, France is a loser in her relationship to England.

> The commerce of England must be more odious to France than that of any other power because the other powers maintain a great commerce with us. So if they extend their commerce to remote places and enrich themselves, we profit from their opulence, whereas England hardly trades with us at all and the riches she acquires are therefore entirely lost from our viewpoint.[96]

Besides Spain and Portugal, the other countries that lose, not just in relationship to one country but to all, are Italy, Hungary, and Poland. Italian city-states are as economically feeble as they were formerly mighty, and Eastern Europe is in a more disadvantageous position still. Lacking entrepreneurs and a working class, suffocated by a feudal society and polity, Poland and Hungary have everything to lose and little to gain from international trade.

> [Poland] has scarcely any of those things which we call the movable effects of the universe, except corn, the produce of its lands. Some of the lords possess entire provinces; they oppress the husbandmen in order to have greater quantities of corn which they send to strangers so as to procure the superfluous demands of luxury. If Poland had no foreign trade, its inhabitants would be happier.

Poland, like her Hungarian neighbor, is

> a state so unhappy as to be deprived of the effects of other countries, and at the same time of almost all its own. . . . This state, wanting all, can acquire nothing; therefore, it would be much better for the inhabitants not to have the least commerce with any nation upon earth, for commercialism in these circumstances must necessarily lead them to poverty.

The imbalance of trade which plagues her economic efforts makes for an elite of feudal autocrats drenched in luxury, while a multitude of peasants are the more impoverished the more they produce. "Let us say, then, that it is not those nations who have need of nothing that must lose by trade; it is those who have need of everything."[97]

Yet even these harsher facts of international trade are not without consolation. Under their authority the policy scientist is armed with arguments which may yet enable him to divert Leviathan from conquest to commerce. A quick perusal is enough to confirm that the list of economic losers coincides exactly with the list of socio-political losers previously adduced by Montesquieu's sociology; the Eastern nations, Spain, Portugal, Hungary, and Poland appear on both inventories of the hapless. Consequently, a nation wishing to take advantage of asymmetry need not follow a policy of conquest. Furthermore, as the history of Spain in America illustrates, the dominion of conquest is undesirable and the dominion of commerce highly desirable from the standpoint of aggrandizement. Spellbound by the violence which saved America for the Spanish empire,[98] Machiavellians always forget that victory over the helpless Indians was also the defeat of Spain as a world power. An abundance of precious metals was a monster that turned on its creator, ravaging him with inflation. Better than anything else could, the example of Spain teaches both the idiocy of conquest and the intimate connection between economics and national power.

"Men should stay where they are." So Montesquieu had bluntly concluded when discussing the colonial issue in the *Lettres persanes*. In that early work the invective he poured on Spain and Portugal, on dreams of conquest and empire, was equalled only by the pleasure he took in watching "the destroyers . . . destroying and consuming themselves from day to day."[99] When he returned to the same topic nearly three decades later, his sympathies had not changed, but he had learned in the meantime that the destroyers often live to boast of their deeds. Yet the feeling of power might entice Leviathan as much as the odor of blood. And power had become an economic phenomenon in the modern age. Most plans of colonization, he could urge in the name of power, should be jettisoned without further ado, and only those few retained which would enable the mother country "to trade on more advantageous conditions than could otherwise be done with neighboring peoples, among whom all advantages are reciprocal." The correct aim of colonization is "the extension of commerce, not the founding of . . . empire."[100]

Nor is it in the interest of wealthy countries to intervene when poor nations begin to develop manufactures. Struggling to keep their infant industries afloat, the underdeveloped countries will fall even more than before into dependence on (and indebtedness to) their opulent neighbors.[101] Moreover, short of a provisional withdrawal from the international market and a radical restructuring of their socio-political systems, Hungary and Poland will not experience enough economic growth to raise the question of competitive manufactures.

Why war? Shrinkage of the world makes aggression foolish, expansion of the world makes it unnecessary. The former has nullified plans of world conquest, the latter has accentuated the growing inequality of nations. Continuation of the arms race, under the circumstances of modern communications, does nothing more than rebalance power at outrageous cost. Armed struggles reward the neutral powers with victory and the victorious powers with defeat. On the other hand, the peaceful economic absorption of strange continents into the orbit of a few European superpowers opens the door to tremendous gains in relative power. Leviathan would do well to melt down its swords and recast them as ploughshares or machinery, because power grows less out of the barrel of a gun than from productive fields, smoke-belching factories, and ships loaded with cargo. Such are the findings of Montesquieu's social science and the policy recommendations of the most astute Machiavellism ever known to the old regime.

What are we to make of Montesquieu the policy scientist? As the greatest social scientist of his age, doubtless he was eminently qualified to advise the prince. But he did not seriously believe it possible to win with economic analysis at court that which had eluded his monarchical model in the provinces. Montesquieu knew perfectly well that what he wrote against Richelieu's *Political Testament* was equally pertinent to his own revised copy of *The Prince:* "scarcely can we flatter ourselves that we shall ever see such a prince and ministers while monarchy subsists."[102]

The record speaks for itself. *Le Prince* was never finished; the *Réflexions sur la monarchie universelle* was no sooner off the press than its author withdrew it from circulation. While writing his magnum opus, Montesquieu complained that political knowledge, which among the Greeks and Romans was obsessively attended to, had come to be neglected in favor of the physical sciences. *De l'Esprit des Lois* is an exception to the rule, one of the few books "not without use in the education of young princes." Or is it? As quickly as he lights the candle of hope, Montesquieu snuffs it out. Commenting further on the practical significance of his work, he sardonically remarks that "in seven or eight hundred years from now there will come some people to whom my ideas will be very useful."[103]

Montesquieu never went to court and never tried to go there. Very likely, he was familiar with the boudoirs of enough well-placed ladies to gain access to court politics, had he so desired. He did not. On the Grand Tour, he grew excited over the thought of serving as an ambassador, but the silent rebuff he met with could not cut short a life of political action which had never entered his own mind. Wanting to be an ambassador was a social, not a political, desire. In aristocratic society, to be a diplomat was to occupy an esteemed position and to enjoy the opportunity of rubbing shoulders with the international literati — but nothing more, certainly nothing political. Montesquieu played at being a policy scientist, and play does not preclude seriousness. Games are real but not "realist"; their charm resides in walling off the normal world and working out their inconsequential internal logic.

However great Montesquieu's achievement as an economist, his sociology explains why trade cannot be substituted for war. The primacy of economic calculations is real in a modern republic but unreal in a monarchy. Honor and religion, nobility and clergy, oppression and arbitrary government are systemic obstacles to a flourishing economy. And were they all removed, which is unlikely to happen short of revolution, the spirit of independence and self-reliance would still be a long time coming. Turning economic analysis into policy does not suffice. Until monarchy becomes republic such advice is irrelevant and then it becomes unnecessary.

Montesquieu's objective in writing a revised copy of *The Prince* was to act as spokesman for "those of us who do not have reasons of state to satisfy our passions."[104] Given this intent, it would be shortsighted to regard his toying with policy science as much ado about nothing. Nevertheless, the only meaningful solution is the making of citizens out of subjects. Most assuredly, that will never occur by addressing a polite "by your leave" to the king.

Of the several policy papers Montesquieu presented to the authorities, the most representative is the *Mémoire contre l'arrêt du conseil*, "a kind of manifesto", suggests an economic historian, "on behalf of the expanding winegrowers of the Bordelais."[105] In this paper Montesquieu attacked the royally imposed stoppage on further vine planting; for, he contended, the individual producer is a far better judge of market and economic conditions than is the government. At one and the same time he defended free trade, combatted mercantilism, and lobbied for his economic interests. Literally and figuratively, he elected to cultivate his own garden.

3. Foreign Affairs in a Post-Heroic Age

Montesquieu's monarchical model and economic theory each demonstrated a limitation of monarchy, but neither struck a decisive blow against imperialism. One last possibility is the historical process. If the cultural causes of imperialism are on the wane, this may mean that norm and fact have finally entered into an alliance against war. If not, "is" and "ought" have definitely parted company, and all of Montesquieu's efforts to squeeze norm from fact have been in vain.

Historically the peace-loving commercial *esprit* is enlarging its sphere of influence; the battle-scarred heroic ethic is in decline.

> Each age has its particular genius: a spirit of disorder and independence took shape in Europe with gothic government; a monastic spirit infected the time of Charlemagne's successors; then the spirit of chivalry reigned; that of conquest appeared with regular troops; and it is the spirit of commerce which dominates today.[106]

Commerce cuts to the quick of the heroic ethos, and the damage it initiates is consummated by the organizational imperatives which have overtaken the military way of life. "This spirit of commerce makes for the desire to calculate everything," and as such rubs abrasively against the heroic temperament, which hates utilitarianism, moderation, and repression of the thirst for *gloire*. The welcome damage that commerce has not done, the dawning age of organization is sure to do. Witness the military machine which has made cogs of the nobles, who were formerly independent to the point of anarchy. As it now stands, "a certain methodical fashion of taking villages and conducting battles [is everything] . . . , all war consisting more in art[ifice] than in the personal qualities of those who battle." Hence no one should be surprised if "what is called 'heroic valor' vanishes in Europe." Louis XIV was already an anachronism. "In a century and a part of the world where heroism had become impossible, it was his foible to search for it."[107]

Personally, Montesquieu was not about to shed tears over the waning of a "false" heroism.[108] "The heroism that morality approves touches few men," he lamented. "It is the heroism which destroys morality which strikes us and arouses our admiration." Extraordinary acts in antiquity were for the welfare of the community, those of modernity against the community. Heroic valor had become "vainglory," or what more commonly answered to the name of "honor." [109]

The temptation to read Comte and Spencer into Montesquieu must be avoided. Appearances to one side, he did not share their belief that industrial societies would necessarily be peace-loving. Should the commercial esprit gain undisputed primacy, it might exert a moderating influence on the international milieu, but it could not guarantee peace. For as long as nations remained in a state of nature, for as long as world government remained impractical, the threat of war would persist.[110] To cite but one example, the arms race which Montesquieu saw and feared was, he knew, as much the outcome of immutable international anarchy as of mutable domestic "honor."

> A new distemper has spread itself over Europe, infecting our princes, and inducing them to keep up an exorbitant number of troops. It . . . of necessity becomes contagious. For as soon as one prince augments his forces, the rest, of course, do the same; so that nothing is gained thereby but the public ruin. Each monarch keeps as many armies on foot as if his people were in danger of being exterminated: and they give the name of peace to this war of all against all.[111]

Seen in perspective, the peace-inducing impact of the upstart commercial esprit is modest at best; and when the aggressive potentialities of science and technology are weighed, it is absurd to judge the new as progress over the old. At any time a breakthrough in weaponry can arm a would-be tyrannical nation with the wherewithal for blackmail and conquest. Offsetting discoveries in military technology may avert immediate disaster, but they stockpile a massive destructive capability waiting for the incident which will start a chain reaction. If science gave us no other inventions than those for efficient killing, we would do well, Montesquieu thought, to banish it along with magic.[112]

Distinct from Comte and Spencer in understanding the compatibility of war and industry, Montesquieu differs from them again in rejecting the inevitability of the transition from militant to industrial society. Open historical possibility is very far from predetermined historical teleology, and it is to the former that Montesquieu consigns industrialism. So far, the advance of the commercial esprit has compromised the simpler forms of heroic display, but has not entailed the loss or even signalled the retreat of honor. Aristocratic society can admit money, the market, and finance to its activities without ceasing to be aristocratic. The speculation fever associated with the name of John Law, the half-baked commercialism of buying and selling offices, and the success of the Bordeaux nobility in viniculture are only a few examples of how readily honor accommodates limited expressions of the commercial esprit without sacrificing itself in the least. An *esprit de commerce,* Montesquieu feels, is what distinguished his age from preceding ages, but it is more absorbed into the pre-existing spirit of honor than a successor to the aristocratic ethos: more a new esprit residing within the old than an end of one esprit and the beginning of another.

Seldom has a political thinker contributed so generously to the theory of international relations as Montesquieu did. After the dust of analytical struggles has settled, it is obvious, nonetheless, that the moral problem of war and conquest is no closer to resolution, and this for the compelling reason that it is irresolvable. The urge to conquer will not die until the last noble has been strangled in the entrails of the last absolute monarch, and even then wars will continue to be fought — possibly more scientifically and therefore more murderously than ever before.

Perhaps something can be salvaged. At least a few of the many clouds of doom and gloom may yet be dispersed if the pattern of English behavior in world affairs proves less pernicious than that of the continental powers. The ugly truths about the foreign policies of monarchy may only be half-truths in the case of the modern republic. Do the blessings of the "system" of liberty have a foreign politics dimension?

Yes and no. Honor has faded into the British past and with it the thirst for blood. In France the new *esprit de commerce* is fatally diluted by the unbudging "principle" of honor, but in England the social "principle" and the new European esprit are one and the same. On the island republic, then, a post-heroic period has come of age, not halfheartedly but completely. Yet England is hardly a political virgin in the international arena. However free the English are from the warlike aristocratic ethos, "at present they demand empire"[113] — an empire of trade, not of guns.[114] Since both are out for all they can get, the difference between France and England cannot be a contrast of empire versus nonempire. No, England is preferable to France simply because her imperialism is less destructive and has some desirable unintended consequences.

England, too, is a Leviathan and the greatest Leviathan in a world of Leviathans. As national power is directly proportional to economic wealth, and England is the wealthiest of nations, it follows that she is the most powerful nation. Dedicated to the welfare of her national economy, England knows when to embrace and when to snub free trade. As Montesquieu insisted, the woolen industry of Walpole's liberal England is excepted from the free play of the international market.[115] In general the English are free traders, but not when free trade runs counter to their interests. Also numbered among the instruments of national economy is the Bank of England, created in 1694 to finance an expensive military struggle. War could no longer be fought without recourse to credit, so England availed herself of a national bank, copied in part from the Bank of Amsterdam. Under the auspices of the Bank, public credit was put on a firm footing and private enterprise stimulated. Because of the Bank, England was a country buzzing with projects, booming with productivity, well on her way to world primacy.

Politically, the significance of the Bank was twofold. First, it entrenched the liberal status quo. There is no arguing with Montesquieu's observation that England's credit institutions solidified the identification of her more affluent citizens with the liberal order of things.[116] In the event of the pretender's return, the debt raised by those who had dethroned him would surely be repudiated and innumerable fortunes lost. Secondly, the Bank was a major factor in the ascendancy of England vis-à-vis the absolute monarchies. Outmanned, undermilitarized, struggling to consolidate a revolution, periodically terrified by Tory plots — real or imaginary — to overturn 1688, England nevertheless bested the absolute monarchies. Every power suffered from an overwhelming debt at the turn of the eighteenth century — the legacy of several European-wide struggles — but England, due to the Bank, was singularly adept at putting her house in order.

In the political rhetoric of the old regime, public banks were synonymous with republicanism. Such institutions had come to be identified with free cities and confederate republics, since they were found in Italian city-states, Hamburg, Holland, and Switzerland. Montesquieu raised this de facto assocation of national bank and non-monarchical politics to the level of a social science generalization. Debt in France was viewed as royal instead of national debt, and not surprisingly. Even Law's scheme began as a *Banque Générale* and ended as a *Banque Royale*. Under absolutism the personalism of government always overrode institutionalization, and credit institutions were no exception. Just as the king forbade private business interests the public influence they enjoyed in England, so was he afraid of a public bank immune to his every whim. "If the state is a republic, the government . . . is in its own nature consistent with its entering into projects of a long duration."[117] With monarchies it was precisely the opposite.

They lived from hand to mouth and somehow had to weather the worst crises in spite of chronic financial insolvency. Anyone investing in crown securities was running a risk and likely to be totalled among those served by the king's ultimate solution to the problem of debts he could not make good on: their repudiation.

Such a profusion of power as England commanded was a great force for good or evil. In the case of England's relationship to Ireland, both the good and the evil are evident. Conquest has nothing to do with consent, Locke had written, but he had no use for Molyneux's effort to adapt this argument to the cause of Irish emancipation. Yet a liberal nation, however guilty of illiberalism abroad, cannot help but export some of her liberalism to those she exploits. England cursed the Irish with foreign domination but blessed them with free institutions. "The subjects there are free and the state itself in slavery. The conquered state has an excellent civil government but is oppressed by the law of nations."[118]

Toward the New World, English policies were less mischievous than those of other Leviathans and sometimes productive of considerable good. Each American colony was made in the image of its parent, and so there was a New Spain and a New England. Adding another province to her absolutist rule, Spain made Spaniards of natives and shipped in native Spaniards who put on aristocratic airs. As miserable as old Spain was, surely there was no need for a new. When Britain exported her institutions and way of life, she came close to reproducing herself. Less an extension of England than a truly new England was the result when institutions of liberalism and self-government were implanted in fresh soil.

> As men are fond of introducing into other places what they have established among themselves, [the British] have given the people of the colonies their own form of government; and this government carrying prosperity with it, they have raised great nations in the forests they were sent to inhabit.[119]

At last we find a ray of hope in the international realm, which affords so very few. From her very selfishness, not from intrinsic virtues, from an unintended consequence, not from conscious design, England's record in foreign affairs is preferable to that of the continental monarchies.

*　　*　　*

The monarchical model underscored the price of imperialism, but it was not the ultimate price of self-liquidation. Economic analysis proved international trade superior to conquest as an imperialistic technique, but Montesquieu could not force monarchical Leviathan to heed a lesson it was unwilling to learn. Republican Leviathan already knew that economics is power, and without fanfare or sound of guns it was steadily carving out an empire. England, too, had committed and was committing imperialistic crimes, but in her case good at last became evident — as a mitigation of evil. Dominating by economics instead of by conquest, England had less blood on her hands than did the monarchies. And, creating colonial settlements in her own image, she unknowingly created new liberal societies and representative political institutions.

During the first World War Lenin adopted an attitude of "revolutionary defeatism": longing for his country's defeat so that she might be made ripe for insurrection. Montesquieu, then, was a "liberal defeatist" when he welcomed the treaty of Aix-la-Chapelle (1748). He hoped that the setback to French ambition had saved France from further illiberalism internally, and, temporarily at least, had saved the world from France.[120]

EPILOGUE
Interpreting the World versus Changing It

1. Society and Politics in a New Mold

Having begun this study with an examination of the revolution Montesquieu forged in the form of political thought, we shall end with an examination of the revolution in content which was likewise his accomplishment. The time has come to give an accounting of England, or more exactly, of the best political and social type that the feudal mother is capable of bearing. Empirical fact, feudal potentiality, and classical ideals all play a part in this imaginative construction of an "ideal-type" truly ideal.

First and foremost among Montesquieu's contributions to the study of the political system was what he had to say about institutions. It will be recalled that it was the problem of institution-building that was the undoing of absolutist thought. (See above, chapter IV, section 2.) Everything Bodin had struggled to build collapsed when confronted by the charge of praetorianism. As Plato and Aristotle had insisted, the government wielding the most absolute power has the shortest life expectancy. In the pattern of reflection conducted under the auspices of the feudal paradigm, Montesquieu lifted the tyrant from the polis and dropped him into the countryside of a territorial monarchy. Instead of the bureaucratic "ideal-type," we get a feudal meditation on Greek tyranny.

Too creative to be content with gloating over the rubble to which the problem of institutionalization had reduced the theory of absolutism, Montesquieu went on to suggest a constitutionalist solution. This second try consisted of unveiling the constitution itself as equal to the challenge of institutionalizing political order. Where the efforts of absolutist theoreticians remained mired in what Weber later termed the traditional, personalized, and weak political system, Montesquieu's idea of the constitution announced the possibility of a "legal-rational," institutionalized, and strong polity.

Under the guidance of constitutionalism, one after another source of instability meets with an institutional remedy. The worst excesses of class conflict are averted, the church separated from the state, and the military subjected to civilian control. Since the upper house of the legislature is drawn from the hereditary nobility and the lower from the commons, classes are checked and balanced against one another. For its part, expulsion of the clergy from the political assemblies eliminates religious fanaticism from politics. And praetorianism can be cured by executive control of military operations, offset by legislative control of military appropriations.

Montesquieu's constitutional ideal is markedly "legal-rational." Separation of government from the household, for Weber the accomplishment par excellence of bureaucracy, is attributed by Montesquieu to the constitution. First under feudal monarchy and then under its absolutist successor, government and the king's household were the same. Constitutionalism, however, takes government out of the royal household and transfigures it into a public entity. Functional differentiation, again for Weber a bureaucratic trait, is likewise proclaimed the achievement of constitutionalism, especially of its distinction between executive, legislative, and judicial branches, and its separation of civilian and military spheres. As for rules and impersonality, they, too, are written large in Book XI, chapter 6, when it provides for the rule of depersonalized law. Indeed, the national holders of judicial office are reduced to machines, to robots, who are "no more than the mouth that pronounces the words of the law, mere passive beings, incapable of moderating either its force or rigor."[1] An earlier bid by Hobbes to claim the legal-rational order for absolutism had proven meaningless, since he could not divest Leviathan of the personalism that made a mockery of legality. Through the constitutional idea, Montesquieu bestows on legality the institutional embodiment conspicuously lacking in Hobbes.*

---

*Classical authors condemned one-man rule as the most impermanent of regimes; Hobbes praised it as the most permanent. All forms of collective rule inevitably lead to instability, Hobbes believed, because "the passions of men, which asunder are moderate, as the heat of one brand, in an assembly are like many brands, that inflame one another." *Leviathan,* ch. 25.

Harrington had put the matter well when he designated administration as the most significant variety of "reason of state."[2] Being the most institutionalized and therefore the best form of administration, constitutionalism must, then, be deemed the most profound reason of state.

All in all, the constitutional ideas set forth by Montesquieu were a remarkable blend of traditionalism and rationalism. Although his starting point was a constitutionalism derived from feudalism, the terms in which he set forth his ideal had the flavor of a classical "blueprint." In common with Polybius, Montesquieu depicted an institutional order which was more the product of a rational design than the outcome of historical accident. Why he chose such a rationalist presentation is a question of grave import.

To begin with, in Book XI, chapter 6, he was drawing a general ideal, and not simply reporting on England. Secondly, the French constitutional tradition had fallen into abeyance since 1614, so that he was invoking a feudal potentiality weakened by prolonged dormancy. Of necessity, then, he abstracted and went beyond the facts. But most telling of all is a third consideration. Above all else, the example of England testified that the constitutionalism of the New Regime could not count on being bolstered by the intermediary bodies which had limited all governments in the past, including the most absolute. Those bodies had perished along with absolutism in the traumatic transition from old to new. Henceforth the government of England, and of any other country following in her revolutionary footsteps, was as centralized after absolutism as it had been before.

Worse than centralized, government was fully aware of its powers — powers frightening in scope now that tradition was broken and voluntarism in command. Upon falling out of love with tradition and organic imagery, absolutists adopted the voluntarism of "policy"; likewise the constitutionalists, no longer under the feudal and Germanic delusion that laws are discovered, not made, were beginning to stress the voluntarism of "legislation." Witness Locke, who placed the legislative power — in the words of a modern commentator — "above all judicial power, above all customary law, subject only to the laws of nature and reason."[3] With the concentration of power and the decline of intermediary bodies, checks and balances could not be left to chance. From now on limited government, in medieval Europe a gift of immediate circumstances, had to be self-consciously planned.

So much for the constitutional notions of Montesquieu, which can be thought of as constituting a theory of formal organization. To this we may add a brief look at the propositions on informal organization which are also present in his thought. Familiar with the outline, at least, of English political debates, Montesquieu knew that the "system of liberty" did not work in the way Book XI, chapter 6, prescribed. Whether this portended good or evil he had to discern.

England was beyond the era of monarchical preponderance, but before the dominance of the House of Commons or the advent of cabinet government. Officially a minister was responsible to the king, and controlled an unwieldy parliament by doling out executive patronage. To Walpole and the "court" party — the protagonists of the liberal status quo — this process was political "influence" and as it should be. To Bolingbroke and the opposing "country" party — radical and reactionary detractors of the established order — it was base "corruption" and proof that England was about to reenact the decline of the Roman republic.[4]

Not given to false analogies, Montesquieu has no use for the specious link Bolingbroke had drawn between Rome and England. Still, the cry of "corruption" could not be dismissed offhandedly. If nothing else, it was further evidence that England had ceased to be a monarchy and was now a republic. In a monarchy sinecures, pensions, and favoritism are "normal," whereas in a republic they are abnormal, if not pathological, because government is — or should be — a public object serving the public interest. Since "placemen" and the like are a sin against the political culture of republicanism, Montesquieu refuses to substitute the apologetic word "influence" for the abusive term "corruption."

More serious, corruption poses the threat of executive encroachment at the expense of the legislature, perhaps eventually upsetting the constitutional balance.[5] Troubled by what he saw, Montesquieu did not abandon hope. From a Machiavellian standpoint, the problem he faced would necessarily call forth counsels of despair. But Montesquieu was no Machiavellian, and he rejected "Old Nick's" belief that corruption at the top always contaminates the entire society. Standing Machiavellism on its head, he asserted that in England the ruled set an example for the rulers to follow. In reply to a query from an English friend, fearful for his country's future, Montesquieu had this to say: "I believe, sir, that what will preserve your government is that, on the whole, the people have more virtue than those who represent them."[6] Constantly switching sides, forever identifying with the weaker party when it is in danger, always independent, rough, and ready, tenaciously adhering to their middle class virtues (so useful to a constitutional system), the English are a people who belie the elite-mass dichotomy.[7]

As he built a constitutional fortress, Montesquieu drew his building blocks from the feudal and classical pasts. Checks and balances were originally a legacy of the classics; representative government, unknown in antiquity, was a distinctively feudal contribution; the rationally idealized version of the constitution was in the classical mode, yet supported by feudal potentiality. But when he upheld the ruled and downgraded the rulers, Montesquieu served notice that he was using the past — classical and feudal alike — in order to destroy it.

Such was the new polity envisioned by Montesquieu. He also had a new society in mind, as we shall presently see.

To the analytical separation of state and society that is presupposed by political sociology, Montesquieu added a normative separation of the same. In so doing, he reversed Aristotle's ethical teachings, which were insistently opposed to allowing the development of a factual distinction between polity and society. Far too many of the educated, Aristotle complained, were withdrawing from the sickly polis, seeking extrapolitical fulfillment: individually in contemplation, associationally in private friendships. Any further aggravation of the divorce between political and social spheres would mean the death of the polis. As for the state in Montesquieu's day, it was both too far removed from society and not far enough removed. Isolated above society, absolutism was socially irresponsible; all-powerful, it threatened every nook and cranny of society. In the constitutional ideal, Montesquieu found a way of shielding society from polity (limited government), while also making polity accountable to society (representative government). At last society was for itself, but what was it to be? Simply stated, a liberal and civic society.

In effect, Montesquieu had learned that Locke's *Second Treatise* did not describe the essence of society in general, as its author suggested, but rather of the liberal and Lockean type of society which Walpole's England had come to be. The individualism and egalitarianism which Locke had set forth on an *a priori* foundation had in fact resulted from the historical crystallization of a liberal society in England. With the decline of intermediary bodies and aristocratic ethos, men were suddenly on roughly the same footing. There being no genuinely privileged order, all left the starting blocks at the same time and ran a competitive economic race which cluttered society with the swarm of individualistic social atoms, each busily engaged in projects large and small. As opposed to the aristocratic ethos, this was all to the good.

And it had other benefits as well. For one thing, high productivity promised that affluence would finally drive out the misery and wretchedness which had thus far been a scourge of human history. Then again, insofar as the economic impulse overturned the "paralogism" which sacrificed the good of the individual to the good of the community,[8] it was welcome a second time. Once and for all, the horror that classical authors felt toward individualism was overcome. As it turns out, the mere particle of "matter," the mass man of the classics, purportedly so drastically in need of guidance from "form," happens to be a sturdy and independent fellow, quite resourceful and capable. Economic activity belies the facile dismissal of the ruled as mindless slaves of habit and passion. It is the rationality par excellence of individual and society, and puts an end to the effort of raison d'état to grant the rulers a monopoly on reason.

All the foregoing is contingent, of course, on the continued well-being of the "system of liberty," for only within it is society creative. Although indispensable, constitutional mechanisms do not exhaust the measures needed to guarantee this freedom. Removal of the clergy from the political assemblies, for instance, is not enough to save the citizen from religious oppression. For if, as in France, criminal law is heavy with the weight of religious fanaticism, then society will remain mired in tutelage to ignorance and in bondage to fear. A major reform in criminal law is therefore necessary. Actions alone are to be punishable and are distinct from words, thoughts, or sins. Furthermore, punishment must be proportional to the crime and rationally administered. Only then is that personal security assured which is directly opposite to despotism's reign of terror.[9]

Liberal on one side, the new society was civic on the other. In monarchies "I" is forever on men's lips, in ancient republics "we."[10] To which may be added that in the modern republic both "I" and "we" are heard. As we have seen, the "I" is bourgeois instead of aristocratic; what concerns us now is the "we," the civic and fraternal dimension of England's existence. Assuredly the sheer size of England is enough to make its civic virtue less intense than that of the polis. Nevertheless, even the right wing of British politics talks in terms of citizenship, virtue, and corruption. Virtually every trace of the authoritarian Toryism of the past has disappeared, replaced by the likes of Bolingbroke, who prided himself on being a better republican than Walpole.

Friendship and fraternity are virtually unknown in monarchies and for several reasons. In the first place, a hierarchical society sets each given social segment apart from the rest. And inside a particular segment, the social communication that once was is no more, since absolute power, extended over time, tends to atomize society.[11] The evil instigated by inequality and absolutism is further nourished by the aristocratic ethos, which trivializes all social relationships by making them a contest in the perpetual one-upmanship of *esprit*. Social intercourse becomes nothing more than a game, an exercise in insincerity in which everything must be turned into a joke. One of the *Persian Letters* is about two wits who seek social pre-eminence by agreeing that each will alternatively act as straight man for the other, allowing him to deliver a prearranged sally. It is in monarchy that society takes on the artificial and shallow aspect of a social contract.[12]

Contrariwise, society in Lockean England is ironically much more than a contract. Because of the levelling of social ranks, there are no obstacles to widespread social intercourse. Moreover, being a republic, England knows an attenuated but nonetheless real rebirth of the civic life which had characterized antiquity. What gave Greek and Roman friendships their supercharged energy, so totally unlike the anemic social bonds of monarchical times, was that they had a public dimension. Whether fighting on the field of battle or delivering a speech in the political assembly, a man lived and died with his comrades. As absolutism falls and the new order rises, political concern is soon as widespread as formerly it was restricted. "In a country [such as England] where the constitution gives each person a share in the government, . . . conversation generally turns on politics."[13] While an individualist, the Englishman is a sociable, fraternal, and publicly concerned individualist.

All this Cicero and Aristotle would have regarded as incomprehensible. Laborers, merchants, and anyone else whose life is spent in economic production they deemed unworthy of citizenship, on the grounds that such men have neither time nor capacity for public affairs. Not even middle class persons can be enlisted in the ranks of the citizenry, since to them all governments are the same, so long as they provide the tranquility of "business as usual." Refuting Cicero by name, and the classical tradition by implication, Montesquieu cites England as living proof that the economic ethos and civic concern are not incompatible.[14] Indeed, there is a great deal of overlap between economic and civic values. "When a democracy is founded on commerce, private people may acquire vast riches without a corruption of morals. This is because the spirit of commerce is naturally attended with that of frugality, economy, moderation, labor, prudence, tranquility, order and rule."[15] Far from being mutually exclusive, the civic and economic ways of life can be mutually supportive.

Something as important as the civic ethos, and as apt to die from neglect, cannot be left to chance. If the citizen spirit is to be effectively inculcated, the modern polity must revive, in part at least, those strategies of political education integral to the ancient polis and written large in the classics. Under monarchy the idea of political education shriveled until it meant the education of just one man. Under the republican version of Machiavellism, it meant the education of a ruling class. But in Montesquieu's vision it was the education of every man. As such it was Enlightenment in its most noble and least self-serving form.

"The judiciary power," wrote Montesquieu the proponent of political education, "should be exercised by persons taken from the body of the people." As de Tocqueville was later to note, quite in keeping with Montesquieu's viewpoint, trial by jury is as much a political as a judicial institution. Politically its most immediate signification is republicanism.

> The institution of the jury may be aristocratic or democratic, according to the class from which the jurors are taken; but it always preserves its republican character, in that it places the real direction of society in the hands of the governed, or of a portion of the governed, and not in that of the government.

Democratic in form, Montesquieu's proposed judiciary presupposes the putting of the legal profession in its place. That is what he means in saying the following: "the judicial power, . . . not being annexed to any particular estate or profession, becomes, so to speak, invisible."

Beyond its use as an obstruction to absolute power, Montesquieu has little sympathy for the French legal caste to which he once belonged.[16]

Earlier than John Adams, Montesquieu had made the democratic point that trial by jury gives the people a share in the execution of the laws. Earlier than de Tocqueville, he upheld the jury as a popular training school in the meaning of justice, a participatory and non-manipulative learning process, a lesson in political education through doing instead of being told what to do. Adams and de Tocqueville, moreover, reported on a democratic judiciary which was fact in America, while Montesquieu offered a democratic idealization of the aristocratic English jury. After stealing the idea of the democratic judiciary from Solonic Athens, he imposed it upon contemporary England.[17] Brushing aside the conservative tactic of waiting on the facts, he evoked the latent possibilities embedded in the empirical.

Before closing this discussion of political education, we pause to interject that it resolves a problem in the interpretation of Montesquieu's thought. At one moment Montesquieu defines liberty "negatively" as an absence of restraints, a second later "positively" as "the power of doing what we ought."[18] Some have charged that the positive definition is inconsistent with Montesquieu's liberal outlook.[19] Once we recognize, however, that his liberalism is neither aristocratic nor straightforwardly Lockean, but rather a democratic and civic liberalism, the insistence on duties as well as rights no longer comes as a surprise.

With the addition of Aristotle to Locke, Montesquieu imagined a brand of liberalism more civic than Locke's. And it is also true that the addition of Locke to Aristotle made for a civic ideal more liberal than Aristotle's. Whereas the civic temperament of classicism had been exclusionary, Montesquieu's was assimilationist. The gates of the polis were thrown open to merchants, laboring classes, women, slaves, and Jews.

With the admission of economic concerns to republican thought, slavery, the subjection of women, and the denigration of the laboring and trading classes lose their rationale. To Montesquieu, who praised "the war of Spartacus . . . [as] the most legitimate ever undertaken,"[20] an end to slavery was a lifelong dream. To the author of the *Lettres persanes*, the liberation of women from patriarchal despotism was also welcome.[21] About the virtues of the producers, real and potential, enough has already been said. Last but not least, he would relieve the

Jews of ghetto exclusion.[22] Liberty, equality, and fraternity can end the domination of the few and the submission of the many.

The modern republic, unlike its city-state forbears, also has the capacity to end the domination of the cities and submission of the rural areas. Inside the city walls, the medieval commune was an improvement over its ancient counterparts inasmuch as slavery had fallen into disuse. Outside the walls, however, its record was less praiseworthy than that of the polis. Ancient democracy, being that of small peasant proprietors, extended beyond the walled enclosure of the city proper. Some two-thirds of all Athenian citizens lived in the countryside, but were citizens nonetheless. By contrast, the medieval commune of professional traders walled out the peasants and treated them as subjects. For all the reputed fraternity within the city, the countryside remained stymied in feudal and patriarchal relationships. Citizenship was a privileged status and the republic a selfish civic island indifferent to the surrounding ocean of corporatism.[23] The contrasting modern republic of Montesquieu's vision, absorbing the urban and rural alike, national in scope and corporate-free,* is a bold and radical ideal.

As Montesquieu evoked the potentiality of the feudal past and used the classics to idealize a possible French future, he groped toward an unprecedented vision: a society unmanipulated by a self-serving political class and unscarred by a dominant social class, parasitically drawing its nourishment and luxury from the other social ranks; a society believed just because it is just, instead of a socially embodied Thrasymachean justice as the interest of the stronger. In other words, Montesquieu approached politics from the bottom up, whereas before it was viewed from the top down. A "Copernican revolution" in political thought, comparable to Kant's "Copernican revolution" in philosophy, transpired several decades in advance of the revolution in politics proper.

2. The Disunity of Theory and Practice

Despite his radical ideals, Montesquieu engaged in few, if any, radical acts. He lived and died a Bordeaux man of affairs, a frequenter of

---

*Free of the old corporations. The status of corporations within the new society was never spelled out by Montesquieu.

Parisian salons, and an international traveller of considerable renown. Apparently quite at home in all these surroundings, he was in every respect a model aristocrat. To speak or write radical thoughts, as he had done, was to act, of course, but Montesquieu knew how adept aristocratic society was in turning truth to its own inconsequential ends. "Truth . . . in conversation is here a necessary point. But is it for the sake of truth? By no means. Truth is requisite only because a person habituated to veracity has an air of boldness and freedom."[24] Inevitably, then, a question of the gap between theory and practice arises. To arrive at an answer, one must weigh how much — or how little — Montesquieu's social science could do to change the world which it had interpreted.

Taking social science to court in the hope of sparking reform from above was a hopeless tactic and Montesquieu knew why. At court, it is true, were the political educator, the policy scientist, and the ideologue, each of whom has joined theory and practice, ideas and action. But Montesquieu said it all when he noted that at first men make institutions but afterward institutions make men.[25] Actually the political educator, policy scientist, and ideologue were the same man, and he was the courtier. All men at court are reduced to courtiers and all ideas at court to the sycophantic pleas of courtiers.

Consider the debasement of reason of state and divine right. Supposedly the carrier of impersonal and public ideals, reason of state was in reality nothing more than the rationalization of princely passions. Equally bad was the capitulation of divine right to the monarch. No matter that divine inspiration had once been understood as pertaining to regal office; now it authorized the personal divine right of the ruler. In consequence, Bossuet's dividing line between absolute and arbitrary monarchy faded; indeed, he himself was guilty on occasion of the most fawning rhetoric: "O Kings, you are as gods on earth!"[26] "Ecclesiastics," Montesquieu observed, "are always the flatterers of princes when they cannot be their tyrants."[27]

Apart from the inevitable spoilage of ideals at court, the politics of bedchamber and throne was notable for having cast the very roles of ideologue and political educator in a distinctive mold. After the French Revolution the target of the ideologue was every man; before the Revolution it was one man only. Likewise with political education. Following the French Revolution de Tocqueville searched for the means of educating every man in the ways of politics; prior to the

Revolution Bossuet's *Politique tirée des propres paroles de l'écriture sainte* and Richelieu's *Testament politique* were the typical educative tracts, and they aimed at a single man. When Montesquieu fulminated against the clerics, charging them with complicity in an effort to keep the people ignorant,[28] he could easily have extended his remarks to the Machiavellians. One of the lessons Richelieu sought to teach the prince was that royalty should never teach subjects, since an educated populace would be presumptuous and disobedient.[29] Because they were courtiers, we may conclude, the ideologue and the political educator were wont to treat the king as everything, everyone else as nothing.

So addicted was court politics to pandering after the reigning monarch that Louis XIV took measures to assure his ghost a place among his son's favorites. The *Mémoires for the Instruction of the Dauphin* was this ghostly presence. Every courtier entered a special plea which, he hoped, would allow him to outdo his rivals, and Louis was no exception. Filmer wrote that an absolute monarch was restrained by the memory of his forefathers,[30] and similarly Louis warned his heir that protracted pangs of guilt awaited a son who failed to heed the written advice of his father.[31] Here we see the recipient of the most outlandish sycophancy numbered among his son's courtiers, trying to outbid them in the courtly battle for access to the prince.

To make a prince see, Montesquieu said, was to be like Descartes, who chased away the shadows of the old philosophy.[32] Unfortunately, a political Descartes is as impossible as a philosophical Descartes was real. Taken to court, Montesquieu's social science would undergo a dissolution until it was another of the shadows of darkness. Reform from above, under the guiding hand of social science, is a chimera.

If not reform from above, is revolution from below more promising? Initially it would seem so. English history proves that such a route to change can succeed. During the Puritan Revolution, England experienced a succession of regimes, finally embracing monarchy once more. But this was not to forsake all that had happened. Above all, it was not a return to the past, for England was henceforth a republic hiding under the form of a monarchy and a liberal society as well. Even at its most successful, a modest improvement is all reform from above can offer. In order for reform to have a chance, the absolute monarch must thrive. Revolution does not depend on the absolute monarch — it eliminates him.

Revolution offers more to gain, then, but the reverse side of the coin is that it threatens greater losses. What Montesquieu dreaded was the "period between the establishment of the new laws and the abolition of the ancient," a period of violence and fanaticism "fatal to the common cause."[33] Throughout his life he fought the extravagance and violence built into the old order and championed the cause of a new constitutional system that would maintain the "relations of things." Faced with the necessity of increasing fanaticism in order to eliminate it, he was caught on the proverbial horns of a dilemma. To appreciate how sharp the horns were we need only repeat in passing that, conceptually, he had torn the *ancien régime* limb from limb, so that one horn was an intense desire to be rid of the established order. The other was his abhorrence of violence and complementary eulogy of moderation. How deep this second half of the dilemma cuts cannot be understood without further elaboration.

In his condemnations of despotism, slavery, Machiavellism, religion, and the heroic ethic, Montesquieu expressed the revulsion and nausea he felt when reviewing the effects of fanaticism and violence. Rica's second last letter is a proclamation of freedom from religious phantoms and an implicit rejection of his despotic native land; his very last utterance is a moving tribute to moderation. "Come, modest men, and let me embrace you. You are the charm and sweetness of life."[34]

As understood by Montesquieu, the old order was guilty of fanaticism, not occasionally and accidentally, but every day and necessarily, because fanaticism was integral to its very nature. Religion is a striking case in point. The impress of religion on legally administered punishment spreads fanaticism throughout society and makes its presence immediate. Often, too, the clergy forced fanaticism upon society from the top down, as when Bossuet and the divine right faction scored their greatest triumph, the Revocation of the Edict of Nantes. Not that Richelieu and the Machiavellian clerics at court were any better. When Montesquieu called priests "eunuchs,"[35] he explicitly had in mind their stunted sexuality and unproductivity, but implicitly, one suspects, he meant something more. Richelieu had advocated the continued recruitment of ministers from the ranks of the clergy on the grounds that priests, wifeless and without children, were unlikely to confound private and public interest.[36] But if, as Montesquieu believed, the clerical ministers are anything but disinterested, if they are desexualized eunuchs in the king's employ, if their Machiavellism is an expression of the eunuch's resentment, then their vindictive manipulation of power must evoke the memory of the eunuch in the *Lettres persanes,* the frustrated, hyperrational and vengeful Machiavellian of the bedchamber.

Directly proportional to his reaction against the excesses of the old regime was the care Montesquieu took to ensure the moderation of the new order. In one fell swoop, he hoped, the bourgeois values of the new republicanism would do away with feudal valor and civic heroism. Since all brands of heroism — civic virtue included — are extravagant and bloodthirsty, this is all to the good. "Shall goodness consist in excess, and all the relations of things be destroyed?" "Who dares say it! Virtue itself has need of limits."[37] Simply to arrive at the new society, then, was to establish the reign of moderation. But only in part, for there are forces in the composition of the new regime which challenge the moderating impact of its values — noxious and powerful forces calling for a timely antidote. Of all such threats the most dangerous is the possibility of intensified class struggle.

Where class oppression is most frequent, class struggles are infrequent; where oppression is least common, struggles are commonplace. Those who suffer from the candid and fierce inequality of feudal society have no expectations to thwart, but those who are politicized by republicanism and accustomed to egalitarian rhetoric press many demands. When social strife gets the upper hand, republican freedom is as exploitative as monarchical unfreedom "because the popular state is the liberty of the poor and feeble and the servitude of the rich and powerful, [while] monarchy is the liberty of the great and the servitude of the small."[38]

Thucydides' account of conflict in ancient Athens and Machiavelli's of the same in modern Florence were read by Montesquieu with great interest. He concluded that "a domineering faction is no less terrible than an enraged prince." Once hostilities have commenced, no neutral sanctuaries are tolerated, and "the moderate man is loathed by both parties." By a political version of Gresham's law, the sensible are either driven out or else devalued until they reach the level of the insensed. Often the object of eloquent praise, liberty is reduced to instrumentality when Montesquieu discusses the republic gone "mad." It is "the good which makes possible the enjoyment of other goods," a modest definition which accords well with his determination to counter the ideological uses of the word "liberty."[39]

Well aware that liberation is not liberty, Montesquieu sought actual and potential curbs against too much freedom. Christianity, his lifelong foe, served him generously in this regard. Dissimilar to paganism, which never penetrated the psyche, Christianity was a "repressive" religion. As such it placed limits not only on the absolute prince but also on the absolute citizens of an overpoliticized republic.[40] For a while Montesquieu feared that if Catholic Spain had too much religion, Protestant England may have had too little.[41] But by the time of the *Esprit des Lois* his doubts were dispelled, and he was prepared to congratulate the British on "know[ing] better than any other people upon earth how to value . . . these three great advantages — religion, commerce, and liberty."[42]

Besides Christianity, the other curb to republican excess was the constitution. Even though England was devoid of a genuine nobility, Montesquieu insisted upon the maintenance of an hereditary upper body. Were it otherwise, those distinguished by birth and riches might discover their enslavement in the common liberty. In the same spirit, the democratic judiciary was to be tempered by the practice of trial by peers. Thus democratic justice could not become a tool of class hostility.[43]

Times of republican trouble, prospective but as yet unreal, clarify Montesquieu's scale of values. Negative freedom gains the ascendancy, at least temporarily, and he can delight in the size of the national republic, seeing in it the provision of a welcome anonymity that acts as insulation against an overheated civic spirit. And once more justice emerges as the most privileged value in his system. There can be too much freedom but never too much justice, if by justice we mean that which balances all values and safeguards "the relations of things."

Summarizing the argument up to this point, reform and revolution are both highly problematic. Given the nature of court politics, reform from above is a self-contradiction resting on the fallacious assumption that corruption can be persuaded to abolish itself. Revolution from below promises radical change, but whether for better or worse is another matter. "Whoever is able to dethrone an absolute prince has sufficient power to make himself absolute."[44] As an unsurpassed enemy of fanaticism and advocate of moderation, Montesquieu could not take lightly the abandonment of his values in a gamble on better achieving them. The fanaticism of the old regime makes the gamble tempting; the uncertain moderation of the new politics, combined with the certain fanaticism of the revolutionary period, dampens political optimism.

Nowhere is Montesquieu's ambivalence more in evidence than when he plots the overthrow of the old order but abstains from putting his scheme into effect. "Suppress the useless monasteries, that is to say all of them."[45] Thus did Montesquieu advise the king in a tentative policy recommendation which never got outside the *Château de la Brède*. Buried underneath this statement's manifest reformism lies the latent germ of revolution, well known to its author but hidden from the eyes of its intended victim. Expropriation of church property is the type of reform initiated from above which can trigger a chain of events culminating in a revolution from below.

"In all spheres, . . ." writes Christopher Hill, "the long-term outcome of the [English] Reformation was the opposite of that intended by the Machiavellians who introduced it": a conclusion in which Montesquieu heartily concurred. *De la politique* (1725) was in complete agreement with Hill's recent evaluation, according to which "the overthrow of papal authority by Henry VIII . . . looks forward to the civil war and the execution of Charles I." Similarly, the *Esprit des Lois* agreed with Hill's contention that "the plunder of the Church . . . stimulated the development of capitalism in England."[46] When Montesquieu considered taking a proposal for monastic confiscations to court, he had the British example in mind. If the point was for France to become like England, then why not follow those British footsteps which ultimately led to the fall of the absolute monarch? Why not promote the Machiavellian reform, whose most outstanding unintended consequence had been death to the monarch, the Machiavellians, and all other partisans of English absolutism?

Corrupt or not, the court might well be interested in a scheme to strip the church of its possessions. In his *Mémoires* Louis XIV had informed his son that "kings are absolute lords and naturally have free and full disposition of all the goods owned by clergymen."[47] Clearly, then, one mood of royalty was favorably disposed to the reception of Montesquieu's proposal. Opportunities abounded, moreover, for pressing the initial advantage of regal receptivity. Of all three estates, Montesquieu contended, the clerical alone was totally parasitical, totally exempted from functional responsibility. Dispossessed, the religious orders would truly live in holy poverty just as they already professed to do, and the church would be purified by its removal from political affairs. Furthermore, Jansenist hatred of the papacy could be counted on to popularize the seizure of church property, especially if tax reforms and other measures favorable to the populace followed. So

Montesquieu argued in notebook entries designed to win over the prince to overt reform and covert revolution.[48]

Yet Montesquieu never sent his proposal to court, nor did he come close to doing so. He abstained because "in politics it is impossible to know what will be the result of the changes one makes." Putting it another way, "reason hardly ever makes reasonable things and one almost never arrives at the reasonable by way of reason."[49] Plundering the church could lead to a "system" of liberty, but an equally dramatic possibility was despotism. Arrested in either the royalist or the revolutionary stage, Montesquieu's scheme could betray him instead of the king.

As supreme feudal lord of France, Louis XIV had occasionally claimed the right to dispose of all lands, lay and clerical, as he saw fit. Too much success, then, might be the paradoxical result of advocating pillage of the church; once whetted, the king's appetite for land might not stop at that owned by the clergy. Remembering that despotism was the government known for a royal monopoly on lands, Montesquieu could only shudder. Always he insisted that change be political as well as social, lest reform of society entail despotism of politics.

Again, despotism will have a chance to realize itself should France fail to emerge rapidly from her revolutionary stage, if and when it is entered. Having broken with the conservative side of the classical tradition, Montesquieu was not traumatized by the vision of "matter" rebelling against "form," mass against elite. Nor did he make the mistake of arbitrarily collapsing the amorphous society and politics of the revolutionary period into the category of despotism. But the danger of despotism is real, so it persists whether or not the attitudes of the classical authors are forgotten. During the violent confrontations of revolutionary politics, a cry will go up for a strong man who can put the shattered world together again. Then the tyrant, more than likely a military dictator, will spring forth from the blood of rape and rampage. A Cromwell (or Napoleon) tyrannizes over his own people and soon over foreign peoples as well, since war is the most ready means of governing a society that has shaken off the yoke of a past government.

Unable to control a revolution, the social scientist is little better at the presumably simpler task of guaranteeing the success of reforms.[50] Indeed, the utility of his wares lies less in planning change than in exposing the planners. "Mr. Law, through ignorance both of a republican and a monarchical constitution, was one of the greatest promoters of absolute power ever known in Europe." Well supplied with good intentions, John Law was, nevertheless, a dangerous man: his projects would suppress the intermediary powers without substituting a national legislature.[51]

No less than the politician, the policy scientist is at the mercy of unintended consequences. Sociology can indeed explain the unintended, but not until it is too late, for its powers are more diagnostic and retrospective than predictive. France's situation is not identical to England's earlier situation, so there is no reason to believe that confiscation of church holdings will lead to the same result. The infinitely complex chain of events, which led in England from reform to revolution to liberal society cannot be duplicated. Nor can chance or Cleopatra's nose be eliminated from the highest political drama. Social science interprets but does not change the world; the social scientist is one man and the politician another. Each has a type of political knowledge, but the nonconceptual "know-how" of the political actor — ruler or revolutionary — is alone relevant to maintaining, reforming, or disrupting the existing order.

Who can fault Montesquieu for doubting that political science can make a difference to the ruled in times of revolution if it has never been able to master the much easier policy chore of ministering to the ruler in times of stability? Guicciardini had punctured the inflated either/or's which Machiavelli presented the ruler by stressing that the correct move is always between the poles of a disjunction, that ruling is improvisation rather than rule-following, art rather than science, risk rather than certainty. Machiavelli had remembered Polybius, whose historical cycle was inevitable, naturalistic, and repetitive: Polybius, whose confusion of society with a natural object encouraged the further mistake of assuming that general principles of political action — a science of policy — can easily be attained. Machiavelli's maxims are written for all time, as befits a history that repeats itself, just as natural events do; Montesquieu's estimate of the life expectancy of maxims of state is twenty years, as befits a history freed from naturalistic preconceptions.[52]

Though sobering, the foregoing reflections are not an excuse for despair. After the revolution is over — provided it does come — one can applaud if its consequences are worthy of applause. In the meantime, however, we usually must wait and let things happen as they may. Should the appropriate circumstances coalesce, action may indeed be indicated, but until then we bide our time and acknowledge the sharp contrast between theory and practice. Montesquieu had interpreted the world, others would have to change it.

NOTES

Notes to Montesquieu refer to the *Oeuvres Complètes*, Roger Caillois, ed., 2 vols. (1949–1951). The only exception is the *Correspondance*, omitted by Caillois. To fill this lacuna, the André Masson edition (1950–1955), vol. III, has been used.

Thomas Nugent's translation of the *Spirit of the Laws*, J. Robert Loy's of the *Persian Letters*, and David Lowenthal's of the *Considerations* have been used — occasionally with slight alterations — when Montesquieu's major works are quoted. All other translations are mine.

Prologue: Montesquieu and Minerva's Owl
1. E.g., F. Ford, *Robe and Sword* (New York, 1965), ch. 12; F. Neumann, "Montesquieu," ch. 4 of *The Democratic and the Authoritarian State* (Glencoe, 1957); A. Mathiez, "La place de Montesquieu dans l'histoire des doctrines politiques du XVIIIe siècle," *Annales historiques de la Révotion française*, VII (1930); L. Althusser, *Montesquieu, la politique et l'histoire* (Paris, 1959). Their view of Montesquieu as a "feudal reactionary" is a refutation of the older understanding of him as an "aristocratic liberal." E.g., É. Carcassonne, *Montesquieu et le problème de la constitution française au XVIIIe siècle* (Paris, 1926); J.J. Chevallier, "Montesquieu ou le libéralisme aristocratique," *Revue Internationale de la Philosophie*, vol. 9 (1955), pp. 330–345.

In *L' Idée de nature en France à l'aube des lumières* (Paris, 1970), esp. pp. 286–300, J. Ehrard has effected a diplomatic compromise between these two schools of interpretation. What is needed, however, is not a synthesis but a fresh start. Those who regard Montesquieu as a "feudal reactionary" are brothers under the skin with those who regard him as an "aristocratic liberal." Both schools assume that his attack on the old regime was limited to its politics. In reality, as I hope to prove, he attacked all of the older order, the entire "system," monarchical politics *and* aristocratic society; and in England he saw, or dreamed of, a new politics and a new society.

2. R.G. Collingwood, *The Idea of History* (Oxford, 1946), Part I, esp. pp. 42–45.

3. K. von Fritz, *The Theory of the Mixed Constitution in Antiquity* (New York, 1954), pp. 12, 30, 59, 74, 333.

4. S. Wolin, *Politics and Vision* (Boston, 1960), p. 390.

5. "One can say of Montesquieu that he is the first thinker to grasp and express clearly the concept of 'ideal types' in history." E. Cassirer, *The Philosophy of the Enlightenment* (Boston, 1951), p. 210.

6. *Pensées,* 2062.

7. R. Aron, *German Sociology* (Glencoe, 1964), p. 72.

8. I. Berlin is wrong, I think, in calling Montesquieu's types "metaphysical." Berlin does so, apparently, because he accepts the myth of "Montesquieu the Cartesian." In truth, Montesquieu's philosophical sympathies lie with empiricism, not rationalism. Descartes the proponent of systematic doubt is, indeed, lauded by Montesquieu. But Descartes the philosopher of "substances" is not.

See chapter V, section 1, of this study. Berlin's comment is to be found in "Montesquieu" (Oxford, 1955), p. 277.

Also mistaken are those who assert that Montesquieu's habit of conceptualizing society in terms of "types" is to be explained by his social position. E.g., Althusser, *op. cit.*, ch. 1, and W. Stark, *Montesquieu: Pioneer of the Sociology of Knowledge* (London, 1960), p. 24. On this view, the aristocratic Montesquieu was, of course, the advocate of a feudal and corporate society, and hence he thought of society in organic metaphors. Our answer is that Montesquieu's outlook was anything but a rationalization of the old order, and that his reputed "organism" must be understood in terms of the intellectual tradition to which he belonged. He stole the idea of the "type," the "whole," the "organism," from the classics and transformed it in the light of Locke's subjective empiricism.

9. *Republic,* 460; *Politics,* 1335b.

10. C.N. Cochrane, *Christianity and Classical Culture* (Oxford, 1944), p. 104.

11. *Art of War,* end of Bk. 7.

12. I have borrowed this phrase from M. Oakeshott, *Rationalism in Politics* (London, 1962).

CHAPTER I
Absolutism and Its Ideologies

1. J. King, *Science and Rationalism in the Government of Louis XIV* (Baltimore, 1949).
2. *Testament politique,* Part I, ch. VIII.
3. *Ibid.* By the time Richelieu made this proposal, it was already becoming a cliché in royalist thought.
4. *Ibid.,* Part I, ch. II.
5. F. Meinecke, *Machiavellism* (New York, 1965), ch. 6.
6. A. Guérard, *France in the Classical Age* (New York, 1965), p. 124.
7. G. Mattingly, *Renaissance Diplomacy* (Baltimore, 1964), p. 126; see also ch. XXIII.
8. *Politique tirée des propres paroles de l'écriture sainte,* Bk. 6, Art. 1, Prop. 1.
9. *Ibid.,* Bk. 7, Art. 5, Prop. 13.
10. J.N. Figgis, *The Divine Right of Kings* (Cambridge, 1922), p. 237.
11. *Politique tirée . . . ,* Bk. 10, Art. 6, Prop. 10; Bk. 4, Art. 2, Prop. 4; Bk. 3, Art. 2, Prop. 4.
12. *Discours sur l'histoire universelle,* Part 3, ch. I; *Politique tirée . . . ,* Bk. 9, Art. 2.
13. *Politique tirée . . . ,* Bk. 1, Art. 5; Bk. 7, Art. 5, Prop. 17.
14. *Ibid.,* Bk. 7, Art. 4, Prop. 9.
15. *Ibid.,* Bk. 7, Art. 3, Prop. 9.
16. W.F. Church, *Richelieu and Reason of State* (Princeton, 1972), has correctly pointed out that Richelieu, living in a religious age, felt compelled to justify raison d'état on the grounds that it served a Christian state. But it would be wrong to conclude that divine right and reason of state got along famously with one another. Sixteen eighty-five proves that these two royalist ideologies were as much enemies as friends.

CHAPTER II
Political Sociology as the Indictment of Absolutism

1. *Testament politique,* Part I, chs. III–IV; *Politique tirée des propres paroles de l'écriture sainte,* Bk. 10.
2. *Politique tirée . . . ,* Bk. 5, Art. 1, Prop. 1.
3. K. Mannheim, *Ideology and Utopia* (New York, 1936), p. 118.
4. *Considérations,* ch. XVIII.
5. *Lois,* III, 5.
6. J. Huizinga, *The Waning of the Middle Ages* (New York, 1954), ch. IV.
7. *Lois,* V, 2.

8. *Ibid.*, IV, 5.
9. *Ibid.*, III, 6.
10. *Lettres persanes*, LXXXIX.
11. *Lois*, III, 6.
12. *Ibid.*, V, 9.
13. *Ibid.*, IV, 2.
14. *Ibid.*
15. *Ibid.*, II, 4; V, 9.
16. *Ibid.*, IV, 2.
17. L. Ducros, *French Society in the Eighteenth Century* (London, 1926), p. 298.
18. *Ibid.*, p. 68.
19. *Lois*, VIII, 6.
20. *Pensées*, 1419.
21. *Ibid.*, 318.
22. *Lois*, XX, 4.
23. *Ibid.*, VII, 1.
24. *Lettres persanes*, XCIX.
25. *Lois*, V, 19; XX, 22.
26. *Lettres persanes*, CVI; *Lois*, XXIII, 15.
27. *Lois*, XX, 23.
28. Ducros, *op. cit.* (n. 17, above), p. 53; cf. *Lettres persanes*, CXXII.
29. *Lois*, VII, 1, 4.
30. *Pensées*, 298, 311; *Lois*, XXIII, 24.
31. *Lois*, II, 4.
32. *Lettres persanes*, XXIV.
33. *Lois*, XIX, 27, p. 580. The argument connecting class stalemate with absolutism is made in reference to English history, not French. But, as will be shown in section 4 of this chapter, Montesquieu regarded the history of England as a preview of the history of France.
34. *Ibid.*, IV, 2.
35. *Ibid.*, VIII, 9.
36. *Ibid.*, III, 5.
37. *Ibid.*, XII, 27.
38. *Ibid.*, XI, 6, p. 397.
39. J. King, *Science and Rationalism in the Government of Louis XIV* (Baltimore, 1949), p. 253.
40. *Lettres persanes*, CXXVII.
41. *Ibid.*, CVII.
42. A. Guérard, *France in the Classical Age* (New York, 1965), p. 230.
43. *Lois*, II, 4; III, 5.
44. *Lettres persanes*, LXXXIX.

45. *Lois,* III, 8.
46. *Ibid.,* IV, 3; XIX, 12.
47. *Ibid.,* III, 10.
48. *Ibid.,* IV, 3.
49. *Ibid.,* V, 14, 15.
50. *Ibid.,* V, 14.
51. *Considérations,* ch. XIV.
52. *Lois,* XVII, 6.
53. *Ibid.,* V, 14.
54. *Ibid.,* V, 13.
55. *Ibid.,* VIII, 10.
56. *Ibid.,* V, 14, where Montesquieu, speaking of the despot, says "he is the law, the state, and the prince."
57. *Ibid.,* IV, 3.
58. *Ibid.,* III, 10.
59. *Lettres persanes,* IX, LXIV, XCVI.
60. *Lois,* II, 5.
61. *Ibid.,* V, 16.
62. *Ibid.,* VI, 1.
63. *Ibid.,* VIII, 19.
64. *Ibid.,* V, 16.
65. *Ibid.,* V, 17, 18.
66. *Ibid.,* V, 14; XIII, 11.
67. *Ibid.,* V, 15.
68. *Ibid.,* III, 9.
69. *Pensées,* 228.
70. *Lois,* V, 14.
71. *Ibid.,* V, 11, 14.
72. *Dossier de l'Esprit des Lois,* vol. 2, p. 996.
73. *The Prince,* ch. 17.
74. *Dossier de l'Esprit des Lois,* p. 1010.
75. *Lettres Persanes,* CXXXVI.
76. *Lois,* XIX, 27, p. 580.
77. *Considérations,* ch. I.
78. *Pensées,* 1661.
79. *Lois,* XX, 21.
80. *Ibid.,* V, 19. The formula of a "republic disguised under the form of a monarchy" may have been borrowed from across the channel. Ever since the Restoration, English republicans had been using similar phrases.
81. *Ibid.,* XX, 4.
82. *Ibid.,* V, 8.
83. *Pensées,* 1428.

84. *Ibid.*, 1434.
85. *Lois*, XIX, 27, p. 583.
86. *Pensées*, 1675.
87. *Lois*, XX, 7.
88. *Ibid.*, XIX, 10.
89. *Ibid.*, XXI, 22. See also Montesquieu's *Considérations sur les richesses de l'Espagne*, vol. 2, pp. 9–18.
90. *Lois*, XXV, 5; *Pensées*, 1977 (fn.), 1995; *Spicilège*, vol. 2, p. 1328.
91. *Lois*, XIX, 9; *Lettres persanes*, LXXVIII.
92. *Lois*, V, 19 (fn.).
93. *Ibid.*, XXI, 22.
94. *Lettres persanes*, LXXVIII.
95. *Pensées*, 311.
96. *Ibid.*, 370.
97. *Lois*, XIX, 27.
98. *Ibid.*, XXV, 13; *Lettres persanes*, XXIX.
99. *Pensées*, 1805, 1806.
100. *Lois*, XXI, 21.
101. *Pensées*, 2053–2059.
102. *Lois*, XX, 10.
103. *Ibid.*, XXI, 22.
104. *Dossier des Lettres persanes*, vol. 1, p. 376.
105. *Lettres persanes*, LXXXVII.
106. *Lois*, XXVIII, 37.
107. *Ibid.*, VIII, 17.
108. *Lettres persanes*, XCII.
109. *Lois*, II, 4; *Pensées*, 1962.
110. *Pensées*, 622.
111. *Lettres persanes*, XLIV.
112. *Ibid.*, LXXVIII.

CHAPTER III
Feudalism and the Problem of the Past

1. Tocqueville, *Democracy in America*, Bradley edition (New York, 1945), vol. 1, pp. 78, 35, 62.
2. M. Bloch, *Feudal Society* (Chicago, 1961), p. 91.
3. Nietzsche, *The Use and Abuse of History* (New York, 1957), p. 21.
4. My remarks on English historiography in the seventeenth century are greatly indebted to J.G.A. Pocock's brilliant study, *The Ancient Constitution and the Feudal Law* (Cambridge, 1957).
5. I. Kramnick, *Bolingbroke and His Circle* (Cambridge, Mass., 1968), pp. 127–136.
6. Pocock, *op. cit.*, p. 25.

7. F. Neumann, *The Democratic and the Authoritarian State* (Glencoe, 1957), p. 110.
8. *Pensées*, 1582.
9. *Lois*, XXX, 10.
10. With exceptions, of course. See, e.g., J. Franklin, *Jean Bodin and the Sixteenth Century Revolution in the Methodology of Law and History* (New York, 1961), and D.R. Kelley, *Foundations of Modern Historical Scholarship* (New York, 1970).
11. See J.N. Shklar, *Legalism* (Cambridge, Mass., 1964).
12. *Lois*, I, 3.
13. *Pensées*, 399.
14. R. Shackleton, *Montesquieu: A Critical Biography* (Oxford, 1961), pp. 333–336.
15. *Lois*, XXVIII, 13, 14.
16. *Ibid.*, XXVIII, 17.
17. *Ibid.*, XXVIII, 19.
18. *Ibid.*, XXX, 11.
19. *Ibid.*, XI, 6.
20. *Ibid.*, XXX, 12.
21. *Ibid.*, XXX, 13.
22. *Ibid.*, XXX, 17.
23. *Ibid.*, XXXI, 2; XVIII, 22.
24. *Ibid.*, XXX, 5, 10, 11.
25. *Ibid.*, XXX, 3.
26. *Ibid.*, XXX, 16, 25.
27. *Ibid.*, XXX, 17.
28. *Ibid.*, XXXI, 8.
29. *Ibid.*, XXXI, 25.
30. *Ibid.*, XXXI, 9.
31. *Ibid.*, XXXI, 7.
32. *Ibid.*, XXXI, 28.
33. *Ibid.*, XXVIII, 20.
34. *Ibid.*, XXVIII, 22.
35. *Ibid.*
36. *Ibid.*, XXX, 11.
37. *Ibid.*, XXX, 2.
38. *Ibid.*, XXXI, 2.
39. *Ibid.*, XXXI, 34.
40. *Ibid.*, XXVIII, 43.
41. *Ibid.*, XXX, 18.
42. *Pensées*, 275.
43. *Ibid.*, 1789; *Lois*, VIII, 5.
44. *Considérations*, ch. XVIII.

45. *Lois,* **XXVIII,** 45.
46. *Ibid.,* **XI,** 8.
47. *Ibid.,* **XXVIII,** 45.
48. *Pensées,* 595, p. 1098.
49. *Lois,* **XXXI,** 3–7.
50. *Ibid.,* **XXXI,** 11.
51. *Pensées,* 595, p. 1096.

CHAPTER IV
Feudalism and the Analysis of the Present

1. *Pensées,* 1963.
2. *Leviathan,* ch. 19.
3. *Lois,* **XXXI,** 16, 33.
4. *Pensées,* 304.
5. *Lois,* **XXXI,** 33.
6. *Ibid.,* **XXXI,** 32.
7. *Pensées,* 399.
8. *Ibid.,* 595, p. 1113.
9. *Ibid.,* 595, p. 1100.
10. *Dossier de l'Esprit des Lois,* p. 996; *Lois,* II, 3; III, 4; V, 8; VIII, 5.
11. *Voyages,* p. 715.
12. *Lois,* **XI,** 6.
13. Z. Fink, *The Classical Republicans* (Evanston, 1945), p. 124.
14. *Lois,* **XI,** 6.
15. *Ibid.,* **VIII,** 5 (fn.); *Pensées,* 1813.
16. *Lois,* II, 3; *Pensées,* 216.
17. *Lois,* V, 8.
18. *Ibid.,* II, 3.
19. *Voyages,* pp. 544–560.
20. *Ibid.,* pp. 722, 916.
21. *Ibid.,* p. 635.
22. *Ibid.,* p. 676.
23. *Ibid.,* p. 617.
24. *Ibid.,* p. 867.
25. *Dossier de l'Esprit des Lois,* p. 1005.
26. *Lois,* **IX,** 1.
27. *Ibid.,* **IX,** 3; *Voyages,* p. 867.
28. *Pensées,* 1986; *Lois,* **XXI,** 21.
29. *Lois,* **XXI,** 21.
30. *Ibid.,* **XX,** 10.
31. *Spicilège,* p. 1379; *Voyages,* pp. 862–874.
32. *Pensées,* 1674.

33. *Voyages,* p. 872.
34. *Spicilège,* p. 1337.
35. *Pensées,* 631.
36. *Ibid.,* 1120, 1441.
37. *Lois,* XIII, 12.
38. *Ibid.,* IX, 2; *Dossier de l'Esprit des Lois,* p. 1006.
39. *Lois,* IX, 3.
40. *Voyages,* p. 858.
41. *Pensées,* 316; *Lois,* XV, 10.
42. *Voyages,* p. 851.
43. *Ibid.,* p. 847.
44. *Lois,* X, 13.
45. *Ibid.,* XVII, 3.
46. *Ibid.,* XIX, 14.
47. *Ibid.,* V, 14.
48. *Ibid.,* XXII, 14; V, 14.
49. *Ibid.,* II, 3.
50. *Ibid.,* VII, 1; XX, 23.
51. *Ibid.,* XI, 5.
52. *Pensées,* 337; *Lois,* XV, 10.
53. *Pensées,* 1977 (fn.), 1995; *Essai sur les causes,* vol. 2, p. 59; *Considérations sur les richesses de l'Espagne,* p. 17; *Spicilège,* p. 1328.
54. *Lois,* XII, 19.
55. *Pensées,* 232.
56. *Voyages,* pp. 878, 880.
57. *Pensées,* 1433.
58. *Considérations sur les richesses de l'Espagne,* p. 10; *Pensées,* 51.
59. *Lois,* II, 4.
60. *Réflexions sur la monarchie universelle,* vol. 2, p. 26.
61. *Pensées,* 1963.
62. *Lois,* XI, 8.
63. F. Ford, *Robe and Sword* (New York, 1965), pp. 121–122; R. Mousnier, *La Vénalité des Offices sous Henri IV et Louis XIII* (Rouen, 1947), p. 623.
64. G. Mosca, *The Ruling Class* (New York, 1939), pp. 80 ff.
65. J.G.A. Pocock, "The History of Political Thought: A Methodological Enquiry," in *Philosophy, Politics, and Society,* second series, eds. P. Laslett and W.G. Runciman (Oxford, 1969), ch. 9.
66. *Lois,* XXX, 25.
67. Bodin, *Six Books of the Commonwealth,* trans. J.M. Tooley (Oxford, n.d.), p. 56.
68. "[A] monarchy with a popular government . . . is the most secure kind of monarchy there is." *Ibid.,* p. 75.

69. *Ibid.*, p. 165.
70. *Ibid.*, 172.
71. *Ibid.*, 173.
72. *Ibid.*, 162, 164.
73. *Ibid.*, 172–173.
74. Dubos, *Histoire critique de l'Établissement de la monarchie française*, Vol. III, Bk. VI, Ch. IV.
75. *Six Books of the Commonwealth*, p. 99.
76. L. Rothkrug, *Opposition to Louis XIV* (Princeton, 1965), pp. 133–138.
77. *Politique tirée des propres paroles de l'écriture sainte*, Bk. 8, Art. 2, Prop. 1.
78. *Testament politique*, Part I, ch. III.
79. *Pensées*, 1921; *Lois*, V, 19; XX, 22.
80. *Lois*, V, 18.
81. *Lettres persanes*, XIX.
82. *Lois*, IX, 4; *Pensées*, 228.
83. *Lois*, XIII, 6, 14.
84. *Ibid.*, X, 16.
85. *Ibid.*, XIII, 10, 12, 13.
86. *Pensées*, 1883; *Lois*, XIX, 27, p. 575.
87. *Lois*, XIX, 27, p. 577.
88. *Pensées*, 2025.
89. *Lois*, XIII, 12.
90. *Ibid.*, VIII, 21.
91. *Ibid.*
92. *Dossier de l'Esprit des Lois*, p. 1010.
93. *Lois*, VIII, 21.
94. Voltaire, *The Age of Louis XIV*, ch. XXXIX.
95. *Lois*, XXV, 8.
96. *Ibid.*, XIX, 17–19.
97. *Pensées*, 315.
98. M. Weber, *The Theory of Social and Economic Organization* (Glencoe, 1964), pp. 324–423.
99. *Lois*, XXXI, 18–28.
100. K. McRae, "The Structure of Canadian History," in *The Founding of New Societies*, L. Hartz et al. (New York, 1964), ch. 7.
101. *Pensées*, 1806.
102. *Lois*, V, 4.
103. *Ibid.*, XVIII, 14, 17, 30; XXX, 3; *Voyages*, pp. 860–861; *Pensées*, 1551.
104. *Lois*, XXIII, 24. See also XXX, 20, where Montesquieu shows that

the judicial powers of the nobility had a foundation in Germanic mores and thus were not totally arbitrary.
105. *Considérations*, ch. XVI.

CHAPTER V
Fiction as a Surrogate for Natural Law

1. *Pensées*, 2060.
2. *Essai sur les causes*, p. 42.
3. *Pensées*, 673.
4. *Ibid.*, 2062, 2093.
5. *Ibid.*, 673.
6. *Ibid.*, 2061.
7. *Essai sur les causes*, pp. 54, 57.
8. *Pensées*, 2064.
9. *Essai sur le goût*, p. 1241.
10. *Lettres persanes*, LIX.
11. *Voyages*, p. 767.
12. Rica expresses his admiration for "nature, which expresses itself in such varied ways and appears under so many forms." *Lettres persanes*, LXIII.
13. *Ibid.*, LXVII.
14. *Lois*, XXVI, 14.
15. *Essai sur les causes*.
16. *Dossier de l'Esprit des Lois*, p. 996.
17. *Lois*, I, 2.
18. *Pensées*, 693, 703.
19. *Lettres persanes*, XCIV.
20. *Lois*, I, 2; *Dossier de l'Esprit des Lois*, p. 996.
21. *Lois*, I, 1.
22. *Pensées*, 2062.
23. *Lettres persanes*, LXXXIII.
24. *Ibid.*, XII, LXXIII.
25. *Ibid.*, XXVIII.
26. A.P. D'Entrèves, *Natural Law* (New York, 1965), ch. I.
27. Montaigne, *Essays*, I, 31.
28. *Lois*, XVII, 5.
29. *Lettres persanes*, CV.
30. *Ibid.*, CVI.
31. *Correspondence*, no. 91.
32. *Lettres persanes*, CXIII.
33. In his early writings, Montesquieu championed something more in

Descartes than the notion of systematic doubt, namely, an antite-leological view of nature. *Discours sur la cause de la transparence des corps; Observations sur l'histoire naturelle,* vol. 1, pp. 27–43. Descartes, so to speak, was the modern who put Lucretius on a scientific footing.

34. *Lois,* XII, 6.
35. *Ibid.,* XIX, 4.
36. *Ibid.,* XVIII, 18.
37. *Ibid.,* XVIII, 31.
38. *Ibid.,* VI, 9.
39. *Lettres persanes,* LXIII.
40. *Ibid.,* XI.
41. *Ibid.,* CXXIX.
42. *Pensées,* 1080.
43. *Lettres persanes,* XII.
44. *Lois,* VII, 9.
45. *Ibid.,* IV, 3.
46. *Ibid.,* XV, 1.
47. *Essai sur les causes,* p. 39.
48. *Quelques Réflexions sur les Lettres Persanes* (1754).
49. *Lettres persanes,* II. One of the few efforts to take the "story" of the *Persian Letters* seriously is that of M. Berman, *The Politics of Authenticity* (New York, 1970), pp. 3–53. Unfortunately, his analysis is flawed by an utterly wrongheaded insistence upon 'discovering' his own romantic individualism in Montesquieu.
50. *Lettres persanes,* IX.
51. *Ibid.,* LXIV.
52. *Pensées,* 121.
53. *Lettres persanes,* LXIV.
54. *Ibid.,* XCVI.
55. *Ibid.,* LXIV.
56. *Pensées,* 121.
57. *Lettres persanes,* III.
58. *Ibid.,* CXLI.
59. *Ibid.,* II.
60. *Ibid.,* XXI.
61. *Ibid.,* VI.
62. *Ibid.,* VII.
63. *Ibid.,* XXII.
64. *Ibid.,* IX.
65. *Pensées,* 121; *Lettres persanes,* IX.
66. *Lettres persanes,* XCVI.
67. *Ibid.,* LXIV.

68. *Ibid.*, IX.
69. *Ibid.*, LXXVI.
70. *Ibid.*, LIII.
71. *Ibid.*, IX.
72. *Ibid.*, XIX.
73. *Ibid.*, XX.
74. *Ibid.*, XXIII.
75. *Ibid.*, XXIV.
76. *Ibid.*, XXV.
77. *Ibid.*, XXVII.
78. *Ibid.*, XXVI.
79. *Ibid.*, XXXI.
80. *Ibid.*, XXXIV.
81. *Ibid.*
82. *Ibid.*, XLVIII.
83. *Ibid.*, XXXVIII.
84. *Ibid.*, LV.
85. *Ibid.*, LVI.
86. *Ibid.*, XXVI.
87. *Ibid.*, XXIV.
88. *Ibid.*, LVIII.
89. *Ibid.*, XCIX.
90. *Ibid.*, LXIII.
91. *Ibid.*, LXXXVI.
92. *Ibid.*, LXXX, CII.
93. *Ibid.*, LXXXVIII–XC.
94. *Ibid.*, XVI–XVIII.
95. *Ibid.*, XXIX.
96. *Ibid.*, XXXV.
97. *Ibid.*, XXXVIII.
98. *Ibid.*, XXXIX.
99. *Ibid.*, XLVI.
100. *Ibid.*, LVII, CXVII.
101. *Ibid.*, XCIII.
102. *Ibid.*, XCVII.
103. *Ibid.*, LXVI.
104. *Ibid.*, CXXXV.
105. *Ibid.*, CXLIII.
106. *Ibid.*, CLV.
107. *Ibid.*
108. *Ibid.*, VIII.
109. *Ibid.*, XLII–XLIII.
110. *Ibid.*, CXLVIII, CLIII.

111. *Ibid.*, CLVII–CLVIII.
112. *Ibid.*, LXII.
113. *Ibid.*, VIII, CLXI.
114. *Ibid.*, XII.
115. *Ibid.*, LXII, CLXI.

CHAPTER VI
Historiography as a Surrogate for Natural Law

1. *Lois*, I, 1.
2. *Lettres persanes*, XIII.
3. *Pensées*, 279.
4. See J.H. Whitfield, *Machiavelli* (Oxford, 1947), for a defense of Machiavelli which has won widespread acceptance. To my mind, the most subtle defense of Machiavelli's amoralism is that of S. Wolin, *Politics and Vision* (Boston, 1960), ch. 7.
5. *Discourses* (New York, 1950), Bk. 1, ch. II.
6. Cf. *Lois*, V, 3.
7. E.g., *The Prince* (New York, 1950), ch. IX; *Discourses*, Bk. 1, ch. V.
8. *Discourses*, Bk. 1, ch. LVIII.
9. *Ibid.*, Bk. 1, ch. LV.
10. Polybius, *Histories*, Bk. VI, 7–8.
11. *Discourses*, Bk. 1, ch. LV.
12. For Machiavelli's view of Venice, see *Discourses*, Bk. 1, chs. V, VI, LV.
13. As Fink has pointed out in *The Classical Republicans* (Evanston, 1945), p. 19.
14. Polybius, *Histories*, Bk. VI, 11–12; cf. Aristotle, *Politics*, 1294b.
15. *Discourses*, Bk. 2, ch. III.
16. *Ibid.*, Bk. 2, ch. VI.
17. *The Prince*, ch. V.
18. *Ibid.*, ch. III.
19. *Discourses*, Bk. 2, ch. XXV.
20. *Ibid.*, Bk. 2, ch. XXI.
21. *The Prince*, ch. V.
22. *Discourses*, Bk. 2, ch. IV.
23. *Ibid.* Bk. 2, ch. XIII.
24. *Ibid.*, Bk. 2, ch. II.
25. *The Prince*, chs. XV, XVIII.
26. Wolin, *op. cit.* (n. 4, above).
27. *History of Florence*, beginning of Bk. V.
28. *Considérations*, ch. IX; *Discourses*, Bk. 2, chs. I, IX, XVII.
29. *Considérations*, Ch. VI.

30. *Ibid.*
31. *Ibid.*, ch. VI.
32. *Ibid.*, ch. IV.
33. *Ibid.*, ch. V.
34. *Ibid.*, ch. VI.
35. *Lois*, V, 5.
36. *Considérations*, ch. III.
37. *Lois*, V, 6.
38. *Considérations*, ch. X.
39. *Lois*, IV, 7.
40. *Ibid.*, XVIII, 17.
41. *Ibid.*, VII, 4.
42. *Ibid.*, VIII, 13.
43. *Ibid.*, VIII, 3.
44. *Ibid.*, VIII, 16.
45. *Considérations*, ch. I.
46. *Lois*, XI, 18–19.
47. *Politics*, 1318b.
48. *Lois*, XV, 16; *Considérations*, ch. XIII.
49. *Pensées*, 338.
50. *Considérations*, ch. IX.
51. *Ibid.*
52. *Ibid.*
53. *Ibid.*, chs. XVIII, XI.
54. *Art of War*, Bk. 1.
55. *Discourses*, Bk. 1, ch. XXXVII; Bk. 3, chs. XXIV, XLIX.
56. *Ibid.*, Bk. 2, ch. XIX.
57. *The Golden Ass*, ch. 5.
58. *Considérations*, ch. XV.
59. *Lois*, VI, 2.
60. *Ibid.*, VI, 8.
61. *Considérations*, chs. XIV–XV.
62. *Ibid.*, ch. XVI.
63. *Ibid.*, ch. XV.
64. *Ibid.*
65. *Lois*, XXIII, 23.
66. *Considérations*, ch. XXII.
67. *Ibid.*, ch. XXI.
68. *Discours sur l'histoire universelle,* Part 3, ch. VI.
69. *Ibid.*, Part 3, chs. VI–VII.
70. C.N. Cochrane, *Christianity and Classical Culture* (Oxford, 1944), ch. XII.

71. *Discours,* Part 3, ch. VIII.
72. *Considérations,* ch. XI.
73. *Discours,* Part 3, ch. II.
74. *Ibid.,* Part 3, ch. VII.
75. *Ibid.,* Part 3, ch. VI.
76. *Ibid.,* Part 3, ch. I.
77. R. Shackleton, *Montesquieu: A Critical Biography* (Oxford, 1961), pp. 157–164.
78. *Lois,* VIII, 16.
79. *Considérations,* ch. V. On Machiavelli, Montesquieu, and Roman history, the reader may wish to consult the following works: R. Oake, "Montesquieu's Analysis of Roman History," *Journal of the History of Ideas,* vol. XVI (Jan., 1955), pp. 44–60; E. Levi-Malvano, *Montesquieu e Machiavelli* (Paris, 1912).

CHAPTER VII
A World of Leviathans

1. *Pensées,* 1483.
2. P. Roberts, *The Quest for Security, 1715–1750* (New York, 1963), p. 1.
3. *Lois,* XIII, 17 (fn.).
4. *Spicilège,* p. 1363; J. King, *Science and Rationalism in the Government of Louis XIV* (Baltimore, 1949), pp. 246–247.
5. *Pensées,* 1484.
6. *Lois,* X, 2, 4. B. Kassem, *Décadence et absolutism dans l'oeuvre de Montesquieu* (Paris, 1960), pp. 125, 143, does Montesquieu a great disservice when he accuses him of jingoism. He has read Montesquieu backwards.
7. *Ibid.,* X, 2.
8. *Pensées,* 1214.
9. *Ibid.,* 617.
10. *Ibid.,* 616.
11. E.g., G. Sabine, *A History of Political Theory,* 3rd ed. (New York, 1961), ch. XXI.
12. *Social Contract,* Bk. I, ch. II.
13. *Lois,* X, 3; cf. G. Mattingly, *Renaissance Diplomacy* (Baltimore, 1964), ch. XXVIII.
14. *History of Florence,* beginnings of Bks. V and VI; *Art of War,* end of Bk. 2.
15. *Rights of War and Peace* (Washington, 1901), Bk. III, ch. V, sect. I; ch. VI, sect. II; ch. VII, sect. I; ch. VIII, sects. I, II.
16. *Lettres persanes,* XCIV.
17. *Social Contract,* Bk. II, ch. II.

18. *Réflexions sur la monarchie universelle*, III; *Lois*, XXVI, 16.

19. J. Wolf, *The Emergence of the Great Powers, 1685–1715* (New York, 1962), p. 20. Earlier, Richelieu had pursued a policy of allying France with Turkey.

20. *Lois*, IV, 2.

21. *Ibid.*, XV, 4.

22. *Dossier de l'Esprit des Lois*, p. 1019.

23. *Pensées*, 617, 1573, 1575.

24. *Ibid.*, 1498; cf. *Lois*, XVII, 4.

25. *Lois*, XIII, 17 (fn.).

26. *Dossier de l'Esprit des Lois*, p. 1007.

27. *Pensées*, 338.

28. *Voyages*, p. 581.

29. *Spicilège*, p. 1305; *Lettres persanes*, CXXI.

30. *Lois*, X, 9.

31. *Ibid.*, VIII, 17.

32. C. Gibson, *Spain in America* (New York, 1967), pp. 58–62.

33. *Lois*, VIII, 17.

34. *Ibid.*, X, 15.

35. *Ibid.*, X, 14.

36. *Ibid.*, VIII, 8.

37. The *Pensées* contains bits and pieces of this proposed work.

38. R. Shackleton, *Montesquieu: A Critical Biography* (Oxford, 1961), p. 146.

39. *Pensées*, 659.

40. *Ibid.*, 595, p. 1117; 652; 1610.

41. *Ibid.*, 658.

42. *Mémoire sur la constitution*, vol. 2, pp. 1217–1221.

43. *Pensées*, 652.

44. *Lois*, XXII, 10, 13, 7.

45. *Ibid.*, XXII, 13.

46. *Considérations*, ch. XXI.

47. *Réflexions*, VII.

48. *Ibid.*, II.

49. *De la politique*, vol. 1, pp. 112–119; *Traité des devoirs*, vol. 1, esp. pp. 110–111.

50. *Pensées*, 1228.

51. *Lois*, IX, 6.

52. *Réflexions*, II.

53. *Lois*, XXIII, 15.

54. *Pensées*, 314; *Lois*, XX, 23; XXIII, 14.

55. *Pensées*, 1977 (fn.).

56. *Lois*, XXIII, 15.
57. *Ibid.*, 1973 (fn.).
58. *Lois*, XXIII, 28; *Dossier de l'Esprit des Lois*, p. 1002.
59. *Pensées*, 311.
60. *Ibid.*, 661.
61. *Lois*, XXI, 22.
62. *Ibid.*, XVIII, 3.
63. *Pensées*, 366.
64. *Ibid.*, 1883.
65. E.g., "Mémoire sur les mines" in *Voyages*, pp. 885–909; *Lois*, XXI, 22.
66. *Lois*, XV, 8.
67. N.E. Devletoglou, "Montesquieu and the Wealth of Nations," *The Canadian Journal of Economics and Political Science*, vol. XXIX, no. 1 (Feb., 1963).
68. *Lois*, XX, 4; XXI, 5.
69. *Ibid.*, XX, 2.
70. *Testament politique*, Part I, ch. IV.
71. *Politique tirée des propres paroles de l'écriture sainte*, Bk. 3.
72. *Lois*, XIII, 7.
73. *Ibid.*, XIII, 2.
74. *Ibid.*, XXI, 20.
75. *Ibid.*, XIII, 2; XXIII, 11; *Pensées*, 1977.
76. Devletoglou, *op. cit.*
77. *Lois*, XXIII, 15; *Réflexions*, II.
78. *Lois*, XXIII, 29.
79. *Ibid.*
80. J.M. Keynes, *Théorie générale de l'emploi, de l'intérêt et de la monnaie* (Paris, 1953), p. 13.
81. *Mémoire sur les dettes de l'état*, vol. 1, pp. 66–71.
82. *Lois*, IX, 9, 10.
83. *Réflexions*, II; *Pensées*, 1773.
84. *Pensées*, 336.
85. *Lois*, XX, 9, 14; *Pensées*, 339, 2032–2033.
86. *Lois*, XXI, 5.
87. *Considérations sur les richesses de l'Espagne*, Art. 1.
88. *Pensées*, 348.
89. *Lois*, XX, 1.
90. E.g., *Voyages*, p. 895.
91. *Lois*, XX, 2; *Pensées*, 1780; *Réflexions*, XVIII.
92. *Lois*, XX, 13.
93. *Ibid.*, XXI, 21.
94. *Ibid.*; *Pensées*, 1486.

95. *Voyages*, p. 895; *Lettres persanes*, XIX; *Lois*, XX, 23; XXI, 21.
96. *Pensées*, 2019.
97. *Lois*, XX, 23.
98. *Pensées*, 1573.
99. *Lettres persanes*, CXXI.
100. *Lois*, XXI, 21.
101. *Pensées*, 337, 1974.
102. *Lois*, V, 11.
103. *Pensées*, 198–200.
104. *Ibid.*, 658.
105. R. Forster, "The Noble Wine Producers of the Bordelais in the Eighteenth Century," *Economic History Review*, 2nd Series, XIV No. 1 (August, 1961), pp. 18–33.
106. *Pensées*, 1228.
107. *Ibid.*, 1226–1228; 595, p. 1123.
108. *Lois*, III, 7.
109. *Pensées*, 1225, 1228.
110. Montesquieu was a friend of Saint-Pierre, author of the *Projet de paix perpetuelle*. But he regarded Saint-Pierre's schemes as ideas which no one would be interested in for centuries. *Pensées*, 198, 408.
111. *Lois*, XIII, 17.
112. *Lettres persanes*, CV-CVI; *Pensées*, 600.
113. *Pensées*, 1664.
114. *Lois*, XIX, 27, p. 578.
115. *Ibid.*, XX, 12.
116. *Ibid.*, XIX, 27, p. 577; cf. I. Kramnick, *Bolingbroke and His Circle*, (Cambridge, Mass., 1968), p. 42.
117. *Lois*, XXII, 18.
118. *Ibid.*, XIX, 27, p. 579; *Dossier de l'Esprit des Lois*, pp. 1002, 1005.
119. *Lois*, XIX, 27, p. 578; *Dossier de l'Esprit des Lois*, pp. 1007–1009.
120. On Aix-la-Chapelle: *Correspondance*, no. 419. On growing illiberalism at home caused by conflicts abroad: *Lois*, XIII, 17.

EPILOGUE
Interpreting the World versus Changing It

1. *Lois*, XI, 6.
2. Harrington, *A System of Politics*, part X.
3. C.J. Friedrich, *The Philosophy of Law in Historical Perspective* (Chicago, 1963), p. 102.
4. I. Kramnick, *Bolingbroke and His Circle* (Cambridge, Mass., 1968), pp. 70–76, 121–124.
5. *Lois*, XIX, 27, p. 575; XI, 6.
6. *Pensées*, 1883.

7. *Lois,* XIX, 27, p. 575.
8. *Ibid.,* XXVI, 15.
9. *Ibid.,* XII.
10. *Pensées,* 233, cf. 1791.
11. *Ibid.,* 604.
12. *Éloge de la sincérité,* vol. 1, pp. 99–107; *Pensées,* 551, 1171; *Lettres persanes,* LIV.
13. *Lois,* XIX, 27, p. 582, and the passages cited in note 12.
14. *Pensées,* 1883.
15. *Lois,* V, 6.
16. *Ibid.,* XI, 6; Tocqueville, *Democracy in America,* vol. 1, ch. XVI.
17. *Pensées,* 1961; *Lois,* XI, 6, "As at Athens."
18. *Lois,* XI, 3.
19. I. Berlin, *Four Essays on Liberty* (Oxford, 1969), p. 147.
20. *Pensées,* 1935.
21. Besides chapter V, section 2, of this book, see my article, "Patriarchalism and Its Early Enemies," *Political Theory: An International Journal of Political Philosophy,* vol. 2 (Nov., 1974), pp. 410–419.
22. *Voyages,* p. 757; *Pensées,* 2029.
23. H. Pirenne, *Early Democracy in the Low Countries* (New York, 1963), pp. 36–38, 53, 156–158; M. Weber, *The City* (New York, 1958), pp. 71, 179.
24. *Lois,* IV, 2.
25. *Considérations,* ch. I.
26. Quoted by M. Gilmore, *The World of Humanism* (New York, 1962), p. 130; W.F. Church, *Constitutional Thought in Sixteenth-Century France* (Cambridge, Mass., 1941), pp. 245, 249, 267–268.
27. *Pensées,* 1317.
28. *Ibid.,* 1339.
29. *Testament politique,* Part I, ch. II.
30. P. Laslett, ed., *Patriarcha and Other Political Works* (Oxford, 1949), p. 103.
31. *Mémoires for the Instruction of the Dauphin* (N.Y., 1970), p. 61.
32. *Pensées,* 1283.
33. *Ibid.,* 616.
34. *Lettres persanes,* CXLIV.
35. *Ibid.,* CXVII.
36. *Testament politique,* Part II, ch. VII.
37. *Lois,* XXIX, 2; XI, 4.
38. *Pensées,* 631.
39. *Ibid.,* 1802, 1797.
40. *Ibid.,* 658, 2152, 2171; *Lois,* XXIV, 2, 13.

41. *Pensées,* 1959.
42. *Lois,* XX, 7.
43. *Ibid.,* XI, 6.
44. *Ibid.,* XIX, 27.
45. *Pensées,* 2030.
46. C. Hill, *Puritanism and Revolution* (New York, 1964), ch. 2; *De la politique,* pp. 112–113; *Lois,* XXIII, 29.
47. *Mémoires,* p. 165.
48. *Pensées,* 2030, 2056, 2057.
49. *Ibid.,* 413, 1199.
50. E.g., *Considérations,* ch. XVII.
51. *Lois,* II, 4; cf. P. Roberts, *The Quest for Security, 1715-1750* (New York, 1963), p. 102.
52. *Pensées,* 1766.

INDEX